D1526571

Jossey-Bass Teacher provides K–12 teachers with essential knowledge and tools to create a positive and lifelong impact on student learning. Trusted and experienced educational mentors offer practical classroom-tested and theory-based teaching resources for improving teaching practice in a broad range of grade levels and subject areas. From one educator to another, we want to be your first source to make every day your best day in teaching. *Jossey-Bass Teacher* resources serve two types of informational needs—essential knowledge and essential tools.

Essential knowledge resources provide the foundation, strategies, and methods from which teachers may design curriculum and instruction to challenge and excite their students. Connecting theory to practice, essential knowledge books rely on a solid research base and time-tested methods, offering the best ideas and guidance from many of the most experienced and well-respected experts in the field.

Essential tools save teachers time and effort by offering proven, ready-to-use materials for in-class use. Our publications include activities, assessments, exercises, instruments, games, ready reference, and more. They enhance an entire course of study, a weekly lesson, or a daily plan. These essential tools provide insightful, practical, and comprehensive materials on topics that matter most to K–12 teachers.

Math Essentials, Elementary School Level:
Lessons and Activities for Test Preparation

Frances McBroom Thompson, Ed.D.

JOSSEY-BASS
A Wiley Imprint
www.josseybass.com

Published by Jossey-Bass
A Wiley Imprint
989 Market Street, San Francisco, CA 94103-1741   www.josseybass.com

Jossey-Bass books and products are available through most bookstores. To contact Jossey-Bass directly call our Customer Care Department within the U.S. at 800-956-7739, outside the U.S. at 317-572-3986, or fax 317-572-4002.

Jossey-Bass also publishes its books in a variety of electronic formats. Some content that appears in print may not be available in electronic books.

Originally published as *Ready-to-Use Math Proficiency Lessons & Activities*, *4th Grade Level* (2003).

Library of Congress Cataloging-in-Publication Data
Thompson, Frances M. (Frances McBroom)
  Math essentials, elementary school level : lessons and activities for test preparation / Frances McBroom Thompson.
      p. cm.
  Includes bibliographical references.
  ISBN-13: 978-0-7879-8880-7 (pbk.)
  ISBN-10: 0-7879-8880-4 (pbk.)
  1. Mathematics—Study and teaching (Elementary)—United States. 2. Mathematics—Study and teaching (Elementary)—Activity programs—United States. 3. Achievement tests—United States—Study guides. 4. Mathematics—Examinations, questions, etc. I. Title.
  QA135.6.T464 2006
  372.7—dc22
                                        2006023716

Printed in the United States of America
FIRST EDITION
PB Printing   10 9 8 7 6 5 4 3 2 1

About This Book

Math Essentials, Elementary School Level is designed to help students review and master all the mathematics concepts they are expected to know and understand by fifth grade. It takes a developmental approach, incorporating manipulative and pictorial lessons, followed by independent practice, and often including multiple-choice exercises that provide practice in standardized testing. *Math Essential, Elementary School Level* covers forty objectives found in typical curriculum for Grades 3 through 5: numeration, computation, graphing, statistics, probability, geometry and spatial reasoning, and measurement, all supporting NCTM Standards.

THE AUTHOR

Frances McBroom Thompson, Ed.D., has taught mathematics full-time at the junior and senior high school levels in Texas and California and has served as a K–12 mathematics specialist in both Georgia and Texas. She holds a bachelor's degree in mathematics education from Abilene Christian University (Texas) and a master's degree in mathematics from the University of Texas at Austin. Her doctoral degree is in mathematics education from the University of Georgia at Athens. She presently serves on the mathematics faculty of Texas Woman's University in Denton, Texas, where she offers undergraduate and graduate courses in mathematics and mathematics teaching.

Dr. Thompson regularly contributes articles on mathematics teaching to professional education journals and conducts workshops for in-service teachers at the elementary and secondary levels. She is the author of *Five-Minute Challenges* and *More Five-Minute Challenges*—two activity books in secondary problem solving—and the coauthor of *Holt Math 1000* (1984) and *Holt Essential Math* (1987)—two general mathematics textbooks for high school students. Her most recent books are *Hands-on Math! Ready-to-Use Games & Activities for Grades 4–8* (Jossey-Bass, 1994) and *Hands-on Algebra! Ready-to-Use Games & Activities for Grades 7–12* (Jossey-Bass, 1998). She has also developed training materials for K–12 mathematics teachers with the Texas Education Agency.

Contents

Section 1:   **NUMERATION AND NUMBER PROPERTIES** **1**

Objectives

Section 2:   **COMPUTATIONAL ALGORITHMS AND ESTIMATION IN PROBLEM SOLVING** **83**

Objectives

Section 3: | **GRAPHING, STATISTICS, AND PROBABILITY** **193**

Objectives

Section 4: GEOMETRY AND LOGICAL OR SPATIAL REASONING 257

Objectives

Section 5: MEASUREMENT 317

Objectives

NOTES TO THE TEACHER

Math Essentials, Elementary School Level: Lessons and Activities for Test Preparation consists of forty key objectives arranged in five sections. These objectives have been selected from the standard mathematics curriculum for Grades 3–5. For each objective, three activities (two developmental lessons and one independent practice) have been included, along with a list of common student errors with respect to problems related to the objective.

A worksheet and an answer key are provided for most activities. Each of the five sections also contains a Practice Test with an answer key.

Description of Activities

Two developmental activities have been included for each objective: the first at the manipulative stage and the second at the pictorial stage. Detailed steps guide the teacher through each of these two activities. Activity 1 usually requires objects of some kind. Materials are described in detail, and necessary building mats, pattern sheets, and worksheets with answer keys are provided. Activity 2 involves pictures or diagrams that closely relate to the actions performed in Activity 1. Worksheets and answer keys are also available for this second activity. The third activity—Activity 3—provides an opportunity for students to practice the objective independently and at the abstract level of thinking. Worksheet items for this third stage will often have multiple-choice responses to provide students with further testing experience.

These three activities may be presented as a connected set, with the manipulative activity leading naturally to the pictorial activity, then the independent practice. Alternatively, each activity may be used separately, depending on the learning needs of the students. All students, however, regardless of intellectual ability or background, need to experience each of the three stages of learning at some point. The natural learning progression that moves from hands-on action to paper-and-pencil drawing and finally to abstract notation is essential for all students to experience and should not be excluded from classroom instruction. Therefore, it is recommended that the three activities be used together.

Common Errors Students Make

When studying any mathematical objective, students will have errors in their work. Test developers know this and usually select item response choices that reflect these errors. Hence, it is helpful if the classroom teacher also is aware of these common errors and can identify them when they occur in a student's work.

To assist teachers with this process, a list of typical errors is given with each objective in this text. Various studies have shown that if students are made aware of their particular mistakes in mathematics, they are more likely to replace them with correct procedures or conceptual understanding. When such errors are not specifically addressed, students are likely to continue making them, no matter how many times the teacher demonstrates the correct steps to use.

Section Practice Tests

A Practice Test, along with an answer key, is provided at the end of each of Sections 1 to 5. For each objective in a section, two multiple-choice test items are provided on the section's Practice Test. The format and level of difficulty of these items are similar to those found in state or national standardized tests for Grades 3–5 students. Where appropriate, the activity worksheets for an objective will reflect the types of problems included in the Practice Test. Otherwise, the activities are designed to give students the conceptual foundation needed to understand the test items.

Instructional Accountability

Teachers must be accountable for what they are teaching to students. The alternative instructional methods and assessment techniques presented in this text will greatly assist teachers as they try to align their classroom instruction with their district and state mathematics guidelines and seek to measure their students' progress.

NUMERATION AND NUMBER PROPERTIES

Objective 1
Order three or more whole numbers up to ten thousands.

Discussion
To be able to compare three or more whole numbers in the thousands or ten thousands and to order them from least to greatest or from greatest to least, students must be able to apply the place value concept. The following activities provide them with experience in making such comparisons.

Activity 1: Manipulative Stage

Materials
Building Mat 1-1a for each pair of students
100 small counters for each pair of students (same color or same style)
Worksheet 1-1a
Regular pencil

Procedure
1. Give each pair of students a copy of Building Mat 1-1a—a base 10 mat that contains columns for thousands, hundreds, tens, and ones (left to right). The columns should be subdivided into three rows under the column headings (see mat illustrations).

2. Each pair also needs a set of 100 small counters. The counters may be the same color and same size.

3. For practice, partners should take turns placing counters in the different spaces within a row on the mat to represent three-digit or four-digit numbers, specifically numbers from 100 to 3,000. These practice numbers should be written on the board for students to build on their mats.

4. After students are comfortable with showing individual numbers on the mat, give each student a copy of Worksheet 1-1a, which contains sets of three numbers listed in mixed order.

5. Students will show each set of three numbers on their mat at the same time, building one number per row. The numbers should be randomly ordered on the mat at first, that is, not placed in any particular row.

6. Students will then compare the quantities of counters in the three rows within the same column to determine which quantity is greatest (or least). The process is repeated for each column until the desired order is found. The final sequence is then recorded in the appropriate box on the worksheet.

7. If numbers are to be ordered from greatest to least, the counters for the greatest number will be placed on the top row, followed by the other two numbers in correct order. If numbers are to be ordered from least to greatest, the counters for the least number will be placed on the top row, followed by the other two numbers appropriately.

8. Guide students through the first exercise before they proceed to the others.

For the first exercise on Worksheet 1-1a, consider the set that contains these three numbers: 2,716; 3,420; 2,585. The numbers are to be ordered from *greatest* to *least*.

Students should place counters in the three rows of Building Mat 1-1a to show the three numbers in some random order.

Here is a possible initial arrangement of the counters for the three numbers as they might appear on the building mat.

THOUSANDS	HUNDREDS	TENS	ONES
▪▪	▪▪▪ ▪▪	▪▪▪▪ ▪▪▪▪	▪▪▪ ▪▪
▪▪▪	▪▪ ▪▪	▪▪	
▪▪	▪▪▪▪ ▪▪▪	▪	▪▪▪ ▪▪▪

First appearance of counters on mat.

After each number has been built on the mat, ask students to look at the counters to find which number has the *most thousands*. Since 3,420 has 3 thousands and the other two numbers both have 2 thousands, have students move the counters for 3,420 to the top row of the mat, exchanging counters with whatever number was built there initially. (Note: If *two* numbers in the set had each had 3 thousands, students would have moved those two numbers to the top two rows of the mat and the third number down to the bottom row. Then the numbers in the top two rows would have been compared in their hundreds columns, and the one having more hundreds counters would be moved to the top row.) In this example, the lower two numbers have the same quantity of counters in their thousands columns, so they must now be compared in their hundreds columns.

The number 2,716 has 7 counters in the hundreds column, which is more than the other number—2,585—has. The counters for 2,716 should then be moved to the second row of the mat (if not already there) and the counters for 2,585 moved to the bottom row.

Have students record their results in the box shown under the given set of numbers on Worksheet 1-1a by writing the number name for the counters in the top row of the mat in the leftmost box, the middle row number in the middle box, and the bottom row number in the rightmost box. Since the top row of the mat was chosen for having the *greatest* number, the recording box shows the numbers sequenced in decreasing or descending order, or *from greatest to least.*

Here is how the final arrangement should appear on the mat, along with the numbers recorded in the box on the worksheet:

THOUSANDS	HUNDREDS	TENS	ONES
▫▫▫	▫▫▫ ▫	▫▫	
▫▫	▫▫▫▫ ▫▫▫	▫	▫▫▫ ▫▫▫
▫▫	▫▫▫ ▫▫	▫▫▫▫ ▫▫▫▫	▫▫▫ ▫▫

Final appearance of counters on mat.

3,420	2,716	2,585

Recording box on student's worksheet.

Repeat this procedure with other sets of numbers on Worksheet 1-1a that must be arranged from *greatest* to *least.* If an exercise requires that a set of numbers be ordered from *least* to *greatest*, students should begin by finding the *least* quantity of counters in the thousands column and moving the corresponding number to the *top row* of the mat. Continue the comparing of the other two numbers to find which one has *fewer* counters in the hundreds column; the counters for this second number identified should then be moved to the middle row of the mat. The third number's counters will end up on the bottom row of the mat. Since the number in the top row is always recorded in the leftmost box, the final recording of the three numbers will list the numbers *from least to greatest.* (Note: If *two* numbers in the set had each had the least thousands, students would have moved those two numbers to the top two rows of the mat and the third number down to the bottom row. Then the numbers in the top two rows would have been compared in their hundreds columns, and the one having fewer hundreds counters would be moved to the top row.)

Answer Key for Worksheet 1-1a

1. 3,420; 2,716; 2,585

2. 3,172; 3,086; 1,843

3. 3,006; 3,530; 4,125

4. 3,618; 4,237; 5,207

5. 3,758; 3,728; 3,258

BUILDING MAT 1-1a

THOUSANDS	HUNDREDS	TENS	ONES

6

WORSHEET 1-1a

Name _____

Ordering Whole Numbers
by Building

Date _____

Use counters on Building Mat 1-1a to order each given set of whole numbers. Then record the final arrangement of the three numbers in the box below the given set, recording from left to right in the required order.

1. Order from greatest to least: 2,716; 3,420; 2,585.

2. Order from greatest to least: 1,843; 3,172; 3,086.

3. Order from least to greatest: 3,006; 4,125; 3,530.

4. Order from least to greatest: 5,207; 3,618; 4,237.

5. Order from greatest to least: 3,258; 3,758; 3,728.

Activity 2: Pictorial Stage

Materials

Worksheet 1-1b
Regular pencil

Procedure

1. Give each student a copy of Worksheet 1-1b. Have students work with partners, but each student will complete her or his own worksheet.

2. For each set of four whole numbers given on Worksheet 1-1b, students will represent the numbers with small circles on the base 10 frame on the worksheet. After they have determined the correct order of the four numbers, they will record the numbers in that order below the base 10 frame.

3. Some sets will be ordered from least to greatest, while others will be ordered from greatest to least.

4. Guide students through the first exercise on Worksheet 1-1b, then allow them to continue with the other exercises.

For the first exercise, consider this set of numbers: 3,425; 5,401; 3,213; 1,140. The first number listed in the set (3,425) should be drawn in the top row of the base 10 frame, the second number in the second row, and so on. To show a number, students should draw small circles in each column of the chosen row to represent each digit of the number.

In this exercise, the numbers are to be ordered *from least to greatest*. The greatest *place value* involved in the four numbers is thousands. Ask students to find the number with the *least* quantity of circles in the thousands column. Have them write #1 to the left of that number's row on the frame. The number is 1,140. Then have students find the number with the *greatest* quantity of circles in the thousands column and write #4 to the left of that number's row. The number is 5,401.

For the two remaining numbers, if their thousands columns differed, students would label the lower amount as #2 and the greater amount as #3. In this example, however, the thousands columns are equal in 3,425 and 3,213. Students must now compare the hundreds columns of the two numbers (they would continue to tens and ones, if necessary). The number with the lower quantity of hundreds (3,213) becomes #2. The remaining number (3,425) becomes #3.

After all four numbers are labeled, students should write the numbers in sequence below the frame, following the labeled ordering. This exercise's final frame and recorded sequence *from least to greatest* are shown here:

	TEN THOUSANDS	THOUSANDS	HUNDREDS	TENS	ONES
#3		○○○	○○○○	○○	○○○○○
#4		○○○○○	○○○○		○
#2		○○○	○○	○	○○○
#1		○	○	○○○○	

Final Order: 1,140; 3,213; 3,425; 5,401

Answer Key for Worksheet 1-1b

1. 1,140; 3,213; 3,425; 5,401

2. 6,119; 5,026; 4,840; 4,385

3. 8,705; 9,235; 12,483; 12,630

4. 32,550; 32,450; 30,859; 30,824

5. 24,800; 24,760; 24,318; 24,035

6. 5,875; 8,860; 10,520; 14,423

WORKSHEET 1-1b

Name _____

**Ordering Whole Numbers
by Drawing**

Date _____

Order each set of four whole numbers by drawing and comparing small circles on the frame provided. Then record the final arrangement of the four numbers below the frame, recording from left to right in the required order.

1. Order from least to greatest: 3,425; 5,401; 3,213; 1,140.

TEN THOUSANDS	THOUSANDS	HUNDREDS	TENS	ONES

Final Order: _____

2. Order from greatest to least: 4,385; 6,119; 4,840; 5,026.

TEN THOUSANDS	THOUSANDS	HUNDREDS	TENS	ONES

Final Order: _____

WORKSHEET 1-1b Continued

Name _____

Date _____

3. Order from least to greatest: 12,483; 8,705; 12,630; 9,235.

TEN THOUSANDS	THOUSANDS	HUNDREDS	TENS	ONES

Final Order: _____

4. Order from greatest to least: 32,450; 30,824; 30,859; 32,550.

TEN THOUSANDS	THOUSANDS	HUNDREDS	TENS	ONES

Final Order: _____

WORKSHEET 1-1b Continued

Name _____

Date _____

5. Order from greatest to least: 24,318; 24,760; 24,035; 24,800.

TEN THOUSANDS	THOUSANDS	HUNDREDS	TENS	ONES

Final Order: _____

6. Order from least to greatest: 14,423; 8,860; 10,520; 5,875.

TEN THOUSANDS	THOUSANDS	HUNDREDS	TENS	ONES

Final Order: _____

Activity 3: Independent Practice

Materials
> Worksheet 1-1c
> Regular pencils

Procedure
Students work independently to complete Worksheet 1-1c. When all are finished, discuss the results.

Answer Key for Worksheet 1-1c
1. 7,351; 5,860; 5,249; 3,085

2. 11,845; 11,860; 12,400; 12,567

3. 9,114; 8,607; 8,549; 7,235; 7,102

4. 8,945; 9,845; 14,000; 20,873; 25,078

5. D

6. C

Possible Testing Errors That May Occur for This Objective
- The numbers are sequenced by size but in reverse order; for example, they are arranged in decreasing order, but the test item requires them to be in increasing order. Students clearly understand how to compare and order numbers, but they may not understand that "from least to greatest" means increasing and that "from greatest to least" means decreasing.

- The first and last numbers listed in the sequence are correct, but the other numbers are randomly ordered between those two numbers. Students focus on the "least" and the "greatest" numbers but disregard any others given in the list.

- The numbers are randomly sequenced without regard for value. Students do not understand the ordering process.

WORKSHEET 1-1c

Name _____

Date _____

In exercises 1 to 4, list each set of whole numbers in the given order:

1. Order from greatest to least: 5,249; 3,085; 7,351; 5,860.

2. Order from least to greatest: 12,400; 11,845; 11,860; 12,567.

3. Order from greatest to least: 8,549; 7,235; 8,607; 9,114; 7,102.

4. Order from least to greatest: 25,078; 9,845; 8,945; 14,000; 20,873.

In exercises 5 and 6, circle the letter of the correct response:

5. Which group of numbers is in order from *least* to *greatest*?

    A. 2,027   2,426   2,409   2,512
    B. 2,409   2,512   2,426   2,027
    C. 2,512   2,426   2,409   2,027
    D. 2,027   2,409   2,426   2,512

6. Which group of numbers is in order from *greatest* to *least*?

    A. 36,943   45,188   37,912   45,395
    B. 37,912   45,395   36,943   45,188
    C. 45,395   45,188   37,912   36,943
    D. 36,943   37,912   45,188   45,395

Objective 2
Identify odd and even whole numbers.

Discussion
Students have difficulty keeping *even* and *odd* numbers separated, mainly because they have never developed the two concepts and do not see the two types as complements of each other. Basically, *even* quantities are quantities that can be separated into two equal sets or amounts without extras being left over.

Hence, we have the idea that things come out *even*, meaning with no leftovers. Using counters arranged in two rows, students can discover for themselves what numbers are considered *even*. Students need to see how even and odd numbers relate to each other in order to be able to apply their general forms ($2N + 1$ and $2N$) later on in algebra and other higher mathematics courses. The following activities are designed to help students differentiate between even and odd numbers and better understand the labels used for them.

Activity 1: Manipulative Stage

Materials
    40 small counters per pair of students (1-inch paper squares, small disks, or
       square tiles)
    Worksheet 1-2a
    Paper and regular pencil

Procedure
1. Give each pair of students a set of 40 counters (for example, 1-inch paper squares, small disks, or square tiles) and two copies of Worksheet 1-2a.

2. The worksheet contains several sets of four different numbers per set (two even and two odd, two large and two small) from 1 to 40. Assign each set to several different pairs of students.

3. For each number assigned to a pair of students, the students should try to arrange that quantity of counters or tiles in exactly *two* equal rows, if possible. Consider a row as going from left to right for this activity.

4. After all numbers have been built with the tiles, ask students to report which of their numbers made two equal rows and which made two unequal rows. Record their numbers in the appropriate column on the classroom board under the headings: "Equal Rows" and "Unequal Rows." Students should also record all reported numbers in the table on Worksheet 1-2a. Do not mention the ideas of *even* and *odd* at this time.

5. Because one tile cannot be arranged in *two* equal rows, the number 1 must be recorded in the "Unequal Rows" column, even though it makes only one row.

6. After all numbers have been recorded, ask students for their observations about the numbers in the different columns. Accept whatever reasonable ideas they might have at this time. Do not rush them to notice the digits in the ones place value position at this time. (Possible observation: In the "Unequal Rows" column for these numbers, one row of tiles had one more tile than the other row had.)

7. Guide students through building arrangements for two examples (5 and 6) before allowing them to build their own assigned set of numbers.

Here are examples for the numbers 5 and 6. Have students draw pictures of the arrangements on Worksheet 1-2a, then record the number 6 in their table under "Equal Rows" and record the number 5 under "Unequal Rows." Remind students that a "row" is considered as going from left to right in this activity.

Here are samples of built, then drawn, tile arrangements:

Two equal rows for 6   Two unequal rows for 5

Answer Key for Worksheet 1-2a Table
Equal Rows: 6, 4, 20, 2, 26, 8, 30, 10, 24, 12, 36, 14, 28, 32, 16, 34
Unequal Rows: 5, 7, 31, 11, 35, 17, 23, 1, 29, 3, 27, 15, 21, 9, 19, 13, 37

16

WORKSHEET 1-2a

Building Equal Rows

Name _____

Date _____

Use small counters or tiles to build a two-row arrangement for each number in one of the given sets. The teacher will assign the set for you to build. Try to build two *equal* rows of tiles each time. On the back of the worksheet, draw a picture of each tile arrangement you build, then record the numbers you used in the appropriate columns of the table.

Examples: 5   6

Row 1   _____   _____

Row 2   _____   _____

Possible Sets to Build:

a. 4, 20, 7, 31   e. 12, 36, 3, 27

b. 2, 26, 11, 35   f. 14, 28, 15, 21

c. 8, 30, 17, 23   g. 2, 32, 9, 19

d. 10, 24, 1, 29   h. 16, 34, 13, 37

Equal Rows	Unequal Rows

Activity 2: Pictorial Stage

Materials

Inch grid paper (8.5 inches by 11 inches)
Colored pencils, regular pencils
Scissors
Tape
Worksheet 1-2a (completed in Activity 1)
Worksheet 1-2b

Procedure

1. Give each pair of students a sheet of inch grid paper, a colored pencil, scissors, and tape. Also give each student a copy of Worksheet 1-2b.

2. Assign each pair of students two different numbers from 10 to 50 (one even and one odd but not consecutive numbers). If possible, give each pair one small number and one large number to make the task easier. Here are suggested number pairs to use: (20, 49), (14, 43), (12, 41), (30, 17), (22, 47), (38, 19), (42, 21), (44, 11), (46, 15), (50, 25), (48, 23), (16, 39).

3. Each assigned number should be colored on the grid paper as two equal rows of squares, if possible. Grid pieces may have to be taped together in order to make some of the larger numbers. The represented number should be written on the colored grid spaces.

4. The arrangement of grid spaces should then be cut out and taped on the board under the appropriate headings: "Equal Rows" and "Unequal Rows." Do not try to order the cutouts by size; allow random placement.

5. Once all the paper cutouts are taped in their proper columns, ask for observations again. Students should notice that all those in the "Unequal Rows" column have one extra square on the end. Tell students that since the cutouts in the "Equal Rows" column do not have the extra square, they will represent *even* numbers (their rows come out "even"). Thus, the numbers represented in the other column (unequal) will *not* be *even* numbers; therefore they will be called *odd* numbers (the extra square makes an "odd-sized" row).

6. Now write the number name beside each paper cutout on the board. Students should also record each of these numbers in the proper column of the table on Worksheet 1-2b. Record in the order shown on the board.

7. Have students take out their completed copies of Worksheet 1-2a. Ask students what they notice about the numbers in the tables of Worksheet 1-2a and Worksheet 1-2b. If necessary, call attention to the different digits in the tens and ones places. Ideally, students will notice that, for numbers in both columns of the two tables combined, the digit in the tens place can be 0 through 5 (since they only went to 50 with their numbers in the two activities), but the newly named *even* numbers have 0, 2, 4, 6, or 8 in the ones place, whereas the *odd* numbers have 1, 3, 5, 7, or 9 in the ones place. Thus, the ones place is really the indicator for even and odd numbers. Have students record their ideas at the bottom of Worksheet 1-2b.

8. Guide students through two examples of coloring grid spaces, cutting the shapes out, taping them on the board, and writing the appropriate numbers beside the cutout shapes before allowing the students to color their assigned amounts.

The following are examples for the numbers 13 and 18 and the column headings where their cutouts will be placed and the numbers recorded:

Equal rows   Unequal rows

              18   13

Answer Key for Worksheet 1-2b
Even Numbers: (unordered in table) 18, 20, 14, 12, 30, 22, 38, 42, 44, 46, 50, 48, 16
Odd Numbers: (unordered in table) 13, 49, 43, 41, 17, 47, 19, 21, 11, 15, 25, 23, 39

WORKSHEET 1-2b
Sorting Even and Odd Numbers

Name _____

Date _____

After cutting out grid shapes for different whole numbers assigned by the teacher, then sorting them on the board, record each number in its correct column in the table below.

Equal Rows (Even Numbers)	Unequal Rows (Odd Numbers)

Describe in your own words how *even* numbers differ from *odd* numbers.

_____

_____

_____

_____

_____

_____

_____

_____

_____

Activity 3: Independent Practice

Materials
Worksheet 1-2c
Regular pencil
Calculators (optional)

Procedure
Students work independently to investigate numbers between 50 and 999 to see which of those amounts can be separated into two equal groups. This will allow students to see that in both even and odd numbers the tens and hundreds places can have 0 through 9. Discuss the idea that separating a quantity of counters into two equal rows can be represented by applying the written algorithm for division to the given number, using 2 as the divisor. If the two rows are equal, the remainder for the algorithm will be 0. If the two rows are unequal, the remainder will be 1. Since this is a discovery lesson, allow students to use the calculator if their division skills are weak. Any needed algorithmic review should occur at another time.

Answer Key for Worksheet 1-2c
1. Even: 98, 86, 574, 128, 432, 700, 980; Odd: 65, 73, 751, 607, 831, 319, 245

2. Answers will vary.

3. Answers will vary.

Possible Testing Errors That May Occur for This Objective
- A set of *consecutive* numbers such as 12, 13, 14, 15 is selected because students do not know the meaning of *even* and *odd* numbers.

- Students know that the two sets of numbers (0, 2, 4, 6, . . . and 1, 3, 5, 7, . . .) are different from each other, but they are confused as to the appropriate label for each set. For example, when the test item asks for a set of *odd* numbers to be identified, students select a set of *even* numbers such as 8, 10, 12, 14. Vocabulary needs to be emphasized.

- When students are asked to select an individual number that represents an *odd* number, they incorrectly select 0 as the *odd* number.

WORKSHEET 1-2c   Name _____

Larger Even and Odd Numbers   Date _____

1. Use division to decide whether each number listed below is even or odd. Write the correct name (even or odd) beside each number.

        98   432

        65   607

        73   700

        86   831

        574   319

        751   245

        128   980

2. Now look at the digits in the hundreds, tens, and ones place value positions of the listed numbers. What do you notice? Describe in your own words a "rule" for deciding when a number is even or odd.

_____

_____

_____

_____

3. Practice: (a) List three *even* numbers between 165 and 483.

_____

_____

_____

(b) List three *odd* numbers between 298 and 352.

_____

_____

_____

Objective 3
Form a generalization of the pattern found in a given ordered set (or sequence) of whole numbers, then generate more members of that set using that generalization.

Discussion
Students need much practice with finding and extending patterns in sequences, particularly as the sequences occur within tables of values. Working with tables of values will provide excellent readiness for the study of functions in algebra in later years. The following activities offer such needed practice. Section 3, Objective 1 will provide additional experience in applying tables to solve word problems.

Activity 1: Manipulative Stage

Materials
> 100 square tiles or 1-inch paper squares for every four students
> Worksheet 1-3a (two-column table)
> Regular pencil

Procedure
1. Give each group of four students a set of 100 square tiles, and give each individual student a copy of Worksheet 1-3a.

2. Have each group build a simple, flat design several times, increasing the tiles according to the same pattern or method each time to gradually enlarge the design. Students should complete the table on Worksheet 1-3a as they build, each time recording which design it is (or position in the sequence) and how many tiles are in the design.

3. After they have built the first four designs, ask them if they can predict how the sixth design will look. They should then continue to build their designs up to the sixth design in order to confirm their prediction.

4. Ask them how the numbers are changing in the left column (increase by 1 each time) and in the right column (increase by 3 each time for the three-wing design and by 4 each time for the tower design shown below).

5. Guide students through the building of the first sequence presented next and the recording of the amounts in the first table on Worksheet 1-3a. Then have them build the second sequence, using the tower design.

   For the first sequence, have students build the following three shapes (three-wing designs) in order with their tiles:

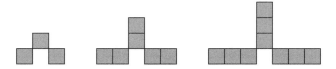

Students should build the fourth design (four tiles per wing), then predict the sixth design. They should then confirm their prediction by building the fifth and the sixth designs. The finished table should show 1, 2, 3, 4, 5, and 6 in the left column and 3, 6, 9, 12, 15, and 18 in the right column.

Ask students how the numbers are changing as they go down the left column. (The numbers are increasing by 1 each time.) Then ask how the numbers are changing as they go down the right column. (The numbers are increasing by 3 each time.) So the next design will need three more tiles to build it than the previous design needed.

Now have students build the second sequence, using a tower design that increases by 4 tiles each time. Here are the first three designs for this second sequence:

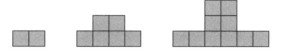

Answer Key for Worksheet 1-3a

1. 3-wing: left column—1, 2, 3, 4, 5, 6

     right column—3, 6, 9, 12, 15, 18

2. Tower: left column—1, 2, 3, 4, 5, 6

     right column—2, 6, 10, 14, 18, 22

WORKSHEET 1-3a   Name _____

Building Sequences of Shapes   Date _____

Follow your teacher's instructions to complete each table below as you build different shapes according to a pattern.

1.

NUMBER OF DESIGN	NUMBER OF TILES

2.

NUMBER OF DESIGN	NUMBER OF TILES

Activity 2: Pictorial Stage

Materials

Worksheet 1-3b (tables)
Regular paper and pencils

Procedure

1. After students have built several sequences of designs with the tiles, have students work with partners to draw several new sequences on their own paper. Give each student a copy of Worksheet 1-3b.

2. Follow the "predict-confirm" procedure described in the Manipulative Stage. Draw three designs of a sequence on the board for students to copy on their own papers, then extend to the sixth design.

3. For each completed sequence, students should complete a table on Worksheet 1-3b.

4. When students are finished with each sequence, ask about the changes in each column (or each row) of the table.

5. Guide students through drawing the first sequence and completing the table before having them continue with the other sequences.

For the first sequence, consider a real-world situation involving shelves and books in a bookcase. Have students draw simple diagrams to represent the objects. In this example, the first "set," or 1 shelf, consists of 4 books. Each new set must increase by 4 books over the previous set. The top row of the table will show "Number of Shelves," so 1 will be the first entry and 2 the second entry. The bottom row will show "Total Books," so 4 will be the first entry there and 8 the second entry. The numbers in the top row of the table will increase by 1 each time, and the numbers in the bottom row will increase by 4 each time. Here are the first three "sets" shown as diagrams ordered from left to right:

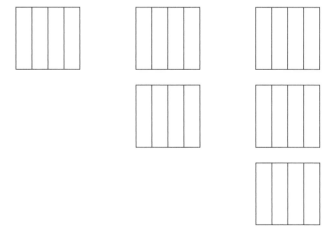

Here are three more sequences (with their first three possible designs) to use for exercises 2, 3, and 4 on Worksheet 1-3b:

2. Number of Clowns vs. Total Balloons (1 balloon per clown)

3. Number of Vehicles vs. Number of Wheels (3 wheels per vehicle)

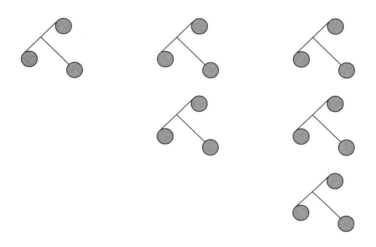

4. Number of Children vs. Number of Cookies (2 cookies per child)

Answer Key for Worksheet 1-3b

1. Top: 1, 2, 3, 4, 5, 6; Bottom: 4, 8, 12, 16, 20, 24

2. Top: 1, 2, 3, 4, 5, 6; Bottom: 1, 2, 3, 4, 5, 6

3. Left: 1, 2, 3, 4, 5, 6; Right: 3, 6, 9, 12, 15, 18

4. Left: 1, 2, 3, 4, 5, 6; Right: 2, 4, 6, 8, 10, 12

WORKSHEET 1-3b

Drawing Sequences

Name _____

Date _____

Follow your teacher's instructions to complete each table below as you draw different shapes or diagrams according to a pattern.

1.

Number of Shelves						
Total Books						

2.

Number of Clowns						
Total Balloons						

3.

Number of Vehicles	Number of Wheels

4.

Number of Children	Number of Cookies

Activity 3: Independent Practice

Materials
  Worksheet 1-3c (tables)
  Regular pencils

Procedure
Students work independently to complete the number sequences and tables on Worksheet 1-3c. Encourage them to look for how the numbers are changing in each row (or column of a table), then use that information to find the missing values.

Answer Key for Worksheet 1-3c
  1. A. 2, 4, 6, 8, 10, 12; B. 3, 6, 9, 12, 15, 18

  2. A. 1, 5, 9, 13, 17, 21; B. 4, 11, 18, 25, 32, 39

  3. Left: 1, 2, 3, 4, 5, 6; Right: 4, 8, 12, 16, 20, 24

  4. Left: 1, 2, 3, 4, 5, 6; Right: 5, 10, 15, 20, 25, 30

Possible Testing Errors That May Occur for This Objective
  * The rate at which the first few numbers in the sequence have changed is not held constant to generate new terms of the sequence. For example, in the given sequence 3, 8, 13, . . ., the rate of change is 5 for the first three terms, but the student uses a rate of 7 to find 20 as the fourth term instead of 18.

  * Only the first new entry for a given sequence is found when the test item asks for the second new entry instead. For example, in the sequence 3, 5, 7, . . ., the student selects the fourth term (9) as the answer instead of the required fifth term (11).

  * The next new entry for a sequence is found by adding 1 to the value of the previous term, even though the rate of change for the first few terms is greater than 1. For example, the rate of change for 5, 8, 11, 14, . . . is 3, but the student selects 15 as the next term after 14.

WORKSHEET 1-3c

Finding Changes in Sequences

Name _____

Date _____

Look for patterns and complete the number sequences in items 1 and 2.

1. A. 2, 4, 6,____,____,____

    B. 3, 6, 9,____,____,____

2. A. 1, 5, 9,____,____,____

    B. 4, 11, 18,____,____,____

In items 3 and 4, find how the numbers change in each column of the table, then complete the blanks with the correct numbers.

3.

Number of Cars	Number of People
1	4
2	8
3	12
5	
	24

4.

Number of Barrels	Number of Gallons
1	5
2	10
	15
	20
5	

Objective 4
Round whole numbers to the nearest ten, hundred, or thousand.

Discussion
Students have great difficulty remembering the rule that is commonly given in the class-room for rounding whole numbers to a given place value. The skill of rounding is important when students need to estimate the answer to a particular computation; they must first round, then apply mental arithmetic to the rounded numbers to obtain the desired estimate. The following activities will help students develop their own rule for the rounding process.

Activity 1: Manipulative Stage

Materials
> 80 small counters in one color (color A)
> 30 small counters in another color (color B) for each pair of students
> Building Mat 1-4a
> Worksheet 1-4a
> Regular pencil

Procedure
1. Have students work in pairs to round numbers to the nearest ten, hundred, or thousand. Give each pair a copy of Building Mat 1-4a and two sets of small counters: 80 in color A and 30 in color B. All the counters should be the same size.

2. For practice, partners should take turns placing counters (color A) in the different spaces within a row on the mat to represent 3-digit or 4-digit numbers, specifically, numbers from 100 to 7,000. These practice numbers should be written on the board for students to build on their mats. For example, to show 3,275 in the first row of the building mat, students should place 3 counters in the thousands column, 2 counters in the hundreds column, 7 counters in the tens column, and 5 ones in the ones column.

3. After students are comfortable with showing individual numbers on the mat, have them build each number listed on Worksheet 1-4a on their mats, using color A counters, and round that number to the stated place value. In each case, they must decide how many *extra* ones, tens, or hundreds counters (color B) are needed to increase the given number to the next higher required place value amount. They must also decide how many *original* ones, tens, or hundreds (color A) must be removed from the building mat to decrease the given number to the nearest lower required place value amount. If the value of the extra counters (color B) needed is less than the value of the counters to be removed, the given number will be rounded up. If the value to be removed is less, the given number will be rounded down. If the two values are equal, we will agree to round up.

4. Guide students through each exercise on Worksheet 1-4a. Once students decide whether to round a number up or down, they should record the rounded result in the appropriate blank on the worksheet.

Here is the procedure to follow for rounding 2,451—the first number listed on Worksheet 1-4a—to the nearest hundred. Ask students to show this number on their mat in the *middle* row with their color A counters. After the number has been built on the mat, ask how many hundreds are really contained in this number. Ideally, students will recognize that there are actually 24 hundreds, but 20 of the hundreds have been traded for the 2 thousands. Discuss the idea that their number on the mat is really more than 24 hundreds but still less than 25 hundreds.

Have students place color A counters for 2 thousands and 5 hundreds in the *top* row of the mat to show the 25 hundreds simplified, then place color A counters for 2 thousands and 4 hundreds in the *bottom* row of the mat to show the 24 hundreds simplified. Students now need to find which amount of hundreds 2,451 is nearest—the 24 hundreds or the 25 hundreds.

Ask them how many tens and ones are needed to increase 2,451 to 2,500—the next hundreds number. Remind them that a trade from ones to tens might be involved. Students should place 9 counters (in color B) in the ones column on or near the line between the top and middle rows. The 9 ones and the single one already in the middle row could be traded for a new ten, but do not remove the ones counters; students must remember the new ten but not show it on the mat. They must be able to see the *extra* ones later. Looking at the 5 tens in the middle row and remembering the new ten, students will need 4 more tens to produce a trade from tens to hundreds. Have students place 4 new counters (in color B) in the tens column on the line between the top and middle rows of the mat. Now students should count the extra counters (in color B) added to the mat: 4 tens and 9 ones. This means that the original number is 49 away from the next higher hundreds number—2,500.

At this point, ask students what color A counters would need to be removed from the middle row to change the original number to the lower hundreds number—2,400. Only the 5 tens and the single one would need to be removed; that is, 2,451 is 51 away from the lower hundreds number. Thus 2,451 is *closer* to the next higher hundreds number, 2,500. Have students complete the statement on Worksheet 1-4a: "2,451 rounds to the hundreds number, *2,500.*"

Repeat this procedure with other numbers on the worksheet, some that will round up and others that will round down. Here is an example of the completed building mat for rounding 2,451 to the nearest hundreds number.

THOUSANDS	HUNDREDS	TENS	ONES
☐ ☐	☐ ☐ ☐ ☐ ☐		▪ ▪ ▪
☐ ☐	☐ ☐ ☐ ☐	▪ ▪ ▪ ▪ ☐ ☐ ☐ ☐ ☐	▪ ▪ ▪ ▪ ▪ ▪ ☐
☐ ☐	☐ ☐ ☐ ☐		

Appearance of counters on mat after extra counters added.

After students are comfortable with rounding *to* the nearest hundreds number, reverse the question. Have them show 3,200 on the top row of the building mat, then ask them to show some number in the middle row on the mat that would round up to 3,200. Have them give reasons for their choices. Repeat this process by having them show 2,500 on the bottom row of the mat. Ask students to show some number on the middle row that would round down to 2,500. Practice rounding to tens or to thousands in a similar manner.

Answer Key for Worksheet 1-4a

1. 2,500	2. 1,700	3. 380	4. 7,000	5. 750
6. 4,000	7. 600	8. 4,360	9. 100	10. 5,070

BUILDING MAT 1-4a

THOUSANDS	HUNDREDS	TENS	ONES

34

WORKSHEET 1-4a

Name _____

Rounding Whole Numbers
on a Building Mat

Date _____

Round each number by building it with counters on the building mat and following your teacher's directions. Complete each sentence by recording the correct answer in the blank.

1. 2,451 rounds to the hundreds number, _____.

2. 1,736 rounds to the hundreds number, _____.

3. 382 rounds to the tens number, _____.

4. 6,500 rounds to the thousands number, _____.

5. 749 rounds to the tens number, _____.

6. 4,380 rounds to the thousands number, _____.

7. 593 rounds to the hundreds number, _____.

8. 4,358 rounds to the tens number, _____.

9. 146 rounds to the hundreds number, _____.

10. 5,073 rounds to the tens number, _____.

Activity 2: Pictorial Stage

Materials

   Worksheet 1-4b
   Regular pencil and red pencil

Procedure

1. Give each student two copies of Worksheet 1-4b and a red pencil. Have students work with partners, but each student will complete her or his own copy of Worksheet 1-4b. The leftmost blank above each frame should be used to number each exercise in order as it is worked.

2. Have students write the following in the exercise blanks on their worksheets (you may fill these in before class):

   1. 3,547, hundred   5. 2,615, thousand
   2. 638, hundred   6. 464, ten
   3. 1,459, ten   7. 5,954, hundred
   4. 750, hundred   8. 4,050, thousand

3. Students should represent each number on the worksheet by drawing small circles in regular pencil in the middle row of the base 10 frame shown below that number.

4. Students should follow the same procedure used in the Manipulative Stage; instead of adding on extra counters, they will draw extra circles on the frame with red pencil. They will record the added value at the right of the top row of the frame. They will then record the value to be removed at the right of the bottom row of the frame.

5. After comparing the amount to be added with the amount to be removed, students will decide which way to round the original number and draw a red path around the small circles, representing the selected rounded amount on the frame. Remind students that if the two amounts are equal, they should round up. The new number will then be recorded in the rightmost blank above the frame.

6. Guide students through the drawing procedure for the first exercise on the worksheet, then have them continue with their partners to complete the other exercises.

   For the first exercise, consider the number 3,547, to round to the nearest hundreds number. Students should draw small circles in regular pencil on the middle row of the first frame on Worksheet 1-4b to represent 3 thousands, 5 hundreds, 4 tens, and 7 ones. Small circles for the next higher hundreds number (3,600) should be drawn on the top row of the frame, and small circles for the nearest lower hundreds number (3,500) should be drawn on the bottom row.

To increase 3,547 to the next higher hundreds number, small circles for 5 tens and 3 ones should be drawn in red pencil between the top and the middle rows of the frame. "+53" should be recorded at the right of the top row of the frame. To change 3,547 to the lower hundreds number (3,500), only 4 tens and 7 ones would need to be removed. "−47" should be recorded at the right of the bottom row of the frame.

Since 47 is less than 53, the original number (3,547) is *closer* to 3,500 than to 3,600. Therefore, it needs to round down to 3,500. Students should draw a red path around the small circles in the bottom row of the frame and record the new number above the frame. The completed frame and blanks are shown here:

1. 3,547 rounded to the nearest hundred is 3,500.

THOUSANDS	HUNDREDS	TENS	ONES	
○○○	○○○ ○○○	●●●●●	●●●	**+53**
○○○	○○○ ○○	○○○○	○○○ ○○○○	
○○○	○○○ ○○			**−47**

After students are comfortable with rounding *to* the nearest hundreds number pictorially, reverse the question. Have them draw 3,000 in the top row of a blank drawing frame, then ask them to draw circles to show some number in the middle row on the mat that would round *up* to the 3,000. Have them give reasons for their choices. Repeat this process by having them draw 1,900 in the bottom row of another blank drawing frame. Ask students to show some number in the middle row that would round *down* to 1,900. Practice rounding to tens or to thousands in a similar manner.

Answer Key for Worksheet 1-4b

1. 3,500	2. 600	3. 1,460	4. 800
5. 3,000	6. 460	7. 6,000	8. 4,000

WORKSHEET 1-4b

Name _____

Drawing Diagrams to Round
Whole Numbers

Date _____

Follow your teacher's directions to round numbers, using the frames provided below.
Fill in the blanks with the results of each exercise.

_____ _____ rounded to the nearest _____ is _____.

Thousands	Hundreds	Tens	Ones

_____ _____ rounded to the nearest _____ is _____.

Thousands	Hundreds	Tens	Ones

38

WORKSHEET 1-4b Continued   Name _____

                                        Date _____

_____ _____ rounded to the nearest _____ is _____.

Thousands	Hundreds	Tens	Ones

_____ _____ rounded to the nearest _____ is _____.

Thousands	Hundreds	Tens	Ones

Activity 3: Independent Practice

Materials
Worksheet 1-4c

Regular pencil

Procedure
Students work with partners on Worksheet 1-4c to explore the rounding of whole numbers further. Ideally, they will discover the rule for rounding that is used in the elementary school curriculum: when rounding to a certain place value, only the digit in the adjacent lesser place value position needs to be considered. Other place value positions to the right do not matter. In the previous two activities, this idea was not presented. After students have completed the worksheet, have them share their conclusions.

Answer Key for Worksheet 1-4c
1. First four numbers round to 3,000; last five round to 4,000; least number to round up is 3,500.

2. 500

3. Hundreds; 5 through 9

4. Tens

5. Ones

Possible Testing Errors That May Occur for This Objective
- If a number is to be rounded to a certain place value, some students will simply change the given digits in the *lesser* place value positions to zeros, regardless of their values. For example, if rounding to the nearest hundred, they would incorrectly change the ones and tens digits in 1,377 to zeros, rounding the number down to 1,300 instead of up to 1,400.

- Students may just change the ones digit in the original number to zero but not actually do the rounding required. For example, 2,485 might be changed to 2,480 instead of being rounded to the nearest thousand.

- The original number may be correctly rounded to a different place value than the one required. Instead of rounding 876 to the nearest ten, for example, students might round it to the nearest hundred—900.

40

WORKSHEET 1-4c   Name _____

Applying Rounding to
Whole Numbers   Date _____

Work with a partner to complete this worksheet. You will need a red pencil.

1. In the following list of numbers, round each number to the nearest thousand by finding which thousands number is *closer* to the given number. In each given number, underline the hundreds, tens, and ones digits with a red pencil; the first number is already underlined. In the rightmost column, write whether the given number was rounded up or down.

Number		Rounded to Nearest Thousand	Rounded Up or Down?
3,340	→	_____	_____
3,375	→	_____	_____
3,484	→	_____	_____
3,499	→	_____	_____
3,500	→	_____	_____
3,501	→	_____	_____
3,575	→	_____	_____
3,684	→	_____	_____
3,699	→	_____	_____

In the list, what is the *least* number that rounds *up*? _____

2. Fill in the blanks with the *least* 3-digit whole number that will cause the completed number to round up to 9,000.

            8, ____ ____ ____

3. When rounding to the nearest thousand, which place value position seems to be the best one to test for whether to round up or round down? What digit values are needed in that position to cause a number to round up?

_____

_____

WORKSHEET 1-4c Continued

Name _____

Date _____

4. Which place value position is best to test when rounding to hundreds?

    _____

    _____

5. Which place value position is best to test when rounding to tens?

    _____

    _____

Objective 5
Represent a proper fraction with various models (physical, pictorial).

Discussion
The concept of relating part to whole is quite difficult for young students. In particular, the ratio format commonly used to name fractional amounts is often confusing to them. Many hands-on experiences are needed, especially in the modeling of word problems.

Activity 1: Manipulative Stage

Materials
Set of 40 colored square tiles or disks per pair of students (two different colors, 20 per color)
Worksheet 1-5a
Regular pencil

Procedure
1. Give each pair of students a set of 40 colored square tiles or disks (two different colors, 20 per color). Tiles and disks are available commercially, or you may use cutout 1-inch paper squares. Also give each student a copy of Worksheet 1-5a, which contains several word problems involving fractions.

2. Each story problem on the worksheet will provide the description of a whole and some fractional part of that whole. Discuss each problem, and have students model the situation with their tiles.

3. As each result is found, students should record their findings as word sentences on their own worksheets. At the Manipulative Stage, use *word* names to describe fractional parts, for example, 3-*fourths* instead of $\frac{3}{4}$ of the whole.

Here is the first exercise on Worksheet 1-5a to consider: "Maury made 12 hamburgers for her party. Eight of the hamburgers were eaten by her guests. What fraction name describes the portion of hamburgers eaten?"

Ask how many hamburgers were in the original set (12). Students should place 12 tiles in one color (for example, red) on the desktop. Ask how many of the hamburgers were eaten (8). Have the students cover 8 of the 12 red tiles with tiles of the second color (for example, blue) to show the amount eaten.

Then, because 8 out of 12 red tiles are covered, the fraction 8-twelfths describes the fractional part of the set that was eaten. Students should write the following sentence on their own worksheets:

"8 hamburgers equal 8-twelfths of 12 hamburgers."

Here is an example of 8 out of 12 tiles being covered:

Answer Key for Worksheet 1-5a

1. 8 hamburgers equal 8-twelfths of 12 hamburgers.

2. 11 broken chairs equal 11-twentieths of 20 chairs.

3. 5 red sectors equal 5-eighths of 8 sectors.

4. 10 eggs equal 10-fifteenths of 15 eggs.

5. 5 uneaten cupcakes equal 5-ninths of 9 cupcakes.

44

WORKSHEET 1-5a   Name _____

Building Parts of a Whole   Date _____

Read and discuss each word problem that follows. Use tiles to build the fractional amount mentioned in the word problem, then write a word sentence to describe the amount.

1. Maury made 12 hamburgers for her party. Eight of the hamburgers were eaten by her guests. What fraction name describes the portion of hamburgers eaten?

    _____

    _____

    _____

2. There are 20 chairs in the classroom. Eleven of the chairs are broken. What fractional part of the total chairs is broken?

    _____

    _____

    _____

3. A circular game spinner contains eight equal sectors. Five of the sectors are red, and the other sectors are green. What fraction of the total spinner sectors is red?

    _____

    _____

    _____

4. There are 15 eggs in a bowl. Ten of the eggs will be used for baking cakes. What fraction of the bowl of eggs will be used for the cakes?

    _____

    _____

    _____

5. Nine cupcakes were on the tray. Luis and his friends ate four of the cupcakes. What fractional part of the original cupcakes was left on the tray?

    _____

    _____

    _____

Activity 2: Pictorial Stage

Materials

Worksheet 1-5b
Regular pencil

Procedure

1. After students have practiced with the tiles to model fractions and to name those fractions, have them draw diagrams to show fractions instead. Give each student a copy of Worksheet 1-5b containing several word problems and with drawing space left between problems.

2. Repeat the procedure followed in the Manipulative Stage, but the recording format will be different. The drawings (squares) should look like the tiles used earlier, but instead of placing new tiles on top of the original tiles to show the parts needed, an X will be marked on those squares that are identified for some special reason. Encourage students to draw their squares to look as "equal" in size as possible.

3. The recording of the results should be written below or beside the drawing on the worksheet. The ratio format for fractions will now be used. The total mentioned in the word problem should always be included with the fraction name.

4. Guide students through the first exercise on Worksheet 1-5b before allowing them to draw models on their own for the remaining exercises on the worksheet. When all students are finished, have them share their results.

The first exercise on Worksheet 1-5b is as follows: "Marion plans to ride his bicycle 10 miles today. After riding 4 miles, he stops to rest. What fraction of the total trip still remains for him to do?"

Here is how the situation might be represented. Ten squares are drawn for the 10 miles, and 4 of those squares are marked with an X to show the 4 miles completed. The 6 remaining unmarked squares represent the miles of the trip Marion still must do. A sentence is written beside the drawing to express the result.

$\frac{6}{10}$ of the 10-mile trip needs to be done.

Answer Key for Worksheet 1-5b (shapes other than squares might be used)

1. ⊠ ⊠ ⊠ ⊠ ☐ ☐ ☐ ☐ ☐
$\frac{6}{10}$ of the 10-mile trip needs to be done.

2. ⊠ ⊠ ⊠ ⊠ ⊠ ☐ ☐
$\frac{5}{7}$ of the 7 spoons are polished.

3. ⊠ ⊠ ⊠ ⊠ ☐ ☐ ☐ ☐ ☐ ☐ ☐
$\frac{4}{12}$ of the 12 runners are from Carter Elementary School.

4. ⊠ ⊠ ⊠ ⊠ ⊠ ⊠ ☐ ☐ ☐ ☐ ☐ ☐ ☐ ☐
Wakoto and her friends make $\frac{6}{14}$ of the 14 children.

WORKSHEET 1-5b

Drawing Models for Fractions

Name _____

Date _____

Draw pictures to represent fractional amounts in the following word problems. Write a word sentence about each fraction shown.

1. Marion plans to ride his bicycle 10 miles today. After riding 4 miles, he stops to rest. What fraction of the total trip still remains for him to do?

2. Esperanza has seven silver spoons she has collected while on different vacations. She wants to polish the spoons and has already polished five of them. What fraction of the seven spoons has she already polished?

3. Twelve students will run in the school race today. Four students are from Carter Elementary School. What fraction of the runners are from Carter Elementary School?

4. Fourteen children will be allowed to attend a special preview of a new movie. Wakoto and five of her friends will go to the preview. What fractional part of the total children at the preview will she and her friends represent?

Activity 3: Independent Practice

Materials
Worksheet 1-5c
Regular pencil

Procedure
Have students work independently to write or apply fraction names for amounts described in diagrams or word problems on Worksheet 1-5c. When all have finished, have them share their results.

Answer Key for Worksheet 1-5c

1. $\frac{4}{7}$ of 7 triangles are shaded.

2. $\frac{4}{6}$ of the whole bar is not shaded.

3. $\frac{2}{10}$ of the 10 pencils are red.

4. 6 cookies total were in the package.

5. Models will vary. Sample: ●○●●

Possible Testing Errors That May Occur for This Objective

- The number of *shaded* parts is compared to the total number of parts in a diagram when the test item asks for *unshaded* parts to be compared to the total instead.

- The number of *shaded* parts (as numerator) is compared to the number of *unshaded* parts (as denominator) instead of being compared to the total number of parts as the denominator.

- The positions of the numerator and the denominator are reversed. The total number of parts (as numerator) is compared to the number of shaded parts (as denominator).

- A pictorial model with unequal parts is matched to a fraction name.

WORKSHEET 1-5c   Name _____

Naming Parts of a Whole or Total   Date _____

Write a word sentence to answer each question that follows. Be sure to include the total or whole amount in any fraction name given.

1. What fraction of the triangles is shaded?

▲▲△△▲△▲

_____

2. How much of the bar is not shaded?

_____

3. Claire has ten pencils in her school box. Five pencils are yellow and two pencils are red. What fractional part of the ten pencils is red?

_____

4. Sam has four cookies, which represent 4-sixths of the total cookies in the original package. How many cookies in all were in the package before it was opened?

_____

5. Draw a diagram in which 3-fourths of the whole diagram is shaded. Remember that all the fourths must be equal in size.

Objective 6
Find equivalent fractions that are less than one.

Discussion
The concept of relating part to whole is quite difficult for young students. In addition, with equivalent fractions they must be able to trade or rename that part and its whole in another way. That is, they need to know how to change the original fraction name to an equivalent fraction name. Many hands-on experiences are needed, especially in the modeling of word problems.

Activity 1: Manipulative Stage

Materials
Set of 40 colored square tiles or disks per pair of students (two different colors, 20 per color)
Worksheet 1-6a
Regular pencil

Procedure
1. Give each pair of students a set of 40 colored square tiles or disks (two different colors, 20 per color), and give each student a copy of Worksheet 1-6a. Tiles and disks are available commercially, or you may use cutout 1-inch paper squares.

2. The worksheet contains several word problems. Each story provides the description of a whole and some fractional part of that whole. Discuss each problem and have students model the situation with their tiles. For two to three problems, students should model only the original fraction in the story.

3. After some practice, have them begin to reduce that fraction to a simpler form (smaller numerator and denominator) or trade or group the given parts differently for a higher count (larger numerator and denominator), depending on the situation. An example of each type will be discussed below.

4. Students should record their findings as word sentences on their worksheets. At the Manipulative Stage, use *word* names to describe fractional parts; for example, 3-*fourths* instead of $\frac{3}{4}$ of the whole.

Here is the first exercise on Worksheet 1-6a to discuss with your students: "Tory made 12 hot dogs for her party. Two-thirds of the hot dogs were eaten by her guests. What other fraction name describes the portion of hot dogs eaten?"

Ask how many hot dogs were in the original set (12). Students should place 12 tiles in one color (for example, red) on the desktop. Ask what portion of the hot dogs was eaten ($\frac{2}{3}$). Do not ask "how many?" because that implies the quantity—8 hot dogs.

Students should separate the 12 tiles into 3 equal groups of red tiles; as a result, 4 connected red tiles will be in each group. Have them cover 2 groups of these red tiles with tiles of the second color (for example, blue) to show the portion eaten. Then, since 8 out of 12 red tiles are covered, the fraction 8-twelfths also describes the fractional part of the set that was eaten. Students should write the following sentence below Exercise 1 on their worksheets: "2-thirds of 12 hot dogs is equal to 8-twelfths of 12 hot dogs."

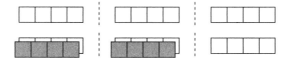

After modeling several stories in which the given simpler fraction is renamed with a larger numerator and a larger denominator, have students begin to reduce some fractions. Exercise 4 on Worksheet 1-6a is an example of the reduction process. Consider the situation: "Eight-twelfths of 12 pencils total have been sold at the school store. What is a simpler fraction name for the portion of pencils sold?"

Students should place 12 red tiles on the desktop, then cover 8 of them with blue tiles. This shows that 8-twelfths of the total pencils have been sold. Ask students if the covered tiles can be grouped 2 at a time and if the uncovered tiles can also be grouped the same way (yes, there will be 4 groups of 2 covered tiles each, blue on red, and 2 groups of 2 uncovered red tiles each). Ask if the blue-topped group and the red group could each be grouped 3 tiles at a time (neither set of tiles can be grouped 3 at a time).

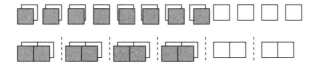

Ask if both can be grouped 4 tiles at a time (yes, the 8 covered or blue-topped tiles can make 2 groups of 4, and the 4 uncovered red tiles can make 1 group of 4). Have students now move their tiles into the larger groups of 4 tiles each, making 2 groups with the covered tiles and 1 group with the uncovered red tiles. Notice that *all* 12 original red tiles are now in 3 groups of 4 red tiles each; 2 of the groups are topped with blue tiles. Discuss the idea that the pencils sold can now be compared to the total pencils by using groups of 4 each instead of counting *individual* pencils; that is, 2 *groups* of pencils out of a total of 3 *groups* of pencils were sold at the school store. A new fraction name for what was sold will be "2-thirds of the 12 pencils total."

Note that the earlier grouping by 2's also allows students to compare 4 groups of 2 covered tiles to a total of 6 groups of 2 tiles each, so "4-sixths of the 12 pencils" would also be a possibility for a new fraction name. Two-thirds and 4-sixths are both reduced forms of 8-twelfths; 2-thirds is just the simplest form. Tell students to look for the lowest possible numbers of groups (that is, the largest group size) when trying to form new groups. Always test for the group size in an orderly way: try groups of 2 tiles each, then groups of 3 tiles each, and so on.

Students should write a sentence below Exercise 4 on the worksheet to record both new fraction names: "8-twelfths of 12 pencils total equals 4-sixths or 2-thirds of 12 pencils."

Answer Key for Worksheet 1-6a

1. 2-thirds of 12 hot dogs is equal to 8-twelfths of 12 hot dogs.

2. 1-sixth of 18 stickers or 3-eighteenths of the stickers are sold.

3. 4-fifths of a 20-gallon container or 8-tenths of the container is filled with water.

4. 8-twelfths of 12 pencils total equals 4-sixths or 2-thirds of the 12 pencils.

5. 4-eighths of a pizza equals 2-fourths or 1-half of a pizza.

6. 5-sixths of a dozen eggs cannot be simplified to lower terms.

WORKSHEET 1-6a

Building Equivalent
Fractions with Tiles

Name _____

Date _____

Build with tiles to solve each exercise that follows. For each exercise, write a word sentence that describes the answer.

1. Tory made 12 hot dogs for her party. Two-thirds of the hot dogs were eaten by her guests. What other fraction name describes the portion of hot dogs eaten?

_____

_____

2. One-sixth of 18 school stickers were sold on the first day of school. What other fraction name tells the portion of stickers that were sold?

_____

_____

3. Only 4-fifths of a 20-gallon container is filled with water. How many tenths of the container is filled with water?

_____

_____

4. Eight-twelfths of 12 pencils total have been sold at the school store. What is a simpler fraction name for the portion of pencils sold?

_____

_____

5. Four-eighths of an 8-slice pizza remains on the buffet tray. What is a simpler fraction name for this uneaten portion of pizza?

_____

_____

6. Joel found 5-sixths of a dozen eggs in the refrigerator. Is there a simpler fraction name for this amount of eggs?

_____

_____

Activity 2: Pictorial Stage

Materials
> Worksheet 1-6b
> Regular pencil and red pencil

Procedure
1. After students have practiced with the tiles to model fractions and to rename those fractions, have them draw diagrams to show fractions instead. Give each student a red pencil and a copy of Worksheet 1-6b containing several word problems and drawing space between problems.

2. Repeat the procedure followed in the Manipulative Stage, but the recording format will be different. The drawings should look like the tiles used earlier, but instead of placing new tiles on top of the original tiles to show the part needed, an X will be marked on those squares that are identified for some special reason. New groups formed will be ringed in red pencil.

3. Some exercises on the worksheet will involve the reduction of a given fraction; others will ask for equivalent fractions that have larger numerators and larger denominators than the original fraction. One example of each type will be discussed below.

Here is the first exercise on Worksheet 1-6b: "Eight-twelfths of 12 cupcakes are eaten at a birthday party. What is the simplest fraction name for the part that is eaten?"

This exercise involves reduction of the given fraction. Students should draw 12 small squares on the worksheet, then make a large X inside each of 8 of the squares to show that 8 out of 12 cupcakes were eaten. Ask students if they can group the X-squares in pairs and then group the plain squares in pairs. (Yes, they can make 4 groups of 2 with the X-squares and 2 groups of 2 with the plain squares.) Lightly drawn tick marks can be made with pencil to show various groupings being tested. Ask if they can group the X-squares to have 3 squares in each group and similarly group the plain squares to have 3 per group. (No, they cannot group by three's.)

Now ask students to try to group the X-squares with 4 in each group and similarly group the plain squares with 4 in a group. (Yes, they will have 2 groups of 4 X-squares each and 1 group of 4 plain squares each.) Because there are only 4 plain squares total, no grouping size larger than 4 will be possible for the plain squares and the X-squares simultaneously.

Have students draw a red path around each group of 4 squares, as shown next. This will show the least number of groups possible when 8-twelfths of 12 cupcakes are eaten. In other words, because 2 groups out of the 3 groups ringed in red pencil contain all X-squares, we can say that $\frac{2}{3}$ of the 12 cupcakes have been eaten.

The recording of the results should be written below or beside the drawing on the worksheet. The ratio format for fractions will now be used, along with products that show the regrouping process used. Multiplication (to show the groupings) is recommended here, instead of the division often shown in elementary textbooks, because it is parallel to the format used in algebra later. Here is the recording for this particular diagram, where 2×4 represents 2 groups of 4 X-squares each and 3×4 represents 3 groups total of 4 squares per group.

$$\frac{8}{12} = \frac{2 \times 4}{3 \times 4} = \frac{2}{3} \text{ of the 12 cupcakes were eaten}$$

Exercise 2 on Worksheet 1-6b is an example of trading to a larger numerator and larger denominator:

"Tom gave 4-fifths of his 15 baseball cards to his friend, Rosie. What is another fraction name for the part he gave to Rosie?"

Have students draw 5 rings in red pencil on the worksheet, then draw equal amounts of small squares inside the rings, using a total of 15 squares. Three squares should be drawn inside each ring. Because 4 groups of baseball cards out of 5 groups total were given to Rosie, have students place a check mark next to 4 of the 5 red rings, then draw a large X inside each square found inside the checked red rings.

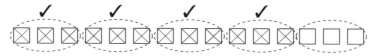

Twelve of the 15 squares are now marked with X, so we can say that $\frac{12}{15}$ of the total baseball cards were given to Rosie. Here is the final recording for this diagram, using 3 squares per group:

$$\frac{4}{5} = \frac{4 \times 3}{5 \times 3} = \frac{12}{15} \text{ of the 15 baseball cards were given away}$$

Answer Key for Worksheet 1-6b

1. $\frac{8}{12} = \frac{2 \times 4}{3 \times 4} = \frac{2}{3}$ of the 12 cupcakes were eaten (diagram given in text).

2. $\frac{4}{5} = \frac{4 \times 3}{5 \times 3} = \frac{12}{15}$ of the baseball cards were given away (diagram given in text).

3.
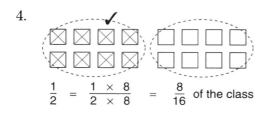

$$\frac{6}{8} = \frac{3 \times 2}{4 \times 2} = \frac{3}{4} \text{ of a pizza}$$

4.

$$\frac{1}{2} = \frac{1 \times 8}{2 \times 8} = \frac{8}{16} \text{ of the class}$$

56

WORKSHEET 1-6b

Name _____

Finding Equivalent Fractions
by Drawing

Date _____

Draw to find the answers to the following exercises. Record your results according to the teacher's instructions.

1. Eight-twelfths of 12 cupcakes are eaten at a birthday party. What is the simplest fraction name for the part that is eaten?

2. Tom gave 4-fifths of his 15 baseball cards to his friend, Rosie. What is another fraction name for the part he gave to Rosie?

3. Sean ate 6-eighths of a pizza cut into 8 slices. Find the fraction in lowest terms that is equivalent to 6-eighths of the pizza.

4. There are 16 students in an art class. One-half of these students also study music. What is another fraction name for the part of the class studying music?

Activity 3: Independent Practice

Materials
Worksheet 1-6c
Regular pencil

Procedure
Students will work exercises on Worksheet 1-6c independently, then share their results with the class. Encourage them to draw diagrams whenever necessary.

Answer Key for Worksheet 1-6c

1. $\frac{10}{15}$ of a whole

2. $\frac{4}{7}$

3. 3 groups; 3 pencils per group

4. [4] in numerator and denominator; 24 as new denominator

5. $\frac{2}{5}$ of the class or $\frac{12}{30}$ of the class; other possible answers are $\frac{4}{10}$ or $\frac{6}{15}$ of the class.

6. $\frac{3}{5}$ of the fabric

Possible Testing Errors That May Occur for This Objective

- A response that is relatively close to the original fraction is given. For example, $\frac{6}{10}$ or $\frac{2}{5}$ is given as equivalent to $\frac{1}{2}$ because 6 is about half of 10 or 2 is about half of 5.

- The common factor is removed from the denominator but not from the numerator, which is simply changed to 1. For example, in $\frac{6}{8}$ the factor 2 is removed from 8 but not from 6, which is just changed to 1. This yields the fraction $\frac{1}{4}$ instead of $\frac{3}{4}$.

- The denominator is multiplied by a certain factor to produce the new denominator, but the original numerator is not multiplied by the same factor. For example, to change $\frac{2}{3}$ to twelfths, students multiply 3 by 4 for the new denominator, but keep 2 as the new numerator, producing $\frac{2}{12}$ as the new but incorrect equivalent fraction for $\frac{2}{3}$.

58

WORKSHEET 1-6c   Name _____

Finding Equivalent Fractions   Date _____

Work the following exercises. Be ready to share your answers with the entire class. Use multiplication to record your steps.

1. Change $\frac{2}{3}$ to fifteenths of a whole.

2. Express $\frac{8}{14}$ as a fraction in lowest terms.

3. Nine red pencils out of 21 pencils total is equivalent to how many *groups* of red pencils out of *7 groups* of pencils total? How many pencils must be in each group?

4. Complete: $\frac{5}{6} = \frac{5 \times [\qquad]}{6 \times [\qquad]} = \frac{20}{?}$

5. Three-fifths of a class of 30 students will attend a band concert. Find two equivalent fraction names for the portion of the class that is not going to the concert.

6. Out of 20 yards of fabric, $\frac{12}{20}$ of the fabric will be used to make a flag. Rename $\frac{12}{20}$ as an equivalent fraction in lowest terms.

Objective 7
Compare and order two proper fractions, using models (physical, pictorial).

Discussion
The concept of relating part to whole is quite difficult for young students. The trading or regrouping process that occurs in finding equivalent fractions is also hard for them to comprehend at this age. Many hands-on experiences are needed, especially in the modeling of word problems that involve the comparison of two fractions.

Activity 1: Manipulative Stage

Materials
Set of 60 colored square tiles or disks per pair of students (two different colors, 30 per color)

Worksheet 1-7a

Regular pencil

Procedure
1. Give each pair of students a set of 60 colored square tiles or disks (two different colors, 30 per color). Tiles and disks are available commercially, or you may use cutout 1-inch paper squares. Also give each student a copy of Worksheet 1-7a, which contains several word problems that require two fractional amounts to be compared. Each story provides the description of a whole and some fractional parts of that whole.

2. Discuss each problem and have students model the situation with their tiles. If the whole is *a set of individual objects* (the "discrete" model), have students physically separate their tiles on the desktop. If the whole is *a single object* (the "continuous" model), have students place the tiles edge-to-edge to form a predetermined bar length. The touching tiles should then be slightly separated to form "sections" of the "whole" bar when new groupings are needed. For example, if students need to find $\frac{1}{2}$ of a whole bar and $\frac{2}{3}$ of another whole bar of the same size, tell students to take 6 tiles ($2 \times 3 = 6$, a common denominator) and make a whole bar that is 6 tiles long. The 6 touching tiles may easily be separated into 2 equal groups or into 3 equal groups when necessary.

3. Students should record their findings as word sentences on their own papers. At the Manipulative Stage, use *word* names to describe fractional parts; for example, 3-*fourths* instead of $\frac{3}{4}$ of the whole.

Here is the first exercise on Worksheet 1-7a to consider: "Cary made 12 hamburgers for her party. Two-thirds of the hamburgers were made with mustard. One-sixth of the hamburgers were made with mayonnaise. Which portion of hamburgers was greater, the portion with mustard or the portion with mayonnaise?"

Ask how many hamburgers were in the original set (12). Students should place 12 tiles in one color (for example, red) on the desktop. (Note: This example uses the discrete model, so the 12 tiles are not touching initially.)

Ask what *portion* of the hamburgers had mustard ($\frac{2}{3}$). Do not ask "how many" at this time; that implies the quantity—8 hamburgers. Students should separate the 12 tiles into 3 equal groups of red tiles; as a result, 4 red tiles will be in each group. Have them cover 2 groups of these red tiles with tiles of the second color (for example, blue) to show the portion made with mustard. Then, since 8 out of 12 red tiles are covered, the fraction 8-twelfths also describes the fractional part of the set that was made with mustard. Students should write the following sentence on their own worksheets: "2-thirds of 12 hamburgers is equal to 8-twelfths of 12 hamburgers, so 8 hamburgers were made with mustard."

Here is a sample of tiles showing "2-thirds of 12 hamburgers" (discrete model):

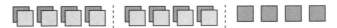

Now repeat the process to show 1-sixth of 12 tiles. Have students put 12 new red tiles on the desktop, leaving the first set of red and blue tiles intact. Separate the new 12 tiles into 6 equal groups; 2 red tiles will be in each group. Because 1-sixth of the hamburgers were made with mayonnaise, have students cover one group of red tiles with blue tiles. Because 2 red tiles are now covered with blue tiles, the fraction 2-twelfths also describes the fractional part of the set that was made with mayonnaise. Students should now write the following sentence: "1-sixth of 12 hamburgers is equal to 2-twelfths of 12 hamburgers, so 2 hamburgers were made with mayonnaise."

Here is a sample of tiles showing "1-sixth of 12 hamburgers" (discrete model):

Discuss the idea that since 8 tiles are more than 2 tiles, we know that 8-twelfths of 12 must also be more than 2-twelfths of 12. Thinking backward to the original portions given, we conclude that 2-thirds of 12 is more than 1-sixth of 12. Students should finally record: "2-thirds of 12 is more than 1-sixth of 12, so more hamburgers were made with mustard than with mayonnaise."

For Exercise 3 on Worksheet 1-7a, the number of wieners in a package is not given. Students will need to build a "continuous" row of tiles (touching tiles) that can be separated into 4 equal groups to show fourths, as well as into 8 equal groups to show eighths. The least amount of tiles that will be able to be separated both ways is 8 tiles. Be sure to discuss with the students the types of separations required by the exercise so they will understand why 8 tiles are being used. A discussion of "least common denominator" is not necessary at this point.

Answer Key for Worksheet 1-7a
Here are suggested sentences to record for each exercise. Complete statements should be encouraged.

1. 2-thirds of 12 hamburgers is equal to 8-twelfths of 12 hamburgers, so 8 hamburgers were made with mustard. 1-sixth of 12 hamburgers is equal to 2-twelfths of 12 hamburgers, so 2 hamburgers were made with mayonnaise. 2-thirds of 12 is more than 1-sixth of 12, so more hamburgers were made with mustard than with mayonnaise.

2. 3-fifths of 15 boxes is equal to 9-fifteenths of 15 boxes, so Jena sold 9 boxes. Susan sold 8-fifteenths of 15 boxes, which is 8 boxes. So 8-fifteenths of 15 boxes is less than 3-fifths of 15 boxes.

3. The north concession stand used 3-fourths of a package of wieners, which is 6-eighths of a package. The south concession stand used 5-eighths of a package. So 3-fourths of a package is greater than 5-eighths of a package. The north concession stand sold more than the south concession stand did.

62

WORKSHEET 1-7a   Name _____

Comparing Fractions with Tiles   Date _____

For each exercise that follows, show each fraction with tiles and compare the two fractions. Write word sentences about what you discover.

1. Cary made 12 hamburgers for her party. Two-thirds of the hamburgers were made with mustard. One-sixth of the hamburgers were made with mayonnaise. Which portion of hamburgers was greater, the portion with mustard or the portion with mayonnaise?

2. On Saturday, Jena sold 3-fifths of her 15 boxes of cookies for her Girls' Club camp fund. On the same day, Susan sold 8-fifteenths of another 15 boxes. Which fractional amount was less, 3-fifths or 8-fifteenths of 15 boxes?

3. Before the football game began, the north concession stand used 3-fourths of a package of wieners to make hot dogs. The south concession stand used 5-eighths of a package. Which concession stand sold the greater part of a package of wieners? (Hint: For a "package of wieners," build a "whole" bar that is 8 tiles long. The tiles should be touching, because the number of wieners in a package is not known.)

Activity 2: Pictorial Stage

Materials

Worksheet 1-7b
Regular notebook paper
Regular pencil and red pencil

Procedure

1. After students have practiced with the tiles to model fractions and to rename and compare those fractions, have them draw diagrams to compare fractions instead. Give each student a red pencil and a copy of Worksheet 1-7b, which contains several word problems. Students will draw their diagrams on their own notebook paper.

2. Repeat the procedure followed in the Manipulative Stage, but the recording format will be different. The ratio format for fractions will now be used, along with products that show the trading or grouping process used.

3. For the discrete model, the drawings should look like the tiles used earlier, but instead of placing new tiles on top of the original tiles to show the portion needed, an X will be marked on those squares that are identified for some special reason. New groups formed will be ringed in red pencil.

4. Guide students through each exercise. The first two exercises will be discussed next. The first exercise involves a discrete model, and the second exercise involves a continuous model. Students need experience with both types.

Consider Exercise 1 on Worksheet 1-7b: "Allen made 12 cupcakes for his party. One-third of the cupcakes were blueberry. Three-sixths of the cupcakes were banana. Which portion of the cupcakes was greater, blueberry or banana?"

We start with "$\frac{1}{3}$ of 12 cupcakes," so students should first draw 12 squares on their own notebook paper. Then red rings will be drawn to form 3 equal groups with the 12 squares. One of the 3 groups is selected by marking an X in each square inside that group. As a result, $\frac{4}{12}$ of the total squares will be marked.

Because 4 squares are found in each ringed group, the change from counting ringed groups to counting individual squares will be recorded below Exercise 1 on Worksheet 1-7b as follows:

$$\frac{1}{3} = \frac{1 \times 4}{3 \times 4} = \frac{4}{12} \text{ of the 12 cupcakes are blueberry}$$

Similarly, "$\frac{3}{6}$ of 12 cupcakes" would be drawn on the notebook paper as follows:

Because 2 squares are in each ringed group, we show the change from counting ringed groups to counting individual squares by also recording the following below Exercise 1 on Worksheet 1-7b:

$$\frac{3}{6} = \frac{3 \times 2}{6 \times 2} = \frac{6}{12} \text{ of the 12 cupcakes are banana}$$

Because $\frac{6}{12}$ is more than $\frac{4}{12}$, we finally record on the worksheet:

$$\frac{1}{3} < \frac{3}{6} \text{, so there are more banana cupcakes.}$$

For the continuous model found in Exercise 2, students will first draw two "whole" bars of the same length (the whole candy bar is a continuous model) on their own notebook paper. At the Manipulative Stage, they were told how many tiles to connect together to form the "whole" bar needed. At this new stage, they will decide how many parts will finally be needed. To compare "$\frac{2}{3}$ of a candy bar" to "$\frac{1}{2}$ of a candy bar," students will subdivide each bar and mark its parts as follows:

Encourage students to carefully subdivide their bars each time so that equal parts are formed within each bar; the parts should at least pass the "eye" test for congruence. After the initial fractional amounts are represented, students must decide how to trade or subdivide each original part shown on each whole bar so that the two whole bars have the same total number of new parts at the end. The new parts should be marked off in red pencil. In the present exercise, if each third in the first bar is changed to *two* new equal parts and each half in the second bar is changed to *three* new equal parts, then each whole bar will contain six new equal parts total. The new markings should be drawn as shown here:

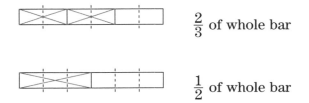

The recordings below Exercise 2 on Worksheet 1-7b for the changes to the two bars will be as follows:

$$\frac{2}{3} = \frac{2 \times 2}{3 \times 2} = \frac{4}{6} \text{ of the whole candy bar}$$

$$\frac{1}{2} = \frac{1 \times 3}{2 \times 3} = \frac{3}{6} \text{ of the whole candy bar}$$

Since we know that 4 parts are more than 3 parts, or $\frac{4}{6}$ of the candy bar is more than $\frac{3}{6}$ of the candy bar, the final comparison should now be recorded on the worksheet:

$$\frac{2}{3} > \frac{1}{2} \text{ of the candy bar}$$

Answer Key for Worksheet 1-7b

1. $\frac{1}{3} = \frac{1 \times 4}{3 \times 4} = \frac{4}{12}$ of the 12 cupcakes are blueberry

   $\frac{3}{6} = \frac{3 \times 2}{6 \times 2} = \frac{6}{12}$ of the 12 cupcakes are banana

   $\frac{1}{3} < \frac{3}{6}$, so there are more banana cupcakes (diagrams shown in text).

2. $\frac{2}{3} = \frac{2 \times 2}{3 \times 2} = \frac{4}{6}$ of the whole candy bar

   $\frac{1}{2} = \frac{1 \times 3}{2 \times 3} = \frac{3}{6}$ of the whole candy bar

   $\frac{2}{3} > \frac{1}{2}$ of the candy bar (diagrams shown in text)

3. Harry:

   Lynn:

   Harry: $\frac{4}{6} = \frac{4 \times 3}{6 \times 3} = \frac{12}{18}$ of the 18 cans

   Lynn: $\frac{5}{9} = \frac{5 \times 2}{9 \times 2} = \frac{10}{18}$ of the 18 cans

   $\frac{4}{6} > \frac{5}{9}$, so $\frac{5}{9}$ of the 18 cans was less.

4. $\frac{4}{10}$ of whole kg

     $\frac{3}{5}$ of whole kg

   $\frac{4}{10}$ is unchanged.

   $\frac{3}{5} = \frac{3 \times 2}{5 \times 2} = \frac{6}{10}$ of a kg

   $\frac{4}{10} < \frac{3}{5}$, so $\frac{4}{10}$ of a kilogram weighs less.

66

WORSHEET 1-7b

WORKSHEET 1-7b

Drawing Diagrams to
Compare Fractions

Name _____

Date _____

For each exercise that follows, draw diagrams on your own notebook paper to compare the two fractions. Follow your teacher's directions to record your results on this worksheet.

1. Allen made 12 cupcakes for his party. One-third of the cupcakes were blueberry. Three-sixths of the cupcakes were banana. Which portion of the cupcakes was greater, blueberry or banana?

2. Joe ate $\frac{2}{3}$ of a candy bar. Phil had the same kind of candy bar but ate $\frac{1}{2}$ of his bar. Who ate more candy, Joe or Phil?

3. Each shipping carton holds 18 cans of vegetables. Harry placed 4-sixths of his carton's cans on the display shelf, and Lynn placed 5-ninths of her carton's cans on the shelf. Which fractional part of the cans was less?

4. Which weighs less: $\frac{4}{10}$ of a kilogram or $\frac{3}{5}$ of a kilogram?

Activity 3: Independent Practice

Materials
Worksheet 1-7c
Regular pencil

Procedure
Students will solve each problem on Worksheet 1-7c independently, using the fraction conversion format developed in Activity 2. When all are finished with the worksheet, have various students explain their results.

Answer Key for Worksheet 1-7c
1. $\frac{15}{16}$ of a whole

2. $\frac{2}{3}$ of a pound

3. <

4. $\frac{3}{8} < \frac{1}{2} < \frac{2}{3}$

5. Charlie

Possible Testing Errors That May Occur for This Objective
- Two fractions are incorrectly considered equal when the same constant is subtracted from both the numerator and the denominator of one fraction to obtain the numerator and the denominator of the second fraction. For example, in $\frac{9}{12}$, 6 is subtracted from 9 and from 12 to get the "fraction" $\frac{3}{6}$; therefore, the student considers $\frac{9}{12}$ equal to $\frac{3}{6}$.

- One shaded amount on a given whole bar is correctly named, but the shaded amount on the second whole bar is not correctly named. The final fraction names found are then compared with the correct inequality sign. For example, students are to compare diagrams that represent $\frac{9}{12}$ and $\frac{2}{3}$ but use $\frac{9}{12}$ and $\frac{5}{6}$ instead, correctly finding $\frac{9}{12} < \frac{5}{6}$ numerically. Students ignore the visual clues in the diagrams that show $\frac{9}{12}$ to be *more than* $\frac{2}{3}$. The test item requires $\frac{9}{12} > \frac{2}{3}$ as the response in order to be correct.

- The unshaded parts are compared to the shaded parts on each whole bar shown instead of the shaded parts being compared to the total parts on each bar. For example, for 9 shaded parts out of 12 parts total on the first whole bar, students incorrectly use $\frac{3}{9}$ as the fraction name. Then for 4 shaded parts out of 6 parts total on the second whole bar, they incorrectly use $\frac{2}{4}$ as the fraction name. The response, $\frac{3}{9} > \frac{2}{4}$, is selected because the first shaded amount (actually $\frac{9}{12}$) looks larger in size than the second shaded amount (actually $\frac{4}{6}$). So the "greater than" sign seems reasonable. The correct response for the test item, however, should be $\frac{9}{12} > \frac{4}{6}$.

68

WORSHEET 1-7c   Name _____

Comparing Proper Fractions   Date _____

Solve the following exercises. Be ready to share your results with the entire class. Record any steps used to change a fraction name to another name.

1. Which is greater: $\frac{7}{8}$ or $\frac{15}{16}$ of a whole?

2. Jose wants to buy either 2-thirds of a pound of fudge or 3-fourths of a pound of peanut brittle. Which portion of a pound weighs less?

3. Complete with <, >, or =: $\frac{3}{5}$ _____ $\frac{7}{10}$ for the same whole.

4. Order from least to greatest, based on the same whole: $\frac{1}{2}$, $\frac{2}{3}$, $\frac{3}{8}$.

5. Each student in Ms. Garza's class has 3 dozen donuts to sell at the school carnival. By noon, Charlie has sold 7-twelfths of his donuts and Maria has sold 10-eighteenths of her donuts. Who has sold more donuts?

Objective 8

Match numerals or number names of decimals involving tenths and hundredths with their equivalent word names (including mixed numbers).

Discussion

Understanding fractional language is difficult for students. It is easier for them to think of 10 ones as 1 ten than to think of a one as 1 out of 10 parts, or 1-tenth of 1 ten. This difficulty extends into the tenths and hundredths place value positions.

Students need practice with fractional language, both orally and in written form. Base 10 blocks are helpful in the development of decimal fractions and provide practice with the naming process.

Activity 1: Manipulative Stage

Materials

Demonstration set of base 10 blocks (1 large cube, 10 flats, 10 rods, and 10 small cubes) for the teacher

Worksheet 1-8a

Regular pencil

For each pair of students, a bag of approximately 60 small counters (centimeter cubes, buttons, and so on, all same color and size)

Building Mat 1-8a (includes ones, tenths, hundredths)

Procedure

1. Use a set of base 10 blocks (1 large cube, 10 flats, 10 rods, and 10 small cubes) to demonstrate to the class the fractional relationship each block has with the next larger size; for example, a flat is 1-tenth of a large cube, a rod is 1-tenth of a flat, and a small cube is 1-tenth of a rod. Then define a flat as the "whole" or "ones block" and discuss what fractional part each smaller block is of this "whole"; for example, a rod will be 1-tenth of the "whole" (10 rods = 1 flat) and a small cube will be 1-hundredth of the "whole." Students should already know that 100 small cubes are equivalent in size to 1 flat, so 100 small cubes should not be necessary for the discussion.

2. Then define a large cube as the *new* "whole" or "ones block" and discuss what fractional part each smaller block is of this "whole." A flat will be 1-tenth of the "whole" (10 flats = 1 large cube), a rod will be 1-hundredth of the "whole" (100 rods = 1 large cube), and a small cube will be 1-thousandth of the "whole" (1,000 small cubes = 1 large cube). Again, the larger amounts of blocks should not be needed. Help students reason through how many total blocks are required. For example, show that 10 rods cover one flat, then reason that 10 flats must represent 10 of 10 rods, or 100 rods, when the flats form the large cube.

3. Discuss the idea that the fractional name of a block changes when the "whole" block changes; for example, the small cube is 1-thousandth *of the large cube*, but it is 1-hundredth *of the flat*. When using fraction language, students must always be aware of what the "whole" is.

4. Now give each student a copy of Worksheet 1-8a. Give each pair of students a bag of approximately 60 small counters (centimeter cubes, buttons, and so on) of the same size and color. Because of limits on the building mat space and the quantities of each kind of block, it is difficult to continue working with the base 10 blocks. Therefore, we must move to nonproportional materials, such as the small counters, in order to show a variety of decimal fractions. Students must now rely on their *understanding* that it takes 10 tenths to make a "whole," 100 hundredths to make a "whole," 10 hundredths to make a tenth of a "whole," and so on. Remind them that each counter placed in the ones column of the building mat now represents the "whole."

5. Students need to practice the different ways amounts of counters on the building mat can be described or named. Have them place one counter in the tenths column. Write its *decimal name* on the board ("0.1"), then read that decimal name as "one-tenth of the whole." Also write "one-tenth of the whole" on the board as the *word name*, and write the equivalent common fraction name ("$\frac{1}{10}$") beside the "0.1" to reinforce the name relationships. Note that both $\frac{1}{10}$ and 0.1 should be *read aloud* as "one-tenth of the whole." Avoid language such as "zero point one" for 0.1 or "one over ten" for $\frac{1}{10}$.

6. Ask students to trade the tenth currently on the building mat for 10 hundredths. To do this, they should remove the counter from the tenths column and put 10 counters in the hundredths column. Now 0.1 has become 0.10. Write the new decimal number on the board, read the number as "ten hundredths of the whole," then write that same phrase on the board as the word name. Also write the common fraction name ("$\frac{10}{100}$") beside the "0.10."

7. Call out different amounts of counters described on Worksheet 1-8a for students to place in the appropriate columns of Building Mat 1-8a. They should make any allowable trades from each column to the adjacent column to the left in order to simplify the amount of counters on the mat. For example, if there are 14 counters in the hundredths column, 10 of the counters should be removed from that column and a new counter placed in the tenths column instead; 4 counters will remain in the hundredths column.

8. Once the initial counters have been simplified, have students record the decimal name, the word name, and the common fraction name (or mixed number name) under the appropriate description on Worksheet 1-8a. Common fraction forms are being included here, even though the objective does not mention them. It is a good time to reinforce equivalent decimal and fraction notations.

9. The first exercise on Worksheet 1-8a will be discussed next.

Consider Exercise 1 on Worksheet 1-8a: "14 hundredths, 7 tenths, 2 ones." The three amounts should be shown with counters on the mat. Ten of the hundredths will trade for 1 tenth. This will leave 4 counters in the hundredths column, 8 counters in the tenths column, and 2 counters in the ones column. Have students record the result on Worksheet 1-8a as the decimal number name (2.84), which directly reflects the amount of counters in each column.

Because the rightmost column of the mat containing counters is hundredths, the final word name will require hundredths as the denominator. Remind students that the 8 tenths can trade for 80 hundredths, so in terms of hundredths, we have 80+4, or 84 hundredths *in value* on the mat. (Do not show the actual trading with the counters because the quantity of counters needed is so large.) Thus, the final amount on the mat should be read as "two and eighty-four hundredths of the whole." This phrase should be written on the worksheet as the word name. The mixed number name, 2 and $\frac{84}{100}$, should also be recorded. Use "and" in the mixed number name at this stage to help students differentiate between whole and fractional notation.

Here is the building mat as it should appear with the initial set of counters and with the final set of counters:

ONES	TENTHS	HUNDREDTHS

ONES	TENTHS	HUNDREDTHS

Answer Key for Worksheet 1-8a

1. 2.84; two and eighty-four hundredths of the whole; 2 and $\frac{84}{100}$

2. 0.43; forty-three hundredths of the whole; $\frac{43}{100}$

3. 1.02; one and two hundredths of the whole; 1 and $\frac{2}{100}$

4. 3.5; three and five tenths of the whole; 3 and $\frac{5}{10}$ (alternatively, since the exercise had hundredths at first: 3.50; three and fifty hundredths of the whole; 3 and $\frac{50}{100}$)

5. 0.21; twenty-one hundredths of the whole; $\frac{21}{100}$

6. 4.2; four and two tenths of the whole; 4 and $\frac{2}{10}$

BUILDING MAT 1-8a.

HUNDREDTHS	TENTHS	ONES

WORKSHEET 1-8a   Name _____
Building Decimal Numbers   Date _____

Show each set of counters listed next on your building mat and simplify the counters. Write the decimal name, word name, and fraction name for each set below its description.

1. 14 hundredths, 7 tenths, 2 ones

2. 3 tenths, 13 hundredths

3. 9 tenths, 12 hundredths

4. 14 tenths, 2 ones, 10 hundredths

5. 11 hundredths, 1 tenth

6. 3 ones, 12 tenths

Activity 2: Pictorial Stage

Materials

Worksheet 1-8b
Regular pencil

Procedure

1. Give each student a copy of Worksheet 1-8b. Repeat the process used in the Manipulative Stage, except have students draw small circles in the columns of base 10 frames on the worksheet instead of using counters on the building mat. This time 0 to 9 circles will be used in each column. Focus on the naming technique without involving any trading.

2. For each exercise on the worksheet, have students draw circles in each column of a base 10 frame according to the amounts stated above the frame.

3. They should write the decimal name below the frame, read its correct name aloud, then write the corresponding word name and common fraction name beside or below the decimal name. Do *not* teach reduction of fractions at this time; it will interfere with the place value study that you are doing here.

4. An example from Worksheet 1-8b will be discussed next.

Consider Exercise 1 from the worksheet: "2 ones, 3 tenths, and 1 hundredth." Students should draw 2 circles in the ones column, 3 circles in the tenths column, and 1 circle in the hundredths column. Using the quantity in each column, they should record 2.31 below the base 10 frame.

Because the rightmost column containing circles is hundredths, the final word name will require hundredths as the denominator. Students should realize that 3 tenths could trade for 30 hundredths, so the tenths and hundredths combined equal to 30 + 1, or 31 hundredths. The word name to be recorded will then be "two and thirty-one hundredths of the whole." The fraction or mixed number name will be 2 and $\frac{31}{100}$.

Here is an example of the completed frame:

ONES	TENTHS	HUNDREDTHS
◯ ◯	◯ ◯ ◯	◯

2.31; two and thirty-one hundredths of the whole; 2 and $\frac{31}{100}$

Answer Key for Worksheet 1-8b

1. 2.31; two and thirty-one hundredths of the whole; 2 and $\frac{31}{100}$

2. 4.07; four and seven hundredths of the whole; 4 and $\frac{7}{100}$

3. 5.6; five and six tenths of the whole; 5 and $\frac{6}{10}$

4. 0.83; eighty-three hundredths of the whole; $\frac{83}{100}$

76

WORKSHEET 1-8b

Name _____

Drawing Decimal Numbers

Date _____

For each exercise, show the given place value amounts by drawing small circles on the base 10 frame. Write the decimal name, word name, and fraction name for the total amount below the frame or on the back of this sheet.

1. 2 ones, 3 tenths, 1 hundredth

ONES	TENTHS	HUNDREDTHS

2. 7 hundredths, 4 ones

ONES	TENTHS	HUNDREDTHS

3. 5 ones, 6 tenths

ONES	TENTHS	HUNDREDTHS

4. 3 hundredths, 8 tenths

ONES	TENTHS	HUNDREDTHS

Activity 3: Independent Practice

Materials
Worksheet 1-8c
Regular pencil

Procedure
Students work independently to complete Worksheet 1-8c. Remind them that the rightmost place value position shown in a decimal number name indicates the denominator when a fractional part is involved. Also encourage them to use the phrase "of the whole" whenever describing a fractional amount. When all are finished, have them share their answers with the class.

Answer Key for Worksheet 1-8c
1. 5.94

2. twenty-five hundredths of the whole

3. 0.60

4. eight and three hundredths of the whole

5. twelve and seven tenths of the whole

6. 1.75

Possible Testing Errors That May Occur for This Objective
- Students recognize the place value required for the denominator of the decimal fraction but ignore the zero in a numeral when naming the numerator. For example, students name 2.40 as "two and four hundredths."

- If a mixed number is changed to an improper fraction before being written in decimal form, the numerator is not correctly aligned with the place value positions. As an example, "one and five hundredths" is changed to $\frac{105}{100}$, but the entire numerator is written to the right of the decimal point as 0.105, instead of as 1.05.

- Students do not know the place value positions to the right of the decimal point. For example, "five and six hundredths" might be written as 5.6 instead of 5.06.

78

WORKSHEET 1-8c   Name _____
Naming Decimal Numbers   Date _____

For each exercise, write the required equivalent name.

1. Write the decimal number name for "five and ninety-four hundredths of the whole."

2. Write the word name for the decimal number 0.25.

3. Write the decimal number name for "sixty hundredths of the whole."

4. Write the word name for the decimal number 8.03.

5. Write the word name for 12.7.

6. What decimal number name is equal to the mixed number name 1 and $\frac{75}{100}$?

Section 1

Name _____

Date _____

NUMERATION AND NUMBER PROPERTIES: PRACTICE TEST ANSWER SHEET

Directions: Use the Answer Sheet to darken the letter of the choice that best answers each question.

1.	◯ A	◯ B	◯ C	◯ D	9.	◯ A	◯ B	◯ C ◯ D
2.	◯ A	◯ B	◯ C	◯ D	10.	◯ A	◯ B	◯ C ◯ D
3.	◯ A	◯ B	◯ C	◯ D	11.	◯ A	◯ B	◯ C ◯ D
4.	◯ A	◯ B	◯ C	◯ D	12.	◯ A	◯ B	◯ C ◯ D
5.	◯ A	◯ B	◯ C	◯ D	13.	◯ A	◯ B	◯ C ◯ D
6.	◯ A	◯ B	◯ C	◯ D	14.	◯ A	◯ B	◯ C ◯ D
7.	◯ A	◯ B	◯ C	◯ D	15.	◯ A	◯ B	◯ C ◯ D
8.	◯ A	◯ B	◯ C	◯ D	16.	◯ A	◯ B	◯ C ◯ D

SECTION 1: NUMERATION AND NUMBER PROPERTIES: PRACTICE TEST

1. Order from greatest to least: 12,500; 11,745; 12,567; 11,760.

   A. 11,745; 11,760; 12,500; 12,567

   B. 12,500; 11,745; 12,567; 11,760

   C. 12,567; 12,500; 11,760; 11,745

   D. 11,760; 11,745; 12,567; 12,500

2. Order from least to greatest: 7,549; 6,235; 7,607; 8,114; 6,102.

   A. 6,235; 6,102; 7,607; 7,549; 8,114

   B. 8,114; 7,607; 7,549; 6,235; 6,102

   C. 6,102; 8,114; 6,235; 7,549; 7,607

   D. 6,102; 6,235; 7,549; 7,607; 8,114

3. Which set contains only even numbers?

   A. 4, 10, 26   B. 5, 6, 7   C. 9, 15, 23   D. 5, 10, 15

4. Which number is an odd number?

   A. 18   B. 27   C. 2   D. 0

5. If the pattern shown in row A continues, what number will be the sixth term in the row?

A	2	4	6		

   A. 8   B. 10   C. 15   D. 12

6. If the patterns shown in row X and row Y continue, what number will be in row Y below the number 4 in row X?

X	1	2		4		6
Y	1	4	7			

   A. 10   B. 4   C. 11   D. 8

Copyright © 2003 by John Wiley & Sons, Inc.

SECTION 1: NUMERATION AND NUMBER PROPERTIES: PRACTICE TEST

7. At the Convention Center, 1,560 parking spaces are being used by people attending a garden show. Estimate to the nearest thousand how many parking spaces are being used.

   A. 1,600   B. 2,000   C. 1,000   D. 1,500

8. What is 3,248 feet rounded to the nearest hundred feet?

   A. 3,000 ft   B. 3,300 ft   C. 3,250 ft   D. 3,200 ft

9. What fraction of the triangles is shaded?

   A. $\frac{2}{5}$ B. $\frac{5}{7}$ C. $\frac{2}{7}$ D. $\frac{2}{3}$

10. George has 15 pencils in his school box. Five pencils are yellow and eight pencils are blue. What fractional part of the 15 pencils is blue?

    A. $\frac{8}{15}$ B. $\frac{5}{8}$ C. $\frac{5}{15}$ D. $\frac{13}{15}$

11. Express $\frac{8}{12}$ as a fraction in lowest terms.

    A. $\frac{4}{12}$ B. $\frac{2}{4}$ C. $\frac{2}{3}$ D. $\frac{4}{6}$

12. Two-fifths of a class of 30 students will attend a band concert. What is an equivalent fraction name for the portion of the class that is not going to the concert?

    A. $\frac{6}{10}$ B. $\frac{6}{15}$ C. $\frac{2}{5}$ D. $\frac{4}{10}$

13. Marge wants to buy either 2-thirds of a pound of hamburger meat or 3-fourths of a pound of fajita meat. Which portion of a pound weighs less?

    A. $\frac{2}{3}$ B. $\frac{5}{7}$ C. $\frac{3}{4}$ D. $\frac{1}{4}$

14. Which statement is correct when each fraction names a part of the same whole?

    A. $\frac{2}{5} = \frac{3}{10}$ B. $\frac{2}{5} < \frac{3}{10}$ C. $\frac{2}{5} > \frac{3}{10}$ D. $\frac{2}{10} = \frac{3}{5}$

15. Write the decimal number name for "five and sixty-three hundredths of the whole."

    A. 563   B. 5.63   C. 0.563   D. 56.3

16. Write the word name for the decimal number 0.09.

    A. Nine   B. Nine thousandths   C. Nine tenths   D. Nine hundredths

Section 1: Numeration and Number Properties: Answer Key for Practice Test

The objective being tested is shown in brackets beside the answer.

1. C [1]

2. D [1]

3. A [2]

4. B [2]

5. D [3]

6. A [3]

7. B [4]

8. D [4]

9. B [5]

10. A [5]

11. C [6]

12. A [6]

13. A [7]

14. C [7]

15. B [8]

16. D [8]

COMPUTATIONAL ALGORITHMS AND ESTIMATION IN PROBLEM SOLVING

Objective 1

Add or subtract whole numbers (two-digit to four-digit) to solve a word problem.

Discussion

Addition or subtraction with two- to four-digit whole numbers should not be difficult for students at this grade level if their regrouping skills are strong and if they have had adequate practice in analyzing word problems. In particular, students need much experience with the "backward trading" aspect of place value in order to perform subtraction of large numbers effectively. The activities described next will provide experience with both addition and subtraction.

Activity 1: Manipulative Stage

Materials

Building Mat 2-1a for each pair of students
100 small counters for each pair of students (same color or same style)
Worksheet 2-1a
Regular pencil

Procedure

1. Give each pair of students a copy of Building Mat 2-1a and 100 small counters. The counters may look alike or be the same color and size. Give each student a copy of Worksheet 2-1a.

2. It is assumed that students have had at least minimal experience in trading 10 ones for 1 ten, 10 tens for 1 hundred, and 10 hundreds for 1 thousand with base 10 blocks or similar materials.

3. Have students use the counters on the building mats to model the word problems on Worksheet 2-1a.

4. For *addition*, only two whole numbers will be involved at this stage. The two needed numbers given in the problem should both be shown on the mat. Students should form groups of 10 counters in each column where possible, beginning with the ones column, then trade each group of counters for a new counter in the next column to the left.

5. For *subtraction*, students should show only the larger amount (called the *minuend*) with counters on the building mat. They will begin with the ones column on the mat and remove the amount of ones counters indicated in the smaller amount (called the *subtrahend*). If there are not enough ones counters there to match what needs to be removed, a counter from the tens column must be removed from the mat and 10 new ones counters placed in the ones column. The removal is then carried out. A similar process is followed to remove tens, hundreds, and thousands counters from the mat, as indicated in the subtrahend.

6. Answers should be recorded on Worksheet 2-1a as complete word sentences below the corresponding exercises.

7. Guide students through each problem before proceeding to the next one.

Consider Exercise 1 on Worksheet 2-1a, which is an example of an *addition* word problem: "At the ticket booth, Kate sold 1,542 tickets to the rock concert for Thursday night. She sold 2,784 tickets for Friday night. How many tickets total did Kate sell for both nights?"

Students should place counters on the mat to show the two numbers as follows:

THOUSANDS	HUNDREDS	TENS	ONES
●	● ● ● ● ●	● ● ● ●	● ●
● ●	● ● ● ● ●	● ● ● ● ●	● ● ● ●
	● ●	● ● ●	

Ask students to join all the ones counters together and, if possible, remove and trade 10 ones for a new counter in the tens column (ones trade not needed here). Then they should join all the tens counters together to get 12 tens. Ten of these 12 tens should be traded for a new counter in the hundreds column. All the hundreds counters are combined for a total of 13 hundreds. Ten of these 13 hundreds should be traded for a new counter in the thousands column.

Finally, there will be 4 counters in the thousands column; no other trades are needed. Three counters remain in the hundreds column, 2 counters remain in the tens column, and 6 counters remain in the ones column. Have various students tell how many counters remain in each column in the following way: 4 thousands, 3 hundreds, 2 tens, and 6 ones. The number name for the sum is 4,326, which students should read as "four thousand three hundred twenty-six."

The answer should be recorded under Exercise 1 on Worksheet 2-1a as follows: "1,542 tickets and 2,784 tickets equal 4,326 total tickets sold." The final mat and counters will appear as shown:

THOUSANDS	HUNDREDS	TENS	ONES
● ● ● ●	● ● ●	● ●	● ● ● ● ● ●

After Exercises 1, 2, and 3 have been worked as examples of addition, discuss Exercise 4 as an example of *subtraction*, followed by the other subtraction word problems. Here is Exercise 4: "Josh counted 3,406 stamps in his collection on Monday. The next weekend, he gave 845 of his stamps to his cousin Sam. How many stamps then remained in Josh's collection?"

Students should place counters on the building mat to show 3,406. The initial counters are shown on the mat given here. Since 845 needs to be removed, have students begin with the ones column and remove 5 counters from the 6 counters, leaving 1 counter in the ones column.

THOUSANDS	HUNDREDS	TENS	ONES
● ● ●	● ● ● ●		● ● ● ● ● ●

Next, 4 tens need to be removed, but there are 0 tens on the mat initially, so 1 counter needs to be removed from the hundreds column and traded for 10 new counters in the tens column. Now 4 tens counters may be removed from the (10 + 0) or 10 counters in the tens column, leaving 6 tens counters on the mat.

There are 3 hundreds currently on the building mat, but 8 hundreds need to be removed. Students must remove 1 counter from the thousands column and trade it for 10 new counters in the hundreds column. There will then be (10 + 3) or 13 hundreds counters, so 8 hundreds counters may be removed from the mat, leaving 5 counters in the hundreds column. No counters need to be removed from the thousands column, so 2 counters remain there.

Finally, the building mat shows 2 thousands, 5 hundreds, 6 tens, and 1 one in counters after all removals have been made. Have various students tell how many counters remain in each column in the following way: 2 thousands, 5 hundreds, 6 tens, and 1 one. The number name for the difference is 2,561, which students should read as "two thousand five hundred sixty-one."

The answer should be recorded under Exercise 4 on Worksheet 2-1a as follows: "3,406 stamps take away 845 stamps equals 2,561 stamps left." The final mat and counters will appear as shown:

THOUSANDS	HUNDREDS	TENS	ONES
● ●	● ● ● ● ●	● ● ● ● ● ●	●

Now guide students through the remaining subtraction exercises on Worksheet 2-1a.

Answer Key for Worksheet 2-1a (possible sentences to use)

1. 1,542 tickets and 2,784 tickets equal 4,326 total tickets sold.

2. 547 miles and 476 miles equal 1,023 miles driven in 2 days.

3. 2,568 fish and 640 fish equal 3,208 fish released in all.

4. 3,406 stamps take away 845 stamps equals 2,561 stamps left.

5. 275 tickets take away 148 tickets sold leaves 127 tickets still to sell.

6. 5,350 new cars take away 2,846 new cars shipped equals 2,504 new cars not shipped.

BUILDING MAT 2-1a

ONES	TENS	HUNDREDS	THOUSANDS

88

WORKSHEET 2-1a

Building with Counters to
Add or Subtract

Name _____

Date _____

Solve the following word problems by placing counters on Building Mat 2-1a. Below each exercise, write a word sentence that states the answer found for that exercise.

1. At the ticket booth, Kate sold 1,542 tickets to the rock concert for Thursday night. She sold 2,784 tickets for Friday night. How many tickets total did Kate sell for both nights?

_____

_____

2. On their vacation, Ned's family drove 547 miles on the first day and 476 miles on the second day. How many miles in all did they drive on the two days?

_____

_____

3. 2,568 fish were released into the public fishing pond. Five hours later, 640 more fish were released. How many fish total were released into the pond?

_____

_____

4. Josh counted 3,406 stamps in his collection on Monday. The next weekend, he gave 845 of his stamps to his cousin Sam. How many stamps then remained in Josh's collection?

_____

_____

5. Sean had 275 tickets to sell for the school play. He sold 148 tickets on Monday. How many tickets were left for Sean to sell?

_____

_____

6. In April and May, 5,350 new cars were manufactured at the local factory; 2,846 of these new cars were shipped out to dealerships in June. How many new cars were not shipped out in June?

_____

_____

Activity 2: Pictorial Stage

Materials
Worksheet 2-1b
Red pencil and regular pencil

Procedure

1. After students are comfortable using the mat and counters to add or subtract, have them work similar word problems with diagrams. Provide each student with a copy of Worksheet 2-1b and a red pencil. Each student should complete the frames on her or his own worksheet but might share results with a partner. Instead of placing counters on the mat to show numbers, students will now draw small circles in the columns of the frames.

2. For *addition*, groups of 10 circles will be formed in each column by drawing a red path around the group. The group of 10 circles will be marked out and a new circle drawn in the next column to the left to show a trade or regrouping. Circles remaining unmarked in the columns after all trades are completed will show the sum. Only two *addends* will be used in each addition problem.

3. For *subtraction*, to show a backward trade between columns, one circle in a column will be marked out with a red X and 10 new circles will be drawn in the next column to the right; a red arrow will be drawn from the old circle to the 10 new circles to indicate the trade. Except for trades, circles will be marked out in pencil to show their removal or subtraction from a column. Circles remaining unmarked in the columns after all trades and removals have been made will represent the difference.

4. Students should write an equation for the sum or difference below the completed frame.

5. Guide students through drawing the diagram for each word problem on Worksheet 2-1b.

6. Finally, help students connect their drawing already shown on each frame to the vertical algorithm for addition or subtraction. Record the notation for each column as you review the combining and trading for addition (or the trading and removal for subtraction) that occurred in that column *on the frame.* The vertical notation might be recorded in the worksheet margin to the right of the corresponding frame or might be recorded on a separate sheet of paper if more writing space is needed. The methods for such recordings will be discussed in specific examples provided next.

Consider Exercise 1 on Worksheet 2-1b as an example of *addition:* "Susan sold 1,408 tickets to the band concert. Robin sold 1,673 tickets to the same concert. How many tickets in all did the two girls sell?"

The two numbers from the word problem should be shown initially with circles on the frame, as follows:

THOUSANDS	HUNDREDS	TENS	ONES
◯	◯◯◯◯		◯◯◯◯◯ ◯◯◯
◯	◯◯◯◯◯ ◯	◯◯◯◯◯ ◯◯	◯◯◯

In the ones column, 10 circles will be grouped together with a red pencil and traded for one new circle in the tens column. There will then be (0 + 7 + 1) or 8 tens. No grouping of tens is needed because there are fewer than 10 tens in the tens column. One individual, or ungrouped, circle remains in the ones column.

In the hundreds column, 10 circles may be grouped with a red pencil and traded for one new circle in the thousands column. No individual, or ungrouped, circles remain in the hundreds column.

There are now (1 + 1 + 1) or 3 circles in the thousands column, which is not enough to make another trade. Have students state how many circles remain ungrouped in each column of the frame: 3 thousands, 0 hundreds, 8 tens, and 1 one. The final sum is 3,081, which students should read aloud as "three thousand eighty-one." Students should finally record an equation below the frame to show the results: "1,408 + 1,673 = 3,081 tickets sold in all." The completed frame with all the groupings or trades marked in red pencil is shown here:

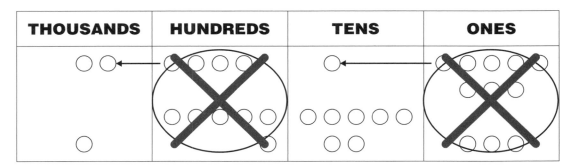

After the frames for Exercises 1 and 2 are completed, help students connect their trading on the two frames to the vertical algorithm for addition. Write the numerical algorithm to the right of each completed frame on Worksheet 2-1b or on a separate sheet of paper. Record the notation for each column as you review the combining and trading that occurred in that column *on the frame*. For example, for Exercise 1, students should notice that a trade was needed in the ones column, so 1 one total should be recorded below the right column of the vertical format and a new 1 ten should be recorded above the tens column. Then 7 tens with 1 new ten make 8 tens total in the tens column, with no trading needed. These two actions will be recorded in the vertical format as follows:

```
      1
   1 4 0 8
 + 1 6 7 3
 ─────────
       8 1
```

Next, in the hundreds column, the 4 hundreds and 6 hundreds combine to make 10 hundreds. The 10 hundreds traded for a new thousand in the thousands column, leaving 0 hundreds in the hundreds column. This action will then be recorded in the vertical format:

```
  1   1
  1 4 0 8
+1 6 7 3
─────────
    0 8 1
```

Finally, in the thousands column, the new thousand, 1 thousand, and 1 thousand combined to make 3 thousands. No trade was needed, so the 3 thousands will be recorded:

```
  1   1
  1 4 0 8
+1 6 7 3
─────────
  3 0 8 1
```

Repeat the process with Exercise 2. Work through the steps slowly, using place value language as shown in the previous narrative. Do *not* allow students to omit place value references in their explanations, as is done in the following example: "1 plus 7 plus 5 equals 13; record the 3 and carry the 1." A correct way to say this might be: "1 new hundred plus 7 hundreds plus 5 hundreds equals 13 hundreds; 10 hundreds trade for 1 new thousand; 3 hundreds remain."

Now consider Exercise 3 on Worksheet 2-1b as an example of *subtraction:* "The candy store has 362 marshmallow bars. 189 of the bars are sold in 5 days. How many bars does the candy store still have after the 5 days?"

Have students draw small circles on the frame to show 362 as follows:

THOUSANDS	HUNDREDS	TENS	ONES
	○○○	○○○○ ○○	○○

Because 189 needs to be removed from the frame, have students begin with the ones column. Nine ones need to be removed, but there are only 2 ones present in the ones column. Therefore, a circle from the tens column must be marked out (X) in red pencil to show a trade is occurring; 10 new circles should be drawn in the ones column to show that 10 new ones have been obtained from the trade. There are now 12 circles in the ones column, so 9 circles should be marked out (/) with regular pencil to show the removal of 9 ones. Three circles remain unmarked in the ones column of the frame.

Five circles remain unmarked in the tens column, but 8 circles need to be removed from the tens column. One circle in the hundreds column must be marked out (X) in red pencil and traded for 10 new circles in the tens column. There are now 15 circles unmarked in the tens column, so 8 of them may be marked out (/) in regular pencil to show removal. Seven circles remain unmarked in the tens column.

Finally, one circle should be marked out (/) in regular pencil from the hundreds column to show removal of 1 hundred, leaving 1 circle unmarked in the hundreds column. The circles remaining unmarked on the frame will be 1 hundred, 7 tens, and 3 ones. The number name is 173, which students should read aloud as "one hundred seventy-three." Below the completed frame, students should record the result as a number sentence or equation: "362 − 189 = 173 marshmallow bars remaining at the candy store." The completed frame should appear as follows:

After students have completed their frames for Exercises 3 and 4, help them connect their tradings on the frames to the vertical algorithm for subtraction. Write the numerical algorithm to the right of each completed frame on Worksheet 2-1b or on a separate sheet of paper. For each subtraction exercise, record the notation for each column as you *review* the trading and removal that occurred in that column *on the frame*. For example, for Exercise 3, students should notice that 1 ten was traded for 10 new ones, leaving 5 tens in the tens column and 12 ones in the ones column. This action, along with the removal or marking out of 9 ones, which left 3 ones, will be recorded in the vertical format as follows:

$$\begin{array}{r} 5\ 12 \\ 3\ \cancel{6}\ \cancel{2} \\ -1\ 8\ 9 \\ \hline 3 \end{array}$$

Next, in the tens column only 5 tens remained, but 8 tens needed to be removed. Another trade from the hundreds column was needed to get 10 new tens. So (10 + 5) or 15 tens became available in the tens column, leaving 2 hundreds in the hundreds column; 8 tens were marked out, leaving 7 tens. This action will then be recorded in the vertical format:

$$\begin{array}{r} 2\ 15 \\ \cancel{5}\ 12 \\ \cancel{3}\ \cancel{6}\ \cancel{2} \\ -1\ 8\ 9 \\ \hline 7\ 3 \end{array}$$

Finally, in the hundreds column, 1 hundred was marked out, leaving 1 hundred in the column. No trade was needed, so the 1 hundred will be recorded as shown:

```
    2 15
      5̶ 12
    3̶ 6̶ 2̶
  − 1 8 9
  ───────
    1 7 3
```

Work through these steps slowly, using place value language as shown in the previous narrative. Do *not* allow students to omit place value references in their explanations, as is done in the following example: "Borrow 1 from 7 to make 15; 15 minus 8 equals 7; then 6 minus 4 equals 2, and 2 minus 1 equals 1." A possible *correct* way to say this would be: "1 ten becomes 10 new ones, and these 10 ones plus 5 ones make 15 ones; 15 ones take away (minus) 8 ones leaves 7 ones; then 6 tens take away 4 tens leaves 2 tens, and 2 hundreds take away 1 hundred leaves 1 hundred."

Answer Key for Worksheet 2-1b

1. 1,408 + 1,673 = 3,081 tickets sold in all.

2. 2,518 + 876 = 3,394 students attending both schools.

3. 362 − 189 = 173 marshmallow bars remaining at the candy store.

4. 2,540 − 1,953 = 587 empty parking spaces.

94

Copyright © 2003 by John Wiley & Sons, Inc.

WORKSHEET 2-1b   Name _____

Drawing Diagrams to Add or Subtract   Date _____

Solve the following word problems by drawing small circles on the given base 10 frames. Use a red pencil to show any trades needed. Below each frame, write the number sentence that states the answer found for that exercise.

1. Susan sold 1,408 tickets to the band concert. Robin sold 1,673 tickets to the same concert. How many tickets in all did the two girls sell?

THOUSANDS	HUNDREDS	TENS	ONES

_____

_____

2. 2,518 students attend East Elementary School, and 876 attend West Elementary School. How many students total attend the two schools?

THOUSANDS	HUNDREDS	TENS	ONES

_____

_____

WORKSHEET 2-1b Continued

Name _____

Date _____

3. The candy store has 362 marshmallow bars. 189 of the bars are sold in 5 days. How many bars does the candy store still have after the 5 days?

THOUSANDS	HUNDREDS	TENS	ONES

4. In the movie theater parking lot, there were 2,540 parking spaces. 1,953 cars filled some of the spaces. How many spaces were still empty?

THOUSANDS	HUNDREDS	TENS	ONES

Activity 3: Independent Practice

Materials
> Worksheet 2-1c
> Regular pencil

Procedure

Have students apply the addition and subtraction algorithms to solve the word problems on Worksheet 2-1c. Exercise 3 will involve three addends. Discuss the idea that the trading process still holds; it is just that more quantities have to be combined within each place value column before one or more trades occur. (Consider a trade as always 10 smaller units for 1 larger unit, so 20 smaller units require two trades.) When all have finished the worksheet, have various students share their answers with the class. Encourage them to use the correct place value language as they describe the computational steps they used to solve the problems.

Answer Key for Worksheet 2-1c

1. $385 - 94 = 291$ marbles saved.

2. $4,380 + 2,134 = 6,514$ miles from city A to city C.

3. $85 + 127 + 209 = 421$ bracelets made in all.

4. $763 - 588 = 175$ more hot dogs sold on Friday.

5. $3,960 + 5,470 = 9,430$ people attended in all.

6. $6,000 - 3,238 = 2,762$ more miles left in trip.

Possible Testing Errors That May Occur for This Objective

Addition

- When three or more addends are involved in a word problem, students will add only the first two numbers given in the problem and ignore the other addends.

- Students fail to regroup their ones, tens, or hundreds when adding two numbers. For example, in $128 + 395$, the 13 ones are recorded as 3 ones only; the other 10 ones are not traded for a new ten. Similarly, the 12 tens (after the ones trade) may be recorded as 2 tens and the other 10 tens ignored.

- Addition fact errors may occur when the sum of two or three numbers is computed, even though regrouping is used correctly. For example, in $49 + 127$, students will use 9 ones + 7 ones incorrectly as 15 ones, recording the 5 ones and trading the other 10 ones correctly for a new ten.

Subtraction

- Students use the correct numbers, but they reverse the digits in order to subtract without regrouping. For example, in 64 – 47, they will use 7 ones – 4 ones instead of 14 ones – 7 ones.

- Students use the correct numbers but fail to decrease the number of tens after they regroup 1 ten to 10 ones in order to subtract in the ones column. As an example, in 64 – 47, along with finding 14 ones – 7 ones = 7 ones, students will use 6 tens – 4 tens = 2 tens, instead of 5 tens – 4 tens.

98

WORKSHEET 2-1c

Name _____

Solving Word Problems with
Addition or Subtraction

Date _____

Solve the following word problems by using addition or subtraction. For each exercise, show all computational steps, then write a number sentence that states the answer. Write on another sheet of paper if more work space is needed.

1. Louise had 385 marbles in her collection. She lost 94 of the marbles through a hole in her bag. How many marbles was she able to save?

2. A map shows that it is 4,380 miles from city A to city B. Then from city B to city C it is 2,134 miles. How many miles is city A from city C if you go through city B on the way to city C?

3. On Monday Liu made 85 friendship bracelets. On Tuesday she made 127, and on Wednesday she made 209 of the bracelets. How many bracelets did she make total for the three days?

4. A concession stand sold 763 hot dogs at the Friday night game but sold only 588 hot dogs at the Saturday game. How many more hot dogs were sold on Friday than on Saturday?

5. 3,960 people attended the high school track meet on Monday, and 5,470 attended the middle school track meet on Thursday. How many people attended the two track meets in all?

6. George has to make a 6,000-mile trip. He has already driven 3,238 miles. How many more miles must he drive to finish the trip?

Objective 2
Multiply two-digit whole numbers by one-digit or two-digit whole numbers (as multipliers) to solve single-stepped word problems.

Discussion
The algorithm for the multiplication of two-digit numbers with one-digit or two-digit numbers needs to be developed well before students are required to independently work story problems requiring multiplication. The algorithm depends heavily on an understanding of multiplication as the repetition of a set. It is also very complex in terms of place value. Many students have difficulty with it because they do not understand how place value changes will cause partial products to be recorded in different columns.

Activities for the development of the algorithm are described next. It is assumed for this objective that the multiplication facts have already been fully developed with manipulative materials.

Activity 1: Manipulative Stage

Materials
Building Mat 2-2a
Set of base 10 blocks per pair of students (4 hundreds, 30 tens, 30 ones)
Worksheet 2-2a
Regular pencil

Procedure
1. Give each pair of students a set of base 10 blocks (4 hundreds, 30 tens, and 30 ones) and a copy of Building Mat 2-2a.

2. Give each student a copy of Worksheet 2-2a. Worksheet Exercises 1 through 3 will involve two-digit multiplicands with one-digit multipliers, and Exercises 4 through 6 will involve two-digit multiplicands with two-digit multipliers.

3. Have students model each exercise with their blocks. Then on Worksheet 2-2a below the exercise have them record a word sentence that shows the results found on the building mat. They should count up their total blocks in the product region (that is, in the interior of the angle of the L-shape) of the mat in order to find their answers. Do not trade any blocks found in the product region. For example, if 10 ones are there, do not exchange them for 1 ten. Always have students use proper place value language when verbally describing their steps to the class.

4. First discuss Exercises 1 through 3 with one-digit multipliers, then discuss Exercises 4 through 6 with two-digit multipliers. An example of each type will be presented in detail.

Here is Exercise 1 to discuss as an example having a *one-digit multiplier:* "The school will use 3 vans to take some students on a field trip. Each van will hold 12 students. How many students can go on the field trip in the vans?"

Have students position Building Mat 2-2a so that the short bar is on the right and vertical. The long bar will be at the bottom of the mat. Have students place 3 ones blocks on the mat aligned with, but to the right of, the vertical bar; these blocks represent the multiplier or the number of vans. Then have students place 2 ones blocks and 1 tens block on the mat below but aligned with the horizontal bar; the ones blocks should be to the right of the tens block. These latter blocks are the multiplicand, or number of students per van.

Tell students that each block along the vertical bar indicates that one row (horizontal) of blocks must be built inside the L-frame in line with that block and that the row must be a copy of the set of blocks already placed on the mat below the horizontal bar of the L-frame. When they finish building the 3 rows of blocks, ask them to describe the blocks now in the product region (interior of the angle of the L-frame) of the mat. They should respond with 3 tens and 6 ones, then with 36.

On their worksheet below Exercise 1, students will write a sentence about their results: "3 vans of 12 students each will carry a total of 36 students." For some story problems, there may be 10 or more ones or 10 or more tens in the product region of the mat. Students should not trade these blocks for a larger block; the arrangement of the blocks must not be changed once they have been placed on the mat.

The final mat for the van problem should appear as follows:

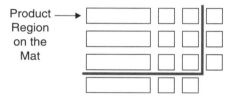

Repeat the process with Exercises 2 and 3.

Here is Exercise 4 to consider as an example having a *two-digit multiplier:* "There are 13 wagons in the parade. Each wagon holds 24 people. How many people total are riding in the wagons?"

Have students place 1 tens block and 3 ones blocks along the vertical bar of the L-frame and then place 2 tens blocks and 4 ones blocks below the horizontal bar of the frame. For both sets, the ones blocks should be placed closest to the corner of the L-frame. The 3 vertical ones blocks indicate that 3 rows of the 2 tens blocks and 4 ones blocks should be built first. The upper vertical tens block indicates that 10 rows of the 2 tens blocks and 4 ones blocks should be built next.

The meaning of the vertical tens block may be new to students, and they need to see the effect it will have on the block placement. First, demonstrate to the class that 10 rows of 1 tens block and 1 ones block, when the rows are pushed together or touching, will occupy the same space on the mat and be equal to 1 hundreds block and 1 tens block. Therefore, the 10 vertical ones blocks may be replaced by 1 vertical tens block, and the 10 touching horizontal tens blocks may be replaced by 1 hundreds block. This direct substitution is called "simplification" of the blocks on the mat. The replacements are shown here:

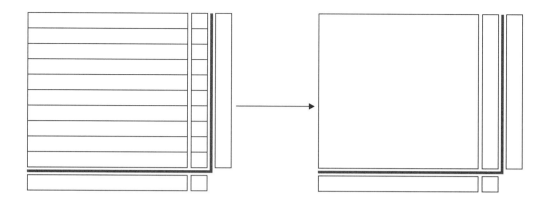

Once students are comfortable with the simplification process (a direct trading of blocks that retains the original block positions on the mat), have them model the story problem of Exercise 4 with their blocks. After simplification, the blocks on the mat should appear as shown:

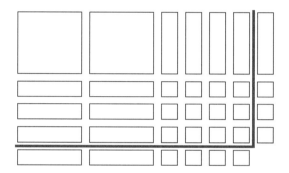

The product now shows 2 hundreds, 10 tens, and 12 ones; a mental trade of the 10 tens for another hundred yields 3 hundreds and 12 ones, or 312. Do not make any *physical* trades with these 10 tens or 12 ones on the mat. Students should write below Exercise 4 on Worksheet 2-2a the following sentence about their results: "13 wagons of 24 people each will hold 312 people in all."

Repeat the process with Exercises 5 and 6.

Answer Key for Worksheet 2-2a (possible sentences to write)

1. 3 vans of 12 students each will carry a total of 36 students.

2. 4 pots of 15 flowers each will hold 60 flowers in all.

3. 5 buses of 20 students each will carry 100 students total on the field trip.

4. 13 wagons of 24 people each will hold 312 people in all.

5. 12 rows of 15 chairs per row will equal 180 chairs total.

6. 21 crates containing 23 vases per crate will hold 483 vases altogether.

102

BUILDING MAT 2-2a

WORKSHEET 2-2a   Name _____

Building Products with Base 10 Blocks   Date _____

Build with base 10 blocks on Building Mat 2-2a to find the product needed for each word problem. Write a word sentence below each exercise to express the answer found.

1. The school will use 3 vans to take some students on a field trip. Each van will hold 12 students. How many students can go on the field trip in the vans?

2. Each of 4 flower pots at the florist's shop contains 15 flowers. How many flowers in all are in the 4 flower pots?

3. At 3 P.M., 5 buses will take students to a museum for a field trip. Each bus will carry 20 students. How many students will go on the field trip?

4. There are 13 wagons in the parade. Each wagon holds 24 people. How many people total are riding in the wagons?

5. At the puppet show, Jimmy saw 12 rows of chairs. Each row had 15 chairs. How many chairs total did Jimmy see at the puppet show?

6. Twenty-one crates are being shipped to Hawaii. Each crate contains 23 ceramic vases. How many vases are being shipped to Hawaii?

Activity 2: Pictorial Stage

Materials

Worksheet 2-2b
Red pencil and regular pencil

Procedure

1. Give each student a copy of Worksheet 2-2b and a red pencil. Students will draw short and long rectangles on L-frames on the worksheet to represent base 10 blocks on a building mat and to find products for the exercises.

2. For each exercise, they will first write a number sentence showing the product found.

3. Students will then label different parts of the product region and transfer the labels to the vertical numerical format for the multiplication algorithm.

4. For each exercise, guide students to find a relationship between the digits of the two factors used and the arrangement of the rectangles in the L-frame.

5. Exercises 1 and 2 will involve one-digit multipliers, and Exercises 3 and 4 will involve two-digit multipliers. An example of each type will be discussed in detail.

Here is a discussion for Exercise 1 and a *one-digit multiplier:* "There are 4 bins of corn. Each bin contains 23 ears of corn. How many ears of corn total are in the 4 bins?"

Drawing the Product Region

Following the repeated row method used in the Manipulative Stage and drawing long and short rectangles to represent the tens and ones, respectively, here is the final frame for Exercise 1:

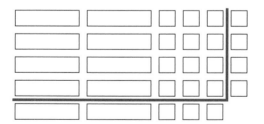

After all students have finished the drawing, have them count the shapes by their value to find the product; 8 tens and 12 ones make 9 tens and 2 ones, or 92. Do not show any trades on the drawing. Write an equation below the frame to show the product found: "4 × 23 = 92 ears of corn in all."

Now follow similar steps to draw rectangles on a frame for Exercise 2.

Labeling Parts of the Product Region

Next, discuss the two parts or smaller regions within the product region in Exercise 1. Separate the tens and ones in the product region by drawing a bar in red pencil between the two groups of shapes. Also label the ones group and the tens group as shown:

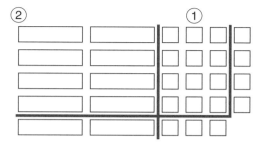

The arrangement of the shapes within each part of the example for Exercise 1 should be described in the following way: "Region 1 has 4 rows of 3 ones, or 12 ones; region 2 has 4 rows of 2 tens, or 8 tens." Students should transfer these descriptions onto the vertical format as shown, to the right of the completed L-frame:

$$
\begin{array}{cc}
\text{T} & \text{O} \\
2 & 3 \\
\times & 4 \\
\hline
1 & 2 \\
8 & \\
\hline
9 & 2 \\
\end{array}
$$

Regions:
(1) 4×3 ones = 12 ones
(2) 4×2 tens = 8 tens

Repeat the process with Exercise 2.

Pattern Search

After both finished frames have been transferred to the vertical format, have students consider Exercise 1 again. Ask students to compare the factors that were used to describe the shape arrangements in the two regions (tens and ones), with the digits in the original two numbers (4 and 23) in Exercise 1. All digits in these two numbers must be unique so that the comparison will be easy for the students. They should notice that the factors in 4×3 and 4×2 use the same digits as those used in the 4 and 23. Now have students draw red arrows on the original numbers to show the connection between these groups of numbers. The arrows should be drawn and labeled for the regions they represent.

$$
\begin{array}{cc}
2 & 3 \\
\times 2\,4 & \\
\hline
1 & 2 \\
8 & \\
\hline
9 & 2 \\
\end{array}
$$

Regions:
① 4×3 ones = 12 ones
② 4×2 tens = 8 tens

Have students examine Exercise 2 in order to see if the digits have the same relationship as shown here. The pattern should hold for both exercises. Thus, students should draw and label arrows on Exercise 2 as they have done on Exercise 1.

Note: It is recommended that the two rows of partial products (for example, the 12 ones and 8 tens used in Exercise 1) not be collapsed into one row at this time. There is no need to do so mathematically, and it will make the transition to two-digit multipliers much easier for the students.

Now consider Exercise 3 with a *two-digit multiplier:* "There are 14 buckets of seashells. Each bucket holds 23 seashells to be made into necklaces. How many shells in all are available for making the jewelry?"

Drawing the Product Region

Students should draw 1 long rectangle and 4 short rectangles (squares) to the right of the vertical bar of the L-frame to show the multiplier, 14. Next, they should draw 2 long rectangles and 3 short rectangles below the horizontal bar of the L-frame to show the multiplicand, 23. The ones (squares) should be drawn closest to the corner of the L-frame.

The 4 vertical ones indicate that four rows of 2 tens and 3 ones need to be drawn in the product region. The long vertical bar (a ten) in the multiplier space indicates that 10 rows of 2 tens and 3 ones need to be drawn as well. Encourage students to draw a large square (a hundred) to show 10 rows of 1 ten instead of drawing the individual horizontal bars (tens); similarly, draw a vertical bar (a ten) for 10 rows of 1 one instead of 10 individual small squares (ones) arranged vertically. In other words, have them "simplify" *as they are drawing shapes* on the L-frame, not afterward.

The completed frame should appear as follows:

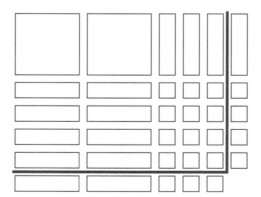

Below the frame, students should write an equation about their results, for example, "14 × 23 = 322 shells in all."

Repeat these steps with Exercise 4.

Labeling Parts of the Product Region

Next, discuss the four parts or smaller regions within the product region in Exercise 3. Separate the hundreds, tens, and ones in the product region by drawing a vertical bar and a horizontal bar in red pencil between the groups of shapes. Also label the four different groups in the order shown (to stay in keeping with the order used in the traditional algorithm):

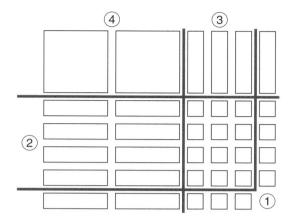

On the finished frame for the example of Exercise 3, the arrangement of the shapes within each region should be described in the following way and order: "Region 1 (lower right region) has 4 rows of 3 ones, or 12 ones; region 2 (lower left region) has 4 rows of 2 tens, or 8 tens; region 3 (upper right region) has 1 row of 3 tens; and region 4 (upper left region) has 1 row of 2 hundreds."

Note that in regions 3 and 4, there is only one row, which is determined by the 1 ten to the right of the vertical bar of the L-frame (which is the 1 ten in the multiplier). Some students will think there are 3 rows in region 3, but these are columns (vertical) and not rows (horizontal), as used in multiplication. Also notice that region 1 always contains *ones*, and that region 3 (or the region above region 1) always contains *tens*. In addition, each region on the left always contains the next-higher place value than that value found in the region immediately to the right. Students should now transfer the descriptions onto the vertical format to the right of the completed L-frame as shown:

$$
\begin{array}{r}
\text{T O} \\
2\ 3 \\
\times\ \ 1\ 4 \\
\hline
1\ 2 \\
8 \\
3 \\
2 \\
\hline
3\ 2\ 2
\end{array}
$$

Regions:

(1) 4×3 ones = 12 ones

(2) 4×2 tens = 8 tens

(3) 1×3 tens = 3 tens

(4) 1×2 hundreds = 2 hundreds

Repeat the process with Exercise 4.

Pattern Search

After the finished frames of Exercises 3 and 4 have been transferred to the vertical format, ask students to look at Exercise 3 again and compare the factors that were used to describe the shape arrangements in the four regions, with the digits in the original two numbers, 23 and 14. All digits in these two numbers were chosen to be unique so that the comparison will be easy for students. They should notice that the factors in 4×3, 4×2, 1×3, and 1×2 use the same digits as those used in the 23 and 14. Now have students draw arrows on the original numbers to show the connection between these groups of numbers. The arrows should be drawn so that they do not cross each other, then labeled for the regions they represent.

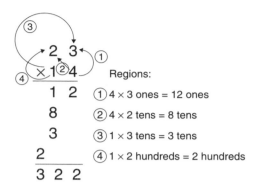

Regions:

① 4×3 ones = 12 ones

② 4×2 tens = 8 tens

③ 1×3 tens = 3 tens

④ 1×2 hundreds = 2 hundreds

Have students examine Exercise 4 in order to see if the digits have the same relationship as found in Exercise 3. The pattern should hold for both exercises. Thus, students should draw and label arrows on Exercise 4 as they have done on Exercise 3.

Note: It is recommended that the four rows of partial products (for example, the 12 ones, 8 tens, 3 tens, and 2 hundreds used in Exercise 3) not be collapsed into two rows at this time. (Regions 1 and 2 are typically written as one row, and regions 3 and 4 are written as a second row.) There is no need to do so mathematically, because students are no longer expected to multiply extremely large numbers by hand. It will also reduce the regroupings students have to do when they add at the end. The traditional multiplication algorithm is quite complex. Students need to go through the stages described here slowly so they will understand the process clearly. This entire development normally requires three or four class periods in order for most students to comprehend all the steps well. Once students see the pattern in the arrows for multiplying two-digit numbers by two-digit numbers, they will be able to extend the pattern to three-digit numbers as well. The arrow-region-simplification procedure reflects the place value changes that occur during multiplication and accounts for the "column shifting" that has been used in the past.

For a more detailed description of this method for developing the whole number multiplication algorithm, please refer to the following resource, which is available at local bookstores: Frances M. Thompson, *Hands-on Math! Ready-to-Use Games and Activities for Grades 4–8* (Jossey-Bass, 1994).

Answer Key for Worksheet 2-2b

1. $4 \times 23 = 92$ ears of corn in all (vertical notation given in text)

2. $3 \times 12 = 36$ eggs in 3 dozen

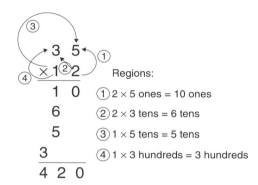

3. $14 \times 23 = 322$ shells in all; vertical notation given in text

4. $12 \times 35 = 420$ seats in all

110

WORKSHEET 2-2b   Name _____

Drawing Products for Word Problems   Date _____

Draw rectangles on each L-frame to find the product for each exercise. Below the frame, write a number sentence that shows the product. Follow your teacher's instructions to finish each exercise.

1. There are 4 bins of corn. Each bin contains 23 ears of corn. How many ears of corn total are in the 4 bins?

2. Charlie used 3 dozen eggs for the school's egg hunt. How many eggs did he use in all?

WORKSHEET 2-2b Continued

Name _____

Date _____

3. There are 14 buckets of seashells. Each bucket holds 23 seashells to be made into necklaces. How many shells in all are available for making jewelry?

4. The auditorium has 12 rows of seats. Each row contains 35 seats. How many seats total are in the auditorium?

Activity 3: Independent Practice

Materials

Worksheet 2-2c
Red pencil and regular pencil

Procedure

On Worksheet 2-2c, students will work several exercises without drawing on L-frames. To check for understanding initially, have them reverse the labeling process used in Activity 2. They should draw the arrows first, then use the arrow information to identify and record the region equations needed to find the partial products of the vertical algorithm.

For the example of a one-digit multiplier in Exercise 1, to work 6×34, arrow #1 will connect the 6 to the 4, which indicates the partial product 6×4 ones = 24 ones. Arrow #1 always represents the ones. Arrow #2 will connect the 6 to the 3, indicating the partial product 6×3 tens = 18 tens. When the 24 ones and 18 tens are recorded and combined, the final product will be 204.

For the example of a two-digit multiplier in Exercise 2, when working 17×32, arrow #1 will connect the 7 to the 2, which indicates the partial product 7×2 ones = 14 ones. Arrow #2 will connect the 7 to the 3, indicating the partial product 7×3 tens = 21 tens. Arrow #3 will connect the 1 to the 2 for the partial product 1×2 tens = 2 tens. In this example, arrow #3 represents the group *above* the ones in the L-frame, and that group is always tens. Arrow #4 will connect the 1 to the 3 for the partial product 1×3 hundreds = 3 hundreds. When the partial products (14 ones, 21 tens, 2 tens, and 3 hundreds) are recorded and combined, the final product will be 544.

The remaining exercises are word problems to be worked using the vertical notation of the algorithm that was developed in Activity 2. Below each word problem, students should record an equation that states the product found. Encourage students to find the partial products mentally, but allow them to continue drawing arrows or writing equations for the partial products if they find that helpful. After they become proficient in finding the partial products, they will no longer need to draw the arrows or record the region equations for the partial products.

Answer Key for Worksheet 2-2c

1. 204 (arrows discussed in text)

2. 544 (arrows discussed in text)

Be sure to keep the multiplier as the first factor in each equation below.

3. $8 \times 24 = 192$ cookies displayed

4. $3 \times 15 = 45$ toy cars total

5. $18 \times 30 = 540$ crates to unload

6. $20 \times 15 = 300$ students total

Possible Testing Errors That May Occur for This Objective

- The correct algorithm for multiplication is applied, but an incorrect multiplication *fact* is used when finding one of the partial products. For example, in 3×27, 3×7 is recorded as the partial product 24 ones instead of 21 ones.

- When the tens digit of the multiplier is used as a factor, the partial product is recorded in the ones column instead of the tens column; that is, students right-justify all the partial products. For example, in 23×45, when finding the partial product for 2×5, students record the amount as 10 ones instead of 10 tens.

- The two original factors in the problem are added instead of multiplied. For example, 13×24 is incorrectly computed as $13 + 24$.

114

Copyright © 2003 by John Wiley & Sons, Inc.

WORKSHEET 2-2c   Name _____

Finding Products in Multiplication   Date _____

To work Exercises 1 and 2, draw arrows with a red pencil, then write equations for the partial products in order to find the partial products and their sum for each exercise.

1.
$$\begin{array}{r} 3\ 4 \\ \times\quad 6 \\ \hline \end{array}$$

2.
$$\begin{array}{r} 3\ 2 \\ \times 1\ 7 \\ \hline \end{array}$$

For Exercises 3 through 6, solve each exercise by using the multiplication algorithm. Show your steps on the back of the worksheet. Below each word problem, write a number sentence that shows the answer.

3. There are 8 display trays at the cooking contest. Each tray holds 24 cookies. How many cookies total are on display at the contest?

4. Luis has 3 boxes of toy cars in his collection. Each box contains 15 cars. How many toy cars does he have in all in his collection?

5. A train has 18 boxcars. Each boxcar contains 30 shipping crates being delivered to a nearby warehouse. How many crates will have to be unloaded from the train at the warehouse?

6. Twenty vans are carrying students to a football game. Each van holds 15 students. How many students are riding in vans altogether?

Objective 3

Divide two-digit or three-digit whole numbers by one-digit whole numbers (as divisors) to solve a single-stepped word problem.

Discussion

The division algorithm for whole numbers needs to be developed carefully for young students. The estimation of quotient digits and the backward trading or regrouping between place values are quite difficult for them. The activities described next will present a method for introducing two- and three-digit dividends with one-digit divisors. It will be assumed here that the multiplication algorithm has already been mastered.

Activity 1: Manipulative Stage

Materials

Set of base 10 blocks per pair of students (4 hundreds, 40 tens, and 40 ones)
Building Mat 2-3a
Worksheet 2-3a
Regular pencil

Procedure

1. Give each pair of students a set of base 10 blocks (4 hundreds, 40 tens, and 40 ones) and Building Mat 2-3a. The building mat should be positioned so that the short bar is vertical and at the left side of the mat and the long bar is horizontal and at the top of the mat.

2. Give each student a copy of Worksheet 2-3a.

3. Have students model each worksheet exercise with their blocks, then record below the exercise a word sentence that shows the results found on the building mat.

4. Students should look at the blocks in each row of the dividend region of the building mat in order to determine the quotient. Always have students use proper place value language when verbally describing their steps to the class.

5. A sample exercise will be discussed next.

Consider Exercise 1 on Worksheet 2-3a as an example: "The school will use 4 buses to take 103 students on a field trip. The same number of students will ride on each bus. How many students will go on the field trip in each bus?"

Have students place 4 ones blocks (or small cubes) on the building mat along the left side of the vertical bar of the L-frame; these blocks represent the divisor or the number of buses. Then have students place 1 hundreds block (or flat) and 3 ones blocks on the building mat in the lower right corner; these blocks are the dividend or total number of students. Tell students that each ones block along the vertical bar indicates that one row (horizontal) of blocks must be built inside the L-frame in line with that block and that a complete row will be equal to the quotient or number of people riding each bus. Here is the initial appearance of the blocks on Building Mat 2-3a:

Ask students if the present single hundreds block is enough to make 4 equal rows (in division, we begin the sharing process with the largest blocks in the dividend). Since it is not, the hundreds block must be traded for 10 tens blocks (or rods); students should then distribute 2 tens blocks to each row. This leaves 2 tens blocks still in the dividend. These must be traded for 20 ones blocks.

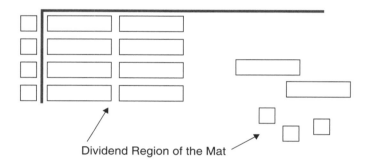

Dividend Region of the Mat

After the trade, there are 23 ones blocks in the dividend; students should distribute 5 ones blocks to each row, leaving 3 ones blocks in the lower right corner of the mat that could not be shared.

When students finish building the 4 rows of blocks, ask them to describe the blocks now in the region directly under the L-frame of the mat. They should respond with 4 rows of 2 tens and 5 ones. This means that the quotient is also 2 tens and 5 ones, or 25. Students should place 2 tens and 5 ones above the horizontal bar of the L-frame, aligned with the other blocks that are similar, in order to show the quotient. The final mat for the bus problem in Exercise 1 should appear as follows:

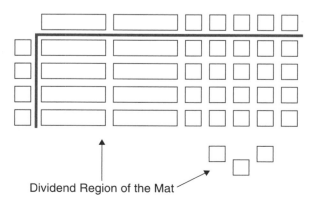

Dividend Region of the Mat

On the worksheet below Exercise 1, students should write a word sentence about their results: "103 students separated equally onto 4 buses makes 25 students per bus, with 3 more students still needing a ride."

For some story problems, there may be 10 or more ones or 10 or more tens in the final block arrangement in the dividend region of the mat. Students should not trade these blocks for a larger block; the arrangement of the blocks must not be changed once the blocks have been shared and placed on the mat.

Answer Key for Worksheet 2-3a (possible sentences to record)

1. 103 students separated equally onto 4 buses makes 25 students per bus, with 3 more students still needing a ride.

2. 45 flowers placed equally into 3 pots makes 15 flowers per pot.

3. 150 circus animals equally placed on 5 trains is 30 animals per train.

4. 34 parade wagons shared equally by 5 clubs makes 6 wagons per club; 4 wagons remain for other groups to use.

5. 72 people sitting at 6 tables equally makes 12 people per table.

6. 212 vases packed equally into 6 crates is 35 vases per crate, with 2 vases left over.

118

BUILDING MAT 2-3a

WORSHEET 2-3a

Building Equal Shares with
Base 10 Blocks

Name _____

Date _____

Build with base 10 blocks on Building Mat 2-3a to find the quotient needed for each word problem. Write a word sentence below each exercise to express the answer found.

1. The school will use 4 buses to take 103 students on a field trip. The same number of students will ride on each bus. How many students will go on the field trip in each bus?

2. The florist's shop has 45 flowers on sale. Equal amounts of the flowers are placed in each of 3 different flower pots. How many flowers are in each of the flower pots?

3. At 3:00 A.M., 5 trains will carry 150 circus animals to the next city for a show. All trains will carry the same number of animals. How many animals will ride on each train?

4. There are 34 wagons available for the Western Day Parade. Each of five local clubs will need an equal number of wagons for their members. The clubs get first choice and will need as many of the wagons as possible. How many wagons will each club be using in the parade? After all the clubs reserve their wagons, how many wagons will still be available for other groups to use?

5. At the banquet, Jimmy saw 72 people sitting at 6 tables. Each table had the same number of people. How many people were sitting at each table?

6. 212 ceramic vases are ready for shipment to stores in Hawaii. Six crates, which hold equal amounts of the vases, will be used to ship the vases. What is the maximum number of vases that can be shipped in each crate?

Activity 2: Pictorial Stage

Materials
Worksheet 2-3b
Red pencil and regular pencil

Procedure

1. Give each student a red pencil and a copy of Worksheet 2-3b.

2. Students will now draw diagrams to find quotients for word problems. The drawings should look just like the finished mat in the example discussed at the Manipulative Stage.

3. After drawing the diagram for each exercise on Worksheet 2-3b, students will write a number sentence or equation below the diagram to record the results found.

4. Then students will label different parts of the shared dividend and transfer the labels to the box format for the division algorithm. For each exercise, the box format will be recorded to the right of the diagram.

5. Students will look for patterns among the digits of the divisor and quotient that will help them identify the partial products involved in the division process.

6. An example of the steps to follow in this discussion will be presented next.

Exercise 1 on Worksheet 2-3b provides this example: "There are 7 bins of corn. 219 ears of corn are to be stored in equal amounts in the bins. How many ears of corn will be in each bin?"

Drawing the Dividend Region

Following the sharing method used in Activity 1 and drawing large squares for hundreds and long and short rectangles to represent the tens and ones, respectively, here is the initial frame for the problem in Exercise 1. Note that the dividend shapes are drawn to the left of the L-frame this time instead of below the L-frame, as was done earlier in Activity 1. This minimizes the need to erase. The 7 ones (short rectangles or squares) drawn immediately to the left of the vertical bar of the L-frame represent the divisor or number of equal shares to be made. A row of shapes must eventually be drawn under the L-frame to correspond to each of the ones in the divisor.

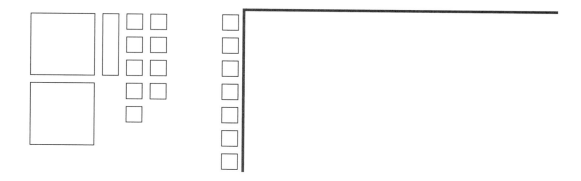

Trades are shown by marking out (X) shapes in red pencil, then drawing new, smaller shapes. Shapes at the left are marked out (/) as they are shared or redrawn under the L-frame.

Beginning with the 2 hundreds as the largest place values, students cannot share or separate the two shapes into 7 rows, so they must trade the hundreds for tens. This is done by marking out the 2 hundreds with red pencil, then drawing 2 new groups of 10 tens in regular pencil nearby. There are now 20 + 1, or 21, tens, which can be shared 7 ways or redrawn equally in 7 rows under the L-frame. As these 21 tens are redrawn under the L-frame, they should be marked out (/) at the left with regular pencil.

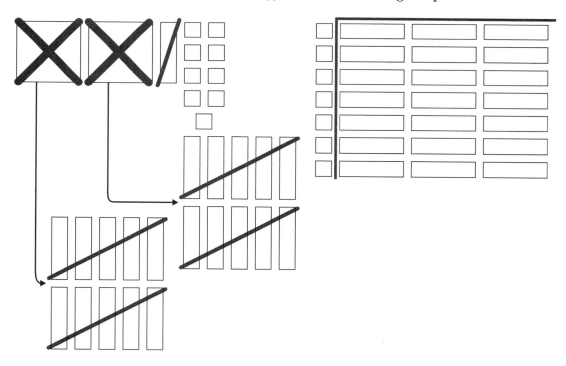

Seven of the 9 ones are then shared by marking them out (/) in regular pencil and redrawing them under the L-frame in the rows with the tens. The two ones left unshared are circled at the left of the frame. One of the finished rows is then copied above the L-frame to show the quotient, which will be 3 tens and 1 one, or 31.

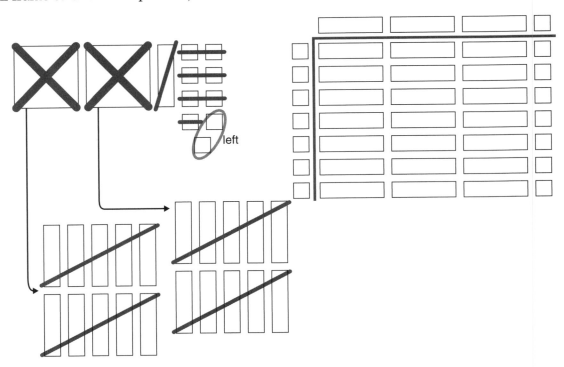

After all students have finished the drawing, have them count the shapes in the quotient above the L-frame; 3 tens and 1 one, or 31 ears of corn will be stored in each bin, with 2 ears left over. Write an equation below the frame to show the results: "219 ÷ 7 = 31 ears of corn per bin with 2 ears left over." Draw frames for the other exercises on Worksheet 2-3b before continuing to the next step of this activity.

Labeling Parts of the Dividend Region

After drawing frames for all exercises on Worksheet 2-3b, return to the frame for Exercise 1. Label and discuss the two parts or regions within the larger dividend region or below the L-frame. Have students draw a vertical red bar to separate the tens and ones below the frame. Label the tens as region 1 and the ones as region 2.

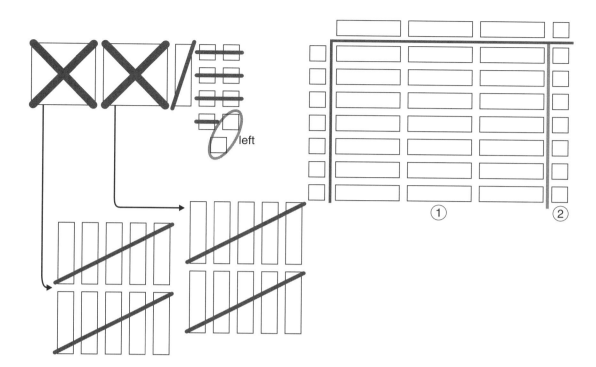

The arrangement of the shapes within each part of the example should be described in the following way: "Region 1 has 7 rows of 3 tens, or 21 tens; region 2 has 7 rows of 1 one, or 7 ones." Students should transfer these descriptions onto the box format to the right of the completed L-frame of Exercise 1 as shown:

$$
\begin{array}{r}
31 \\
7\overline{)219} \\
-21 \\
\hline
09 \\
-7 \\
\hline
2
\end{array}
$$

Regions:
① 7 × 3 tens = 21 tens used

② 7 × 1 ones = 7 ones used

   ones left unshared

Because 2 hundreds could not be shared 7 ways but 21 tens could, the 2 and 1 in the dividend should be underlined in red pencil. This will indicate where the quotient begins. Now repeat the labeling and transfer process for the other exercises on Worksheet 2-3b.

Pattern Search

After all finished frames have been transferred to the box format, return to Exercise 1. Ask students to compare the factors that were used to describe the shape arrangements in the two regions (tens and ones) with the digits in the divisor and quotient (7 and 31) in the example. All digits in these two numbers are unique, so the comparison should be easy for the students. They should notice that the factors in 7 × 3 and 7 × 1 use the same digits as those used in the 7 and 31. Now have students draw arrows on the divisor and quotient to show the connection between these groups of numbers. The arrows should be drawn and labeled for the regions they represent.

$$
\begin{array}{r}
31 \\
7\overline{)219} \\
-21 \\
\hline
09 \\
-7 \\
\hline
2
\end{array}
$$

Regions:

① 7 × 3 tens = 21 tens used

② 7 × 1 ones = 7 ones used

2   ones left unshared

Have students examine all the other exercises on Worksheet 2-3b that they have worked at this stage of development, in order to see if their digits have the same relationship as shown in the example. The pattern should hold for all the problems. Thus, students should draw and label arrows on the rest of the exercises as they have done for Exercise 1.

At this point, discuss how division is different from the other three operations in that students must *estimate* the first digit or leftmost digit of the quotient, then compare the product of that digit and the divisor against the first leftmost digits within the dividend. As in the case of Exercise 1, students will have to look at the 21 tens available to fill region 1 and decide what the other factor must be to pair with the divisor, 7, so that their product equals to the 21 tens. The factor that works may not use up all 21 tens (here it does). Then the extra tens must be traded for ones and used in region 2 instead.

The traditional division algorithm is quite complex. Students need to go through the stages described here slowly so they will understand the process clearly. When the division algorithm is taught for the first time, this entire development usually requires three or four class periods in order for most students to comprehend all the steps well.

For a more detailed description of the method for developing the whole number division algorithm, including two-digit divisors, please refer to the following resource, which is available at local bookstores: Frances M. Thompson, *Hands-on Math! Ready-to-Use Games and Activities for Grades 4–8* (Jossey-Bass, 1994).

Answer Key for Worksheet 2-3b

1. 219 ÷ 7 = 31 ears of corn per bin with 2 ears left over (diagram and box format shown in text)

2. 48 ÷ 3 = 16 eggs per box

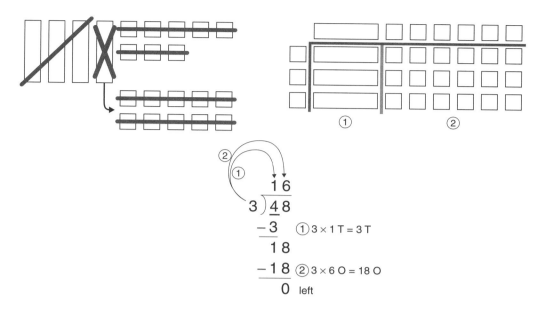

3. $120 \div 5 = 24$ seashells per box

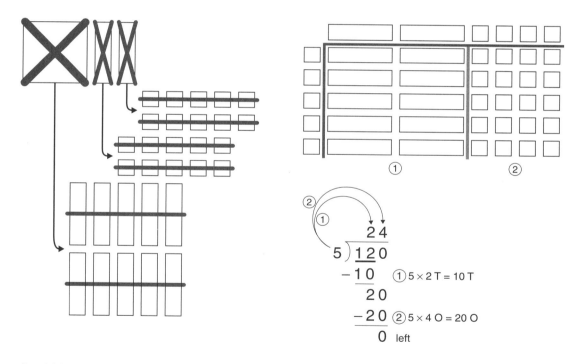

4. $132 \div 6 = 22$ people per table

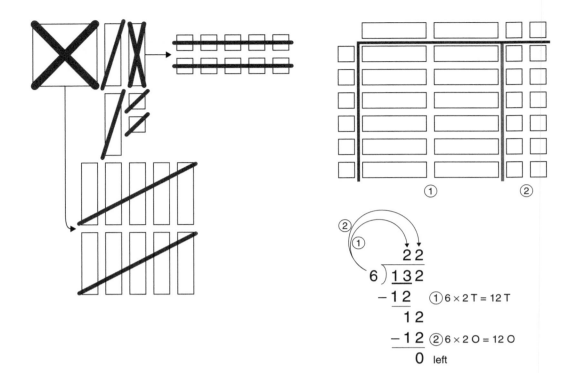

① 6 × 2 T = 12 T

② 6 × 2 O = 12 O

WORKSHEET 2-3b

Drawing to Make Equal Shares

Name _____

Date _____

Draw rectangles on each L-frame to find the quotient for each exercise. Below the frame, write a number sentence that shows the results. Follow your teacher's instructions to finish each exercise.

1. There are 7 bins of corn. 219 ears of corn are to be stored in equal amounts in the bins. How many ears of corn will be in each bin?

2. Charlie used 48 eggs for the school's egg hunt. He stored the eggs in equal amounts in 3 boxes. How many eggs did he put in each box?

WORKSHEET 2-3b Continued

Name _____

Date _____

3. Jamie has 120 seashells to sell at the craft fair. She plans to put equal amounts into 5 buckets, which she will sell for $8 a bucket. How many shells will be in each bucket?

4. 132 people need to be arranged equally at 6 banquet tables. How many people will be placed at each table?

Activity 3: Independent Practice

Materials

Worksheet 2-3c
Red pencil and regular pencil

Procedure

Give each student a red pencil and a copy of Worksheet 2-3c. Students will work several problems without drawing on frames. Exercise 1 will show the quotient already written over the dividend but no partial products recorded below the dividend. Students should first draw the arrows. Then using those arrows, they should write the region factor equations to the right of the problem and write the region products under the dividend to subtract. Finally, Exercises 2 through 4 will be word problems to be worked with the box format. Encourage students to find the region factor equations mentally, but if necessary, allow them to continue drawing arrows and writing the equations beside the division box. In all exercises, have students underline in red pencil the leftmost digits in the dividend that represent the first amount to be shared. For example, in 219 ÷ 7, 21 should be underlined in red to show that 21 *tens* are the first amount to be separated equally into 7 rows or groups. Hence, the leftmost digit in the quotient must begin in the tens place.

Answer Key for Worksheet 2-3c

1.

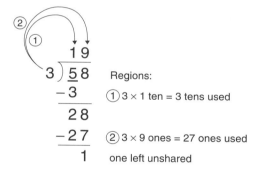

Regions:
① 3 × 1 ten = 3 tens used

② 3 × 9 ones = 27 ones used

one left unshared

2. 192 ÷ 8 = 24 cookies per tray

3. 45 ÷ 3 = 15 toy cars per box

4. 231 ÷ 6 = 38 children per group, with 3 on the waiting list

Possible Testing Errors That May Occur for This Objective

- After subtracting the first partial product found and getting a remainder, students drop that initial remainder when finding the second partial product. For example, in 229 ÷ 7, after dividing 22 tens by 7, 1 ten will remain; this ten is ignored, and only the 9 ones are divided by 7 instead of the 19 ones.

- Students do not apply the division or separation process described in the story situation. Rather, they use multiplication to solve the problem.

- An incorrect multiplication fact is used to find a partial product during the division process.

130

WORKSHEET 2-3c   Name _____

Finding Quotients in Division   Date _____

To work Exercise 1, draw arrows with a red pencil, then write factor equations in order to find the partial products to subtract during division.

1.
$$3\overline{)\,5\,8}$$
with quotient $1\,9$ written above

For Exercises 2 through 4, solve each exercise by using the box method of the division algorithm. Show your steps on the back of the worksheet. Below each word problem, write a number sentence that shows the answer.

2. There are 192 cookies displayed equally on 8 trays at the cooking contest. How many cookies will each tray hold?

3. Luis has 45 toy cars in his collection. The cars are stored in equal amounts in 3 boxes. How many toy cars does Luis have in each box?

4. 231 children have applied to attend a summer camp. At the camp, the children are to be equally assigned to 6 groups. Any children not assigned to a group will be put on a waiting list. How many children will be assigned to each group, and how many must be put on the waiting list?

Objective 4

Solve multistepped word problems, using addition, subtraction, multiplication, or division of whole numbers.

Discussion

Some multistepped problems require students to actually compute to find the answer, whereas other multistepped problems focus on notation and require the students to set up the series of equations needed or to find a single equation that combines all the steps together. The activities presented here will focus on the written notation for combined steps and how to interpret it. Problems involving two steps will be used. It is assumed that students already know the meaning of each of the four basic operations, as well as the notation used for each operation.

Activity 1: Manipulative Stage

Materials

Set of 21 number cards per pair of students (use 0 to 20, one number per card)
Set of 8 operation cards per pair of students (1 operation symbol per card, two
    cards per symbol: +, −, ×, ÷)
1 blank card and 2 Popsicle sticks (or pipe cleaners) per pair of students
Worksheet 2-4a
Regular pencil

Procedure

1. Give each pair of students a set of cards numbered 0 through 20, one number per card. Also have operation cards ready. Each card should have one of the four basic operation symbols on it. Partners would have 2 cards for each of the 4 operations, or 8 operation cards total, as well as the number cards. Make card sets with 3×5 blank index cards, using the longer edge as the height of a card.

2. Give each pair one blank card to use as a space holder or unknown when needed and 2 Popsicle sticks (or pipe cleaners) to serve as parentheses.

3. Give each student a copy of Worksheet 2-4a.

4. Have students use the cards and sticks to model the equations needed to solve each word problem on Worksheet 2-4a. Students will be analyzing, not computing, in this activity. Discuss each problem with the class before continuing to the next problem.

5. For each two-stepped problem, students should put down on the desktop the cards for the two numbers and the operation needing to be computed first, if possible. These cards should be blocked on each side with the Popsicle sticks (or pipe cleaners). Students should then put down the third number and the second operation beside the other three cards in the appropriate order from left to right to reflect the second computation needed to find the solution.

6. Remind students that they may need to use "backward thinking" here; that is, they may have to think of the second or final step first before they can decide what the first step should be. This is where the blank card will be helpful.

7. Once they have the correct arrangement of cards, students should write the complete expression in equation form on Worksheet 2-4a, using N as the final answer.

8. Exercise 1 on Worksheet 2-4a will be discussed next.

Exercise 1 on Worksheet 2-4a is as follows: "Ellie bought 12 bushes and 4 trees for her new yard. On Friday, she planted 7 bushes. How many bushes and trees are left to be planted on Saturday?"

Ask students to describe what they are really wanting to find (remaining bushes and remaining trees to plant). To show this, they should place the 4-card, the plus-card, and the blank card left to right on the desktop; the blank card holds a space for the number of remaining bushes. Because this actually represents the final step, "backward thinking" must be used in this problem.

Ask students how to find the remaining bushes. Below the first 3 cards, they should show left to right the 12-card, minus-card, and 7-card. These last 3 cards show the remaining bushes, but they actually represent the first computation step needed.

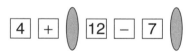

The 3 new cards should be substituted for the blank card in the first 3 cards. After the substitution is made, to identify the first computation step, students should place one Popsicle stick on each side of the two numbers, 12 and 7, involved in that first step. This will show that the subtraction, 12 − 7, is done first. The final arrangement of the cards is shown here.

$$\boxed{4}\ \boxed{+}\ \big(\ \boxed{12}\ \boxed{-}\ \boxed{7}\ \big)$$

Students should record their final card set on Worksheet 2-4a below Exercise 1 as follows: "4 + (12 − 7) = N," where N represents the final answer. If some students originally placed their blank card to the left of the 4-card, their equation will be the following: "(12 − 7) + 4 = N." Continue this process with the other word problems. Remind students that there may be more than one way to set up their combination equation for a problem.

Answer Key for Worksheet 2-4a (possible equations to use)

1. $4 + (12 - 7) = N$

2. $14 - (7 + 4) = N$ or $(14 - 7) - 4 = N$

3. $(2 \times 8) + 5 = N$

4. $(18 - 10) - 5 = N$ or $18 - (10 + 5) = N$

5. $(12 \div 2) + 3 = N$

WORKSHEET 2-4a

Name _____

Building the Steps for
Multistepped Problems

Date _____

Use number and operation cards to build the computation steps needed for the given word problems. Write the final combination equation below each exercise.

1. Ellie bought 12 bushes and 4 trees for her new yard. On Friday she planted 7 bushes. How many bushes and trees are left to be planted on Saturday?

2. Tommy rode his bicycle along three different streets last Saturday. He rode a total distance of 14 kilometers. He rode 7 kilometers along Jackson Street and 4 kilometers along Duke Avenue. How many kilometers in all did he ride on Morris Street?

3. Mario mowed 2 lawns last week and earned $8 for each lawn. He also earned an additional $5 for weeding a flower garden. How much in all did he earn last week?

4. Liu had $18 in her savings. She decided to buy a new CD for $10 and to go to a movie for $5. How much did she have left in her savings?

5. George and Henry shared a dozen donuts equally. George then ate 3 more donuts. How many donuts in all did George eat?

Activity 2: Pictorial Stage

Materials
Worksheet 2-4b
Red pencil and regular pencil

Procedure
1. Give each student a copy of Worksheet 2-4b and a red pencil.

2. Repeat the process used in the Manipulative Stage, but instead of using actual cards, have students *draw boxes* on Worksheet 2-4b to represent the cards. Numbers and operation symbols should be written inside the boxes. Students will have to decide which pair of numbers to draw first and whether to draw the pair to the left or to the right on their papers, particularly with respect to division or subtraction. Have students draw a red ring around two numbers to represent pairing the numbers for the first computation step.

3. For each exercise on Worksheet 2-4b, the final combination equation should be recorded below the drawing of the boxes.

4. As an example, Exercise 1 will be discussed next.

Exercise 1 on Worksheet 2-4b is as follows: "Oliver had 10 hat pins in his collection at first. On Monday, he gave 6 pins away to a friend. He then tripled what he had left by trading some of his stamps for more pins. After the trading, how many hat pins did Oliver have in his collection?"

To show the removal of 6 pins from 10 pins, students should draw three boxes on the worksheet and fill them with the appropriate symbols. Since these boxes represent the first computation step needed, students should draw a red ring around them as follows:

Once students know how many hat pins are left, they need to triple this amount, that is, multiply the amount by 3. Three is the multiplier in this case, so it should be drawn to the left of the ringed group. The multiplication represents the second computation step in solving the problem.

Students should now record the final combination equation below the drawing on the worksheet: "$3 \times (10 - 6) = N$."

Answer Key for Worksheet 2-4b

1. $3 \times (10 - 6) = N$

2. $(35 - 18) + 10 = N$

3. $(10 + 18) \div 2 = N$

4. $(4 \times 8) + 15 = N$

136

WORSHEET 2-4b

Name _____

Drawing the Steps for
Multistepped Problems

Date _____

Draw number and operation cards to show computation steps needed for the given word problems. Circle in red pencil the first step to be done in each situation. Write the final combination equation below the drawing for each exercise.

1. Oliver had 10 hat pins in his collection at first. On Monday, he gave 6 pins away to a friend. He then tripled what he had left by trading some of his stamps for more pins. After the trading, how many hat pins did Oliver have in his collection?

2. Tara had $35 in her savings account. She took out $18 to spend at a theme park. A week later, she received $10 for a birthday gift and put it into her savings account. How much money was finally in her savings account?

3. Harry earned $10 for cutting a neighbor's lawn and $18 for helping to paint a house. He then gave half of his total earnings to his sister as a graduation gift. How much did he give to his sister?

4. Luisa earned $8 each week for 4 weeks as a babysitter. She also earned $15 working at her aunt's candy store. How much did Luisa earn total from both jobs?

Activity 3: Independent Practice

Materials
Worksheet 2-4c
Regular pencil

Procedure
Give each student a copy of Worksheet 2-4c. Exercises 1 and 2 require students to rewrite a combination equation as the two separate equations that represent the two steps involved in solving the problem. Do not allow students to write a "run-on" equation like "$18 - 6 = 12 \div 4 = 3$," where clearly the left expression ($18 - 6$) does not equal the right expression (3). Exercises 3 through 5 require students to write a combination equation for solving the problem. Remind students that the parentheses in a combination equation indicate the computation step that needs to be done first.

Answer Key for Worksheet 2-4c
1. $18 - 6 = 12$; $12 \div 4 = 3$; $N = 3$

2. $5 \times 3 = 15$; $9 + 15 = 24$; $N = 24$

3. $20 - (3 \times 2) = N$

4. $(25 - 7) - 3 = N$

5. $(36 \div 12) - 1 = N$

Possible Testing Errors That May Occur for This Objective
- If subtraction is involved, students forget to decrease their tens or hundreds after a regrouping is performed. For example, in $80 - 64$, after they trade a ten for 10 ones, students use 10 ones – 4 ones but use 8 tens – 6 tens instead of 7 tens – 6 tens. A similar regrouping error may occur with addition.

- A fact error is made for one of the operations involved in the problem. For example, in finding 3×28, $3 \times 8 = 21$ ones might be used instead of $3 \times 8 = 24$ ones.

- In a two-step problem, students may use only two of the three given numbers; that is, they perform only one of the required steps.

- The wrong operations are applied. For example, if multiplication and subtraction are needed, students might use multiplication and addition. This is generally caused by a misunderstanding of the meanings of the operations.

138

WORKSHEET 2-4c
Writing Equations for
Multistepped Problems

Name _____

Date _____

For Exercises 1 and 2, rewrite the given combination equation as two equations to show the two steps involved in the original equation. Use the computed answer for step 1 in the equation for step 2. State what N finally equals.

1. $(18 - 6) \div 4 = N$

2. $9 + (5 \times 3) = N$

For Exercises 3 through 5, write the final combination equation that represents the two steps needed to solve the problem.

3. A bakery had 20 brownies for sale. Three sacks were already prepared with 2 brownies per sack. The sacks were sold first. How many brownies then remained to be sold?

4. Twenty-five school desks were in storage. Seven of the desks were small desks. The rest were large desks. Three of the large desks were broken, so they were thrown away. How many large desks still remain in storage?

5. Three dozen donuts were shared equally by Joel and 11 other students. Joel gave one of his donuts to his sister. How many donuts did Joel actually have to eat?

Objective 5
Estimate a solution to a word problem, using rounding and whole number addition with two or more addends.

Discussion
When using estimation, the general principle is to have students round numbers to levels that will allow them to apply addition facts in only one place value column. For example, if four-digit numbers are used in an addition problem, generally thousands would be the best level to choose for rounding. However, if one number is in the thousands and the other is only in the hundreds, then both numbers should be rounded to the nearest hundred in order to keep the same degree of accuracy for both numbers. For example, 1,520 + 3,425 would become 2,000 + 3,000 to use the fact 2 + 3 in the thousands column, but 1,520 + 865 would become 1,500 + 900, requiring regrouping in the hundreds column.

Activity 1: Manipulative Stage

Materials
Building Mat 2-5a for each pair of students
50 small counters for each pair of students (same color or same style)
Worksheet 2-5a (word problems)

Procedure
1. Provide each pair of students with a building mat, counters, and two copies of Worksheet 2-5a, which involves only two- and three-digit numbers at this stage.

2. The two numbers needed for each problem should be shown on the mat and then rounded.

3. Once the numbers are rounded, students will perform the required computation mentally, if possible, or with the appropriate written algorithm, if preferred.

4. A word sentence should be recorded to show the estimated work.

5. Also have students use three-digit numbers as endpoints and describe a numerical *interval* that contains the estimate they have found. (Intervals will vary.)

6. Guide students through Exercise 1 before they proceed to the others.

Here is Exercise 1, followed by a discussion of how to guide students through the problem: "Janice sold 375 tickets to the school play one weekend. She sold 241 more tickets the next weekend. Find a reasonable estimate for the total number of tickets sold."

Students should place counters on the mat to show the two given numbers; the initial amount, 375, should be shown on the top empty row, and the second amount, 241, should be shown on the bottom empty row.

HUNDREDS	TENS	ONES
● ● ●	● ● ● ● ● ● ●	● ● ● ● ●
● ●	● ● ● ●	●

We want to use only one addition fact, if possible, so the largest place value of the *smaller* number is where the addition must occur. For both numbers in this example, that will be the hundreds place. Ask students to look at the top number (375) and observe that there are already 3 hundreds. The tens and ones columns in 375 together show an additional 75. Ask students whether 75 is closer to another hundred or closer to 0. Because 75 is closer to another hundred, have students remove the counters for 75 from the mat and place a new counter beside the original 3 counters in the hundreds column to show an extra hundred. 375 has now been "rounded up to the nearest hundred," which is 400. Repeat the process with 241 in the bottom row of the mat. Discuss the 2 hundreds, then look at the extra 41 shown in the tens and ones columns. Ask whether the 41 is closer to another hundred or closer to 0. In this case, 41 is closer to 0; therefore, a new hundred will not be added, but the counters for 41 will be removed from the mat to show 0 instead. Hence, 241 has been "rounded down to the nearest hundred," which is 200.

The mat now shows 400 on top and 200 on bottom. Students should now compute, using 400 estimated tickets and 200 estimated tickets sold. The addition fact used will be 4 + 2 = 6. A final word sentence should be recorded on the worksheet by each student as follows: "375 + 241 is estimated by 400 + 200 = 600 tickets total sold."

Also ask students to describe an interval that would contain their answer (600); for example, "600 is between 550 and 650." Other possible intervals might be "between 500 and 700" or "between 575 and 660." Record this interval on the worksheet as well (intervals will vary). The interval practice is intended to give students a keener understanding of a number's position among other, similar numbers. In general, if rounding has been to hundreds, each endpoint of the chosen interval should be at most 100 points from the estimated answer. Discourage extreme values, as in "600 is between 0 and 1,000." The final mat and counters will appear as shown.

HUNDREDS	TENS	ONES
● ● ●　●		
● ●		

Answer Key for Worksheet 2-5a

1. 375 + 241 is estimated by 400 + 200 = 600 tickets sold; interval example: 600 is between 550 and 650.

2. 535 + 360 is estimated by 500 + 400 = 900 ounces sold; interval example: 900 is between 875 and 950.

3. $326 + $139 is estimated by $300 + $100 = $400 saved by both; interval example: $400 is between $300 and $500.

4. 144 + 87 is estimated by 140 + 90 = 230 cards total; interval example: 230 is between 200 and 280.

5. 815 + 134 is estimated by 800 + 100 = 900 people total at the game; interval example: 900 is between 800 and 950.

BUILDING MAT 2-5a

ONES	TENS	HUNDREDS

WORKSHEET 2-5a

Addition by Estimation

Name _____

Date _____

Use counters on the estimation building mat to solve the given problems. For each problem, write a word sentence that describes the estimation used and describe a numerical interval that contains the answer found.

1. Janice sold 375 tickets to the school play one weekend. She sold 241 more tickets the next weekend. Find a reasonable estimate for the total number of tickets sold.

2. Charla sold 535 ounces of fudge at her candy store sale on Monday. By Thursday afternoon, she had sold another 360 ounces. Estimate the total number of ounces of fudge she sold during the four days.

3. Kari has saved $326 for her vacation. Her brother Jonathan has saved $139. Find the best estimate of the amount of money that Kari and Jonathan have saved altogether.

4. Jose wants to buy 144 more baseball cards for his collection. He already has 87 cards. About how many cards does he want to have in all in his collection? Estimate to the nearest ten.

5. On Saturday, 815 people arrived at the soccer game on time. 134 more people arrived late for the game. Approximately how many people in all attended the game?

Activity 2: Pictorial Stage

Materials

Worksheet 2-5b (frames)
Worksheet 2-5c (word problems)
Regular pencils

Procedure

1. Provide each student with one copy of Worksheet 2-5b, which contains small frames that look like the earlier building mat, but each frame now includes a thousands column. Above each frame is a small box and a blank writing space. The small box is for recording the number of the word problem being solved on the frame, and the blank is for recording the initial numerical setup obtained from the problem, for example, 4,365 + 1,048 = ?

2. Each student will solve problems by completing the frames on her or his own worksheet but might share results with a partner. Instead of placing counters on the mat to show numbers, students will now draw circles in the columns of the frames. If a number must round up to the next thousand, students should mark out the extra hundreds, tens, and ones and draw a new circle in the thousands column. If a number must round down to the nearest thousand, the extra hundreds, tens, and ones should just be marked out.

3. Give each student a copy of Worksheet 2-5c, which contains several word problems involving three- and four-digit numbers. Below each word problem, students will record the equation used to estimate the sum and will describe an interval that contains the estimate found. Interval descriptions will vary.

4. Guide students through Exercise 1 before allowing them to proceed to others independently.

Here is Exercise 1 to discuss with students as an example: "There were 2,780 tickets sold to a Friday night rock concert, and 1,425 tickets were sold for the Saturday night concert. Estimate the total number of concert tickets sold for both concerts."

Students need to round to the nearest thousand to estimate the total number of tickets sold, since both numbers are in the thousands. By rounding both numbers to thousands, only one addition fact will be needed to find an estimate. (If the smaller number were in the hundreds, both numbers might need to be rounded to the nearest hundreds in order to use an addition fact.) In 2,780, 780 is closer to a new thousand than to 0, so 2,780 rounds up to 3,000. In 1,425, 425 is closer to 0 than to a new thousand, so 1,425 rounds down to 1,000. The rounding will appear on the pictorial frame, along with its final addition equation, as follows:

THOUSANDS	HUNDREDS	TENS	ONES
⬭⬭ ⬭	⊖⊖⊖⊖⊖ ⊖⊖	⊖⊖⊖⊖⊖ ⊖⊖⊖	
⬭	⊖⊖⊖⊖	⊖⊖	⊖⊖⊖⊖⊖

Estimate: 3,000 + 1,000 = 4,000 estimated total tickets sold

The addition fact used was $3 + 1 = 4$. Also ask students to describe an interval that contains their estimate of 4,000; for example, "4,000 is between 3,800 and 4,400." Intervals will vary, but endpoints should be at most 1,000 points from the estimate (4,000), since rounding was to thousands.

Answer Key for Worksheet 2-5c

1. $2,780 + 1,425 = ?$; $3,000 + 1,000 = 4,000$ estimated total tickets sold; interval example: 4,000 is between 3,500 and 4,500.

2. $6,410 + 2,685 = ?$; $6,000 + 3,000 = 9,000$ estimated bushels shipped; interval example: 9,000 is between 8,000 and 10,000.

3. $1,340 + 635 = ?$; $1,300 + 600 = 1,900$ estimated people attended; interval example: 1,900 is between 1,850 and 1,950.

4. $1,278 + 842 = ?$; $1,300 + 800 = 2,100$ estimated tickets sold; interval example: 2,100 is between 2,000 and 2,200.

146

WORSHEET 2-5b
Estimating to Add

Name _____

Date _____

Base 10 Drawing Frames

□ _____

THOUSANDS	HUNDREDS	TENS	ONES

□ _____

THOUSANDS	HUNDREDS	TENS	ONES

□ _____

THOUSANDS	HUNDREDS	TENS	ONES

□ _____

THOUSANDS	HUNDREDS	TENS	ONES

WORKSHEET 2-5c
Estimating to Add

Name _____

Date _____

To solve each word problem, draw circles on a frame on Worksheet 2-5b to show each number, then round as needed in order to add. Below the word problem on this worksheet, record the final estimating equation and an interval that contains the answer.

1. There were 2,780 tickets sold to a Friday night rock concert, and 1,425 tickets were sold for the Saturday night concert. Estimate the total number of concert tickets sold for both concerts.

2. In 1998, Joe's Fruit Company shipped 6,410 bushels of apples to grocery stores. 2,685 bushels were shipped to individuals. Estimate how many bushels total were shipped to stores and individuals.

3. 1,340 people attending the rock concert at the park sat on the grass. 635 other people attending had reserved seats. About how many people in all attended the concert? (Hint: Round to nearest hundreds.)

4. Students had sold 1,278 tickets for the school raffle by Wednesday. By Friday, they had sold 842 more tickets. Find a reasonable total for the number of tickets sold.

Activity 3: Independent Practice

Materials

Worksheet 2-5d (word problems)
Regular pencils

Procedure

Students work independently to complete Worksheet 2-5d. When all are finished, discuss the results.

Answer Key for Worksheet 2-5d

1. A

2. E

3. D

4. B

5. B

Possible Testing Errors That May Occur for This Objective

- One or both numbers are rounded incorrectly; for example, 7,740 might be rounded to 7,000 instead of to 8,000.

- An addition fact error is made, such as in $1,500 + 800 = 2,400$, where the incorrect fact $5 + 8 = 14$ is used.

- A number that is an extraneous value in the problem, such as the year 1998, is used as an addend instead of as an intended number.

WORKSHEET 2-5d
Estimating to Add

Name _____

Date _____

Show your work on another sheet of paper. Circle the best answer choice for each problem on this worksheet. Be ready to discuss how you solved each problem with the other students in your class.

1. Amy sold 321 school-spirit buttons. She later sold 178 more buttons. She also sold 65 of the school pennants. Find the best estimate of the total number of spirit buttons sold.

   A. 500   B. 400   C. 300   D. 200   E. 100

2. Mrs. Josey bought a digital camera on sale for $403. The discount was $194. Which is the best estimate of the original price of the camera?

   A. $200   B. $300   C. $400   D. $500   E. $600

3. Jo's two highest scores on her favorite computer game are 4,950 and 3,050. Which is the best estimate of the sum of her two scores?

   A. Less than 2,500

   B. Between 2,500 and 5,000

   C. Between 5,000 and 7,500

   D. Between 7,500 and 9,000

   E. More than 9,000

4. Elm Farm grew 1,450 pumpkins last year. That same year, Greer Farm grew 680 pumpkins and Shorty's Farm grew 941 pumpkins. Estimate how many pumpkins Greer Farm and Elm Farm grew in all.

   A. 1,900   B. 2,200   C. 2,400   D. 2,500   E. 2,800

5. On Friday 4,428 people attended a band concert at the Hughes Conference Center, and on Saturday 5,740 people attended a stage musical there. What is a reasonable estimate for the total number of tickets taken up at the two events?

   A. More than 12,000

   B. Between 9,000 and 12,000

   C. Between 6,000 and 9,000

   D. Between 2,500 and 6,000

   E. Less than 2,500

Objective 6
Estimate a solution to a word problem, using rounding and subtraction of whole numbers.

Discussion
When using estimation, the general principle is to have students round numbers to levels that will allow them to apply subtraction facts and not have to regroup. For example, if four-digit numbers are used in a subtraction problem, generally thousands would be the best level to choose for subtraction. However, if one number is in the thousands and the other is only in the hundreds, then both numbers may be rounded to the nearest hundred in order to subtract. For example, $1,520 - 865$ would become $1,500 - 900$, in order to use the subtraction fact $15 - 9 = 6$.

Activity 1: Manipulative Stage

Materials
   Building Mat 2-6a for each pair of students
   50 small counters for each pair of students (same color or same style)
   Worksheet 2-6a (word problems)

Procedure
1. Provide each pair of students with a building mat, counters, and two copies of Worksheet 2-6a, which involves only two- and three-digit numbers at this stage.

2. The two numbers needed for each problem should be shown on the mat and then rounded.

3. Once the numbers are rounded, students will perform the required computation mentally, if possible, or with the appropriate written algorithm, if preferred.

4. A word sentence should be recorded to show the estimated work. Also have students use three-digit numbers as endpoints and describe a numerical *interval* that contains the estimate they have found. (Intervals will vary.)

5. Guide students through the first exercise before they proceed to the others.

   Following is an example of how to guide students through Exercise 1 on the worksheet: "Juan had 375 tickets to sell for the school play. He sold 241 of the tickets. Find a reasonable estimate for the number of tickets remaining to be sold."
   Students should place counters on the mat to show the two given numbers; the initial total, 375, should be shown on the top empty row, and the amount sold, 241, should be shown on the bottom empty row.

HUNDREDS	TENS	ONES
● ● ●	● ● ● ● ● ● ●	● ● ● ● ●
● ●	● ● ● ●	●

We want to use only one subtraction fact, if possible, so the largest place value of the *smaller* number is where the subtraction must occur. In this example, that will be the hundreds place for either number. Ask students to look at the top number, 375, and observe that there are already 3 hundreds. The tens and ones columns in 375 together show an additional 75. Ask students whether 75 is closer to another hundred or closer to 0. Because 75 is closer to another hundred, have students remove the counters for 75 from the mat and place a new counter beside the original 3 counters in the hundreds column to show an extra hundred. 375 has now been "rounded up to the nearest hundred," which is 400. Repeat the process with 241 in the bottom row of the mat. Discuss the 2 hundreds, then look at the extra 41 shown in the tens and ones columns. Ask whether the 41 is closer to another hundred or closer to 0. In this case, 41 is closer to 0; therefore, a new hundred will not be added, but the counters for 41 will be removed from the mat to show 0 instead. Hence, 241 has been "rounded down to the nearest hundred," which is 200.

The mat now shows 400 on top and 200 on the bottom. Students should now compute, using 400 estimated total tickets and 200 estimated tickets sold. The subtraction fact used will be 4 – 2 = 2. A final word sentence should be recorded on the worksheet by each student as follows: "375 – 241 is estimated by 400 – 200 = 200 tickets remaining to be sold."

Ask students to describe an interval that would contain their answer (200); for example, "200 is between 150 and 250." Other possible intervals might be "between 100 and 300" or "between 175 and 260." Record this interval on the worksheet as well (intervals will vary). The interval practice is intended to give students a keener understanding of a number's position among other similar numbers. In general, if rounding has been to hundreds, each endpoint of the chosen interval should be at most 100 points from the estimated answer. Discourage extreme values, as in "200 is between 0 and 1,000." The final mat and counters will appear as shown.

HUNDREDS	TENS	ONES
● ● ● ●		
● ●		

Answer Key for Worksheet 2-6a

1. 375 – 241 is estimated by 400 – 200 = 200 tickets to sell; interval example: 200 is between 150 and 250.

2. 535 – 360 is estimated by 500 – 400 = 100 ounces to sell; interval example: 100 is between 75 and 150.

3. $326 – $139 is estimated by $300 – $100 = $200 saved by Jonathan; interval example: $200 is between $100 and $300.

4. 144 – 87 is estimated by 140 – 90 = 50 more cards; interval example: 50 is between 30 and 80.

5. 815 – 134 is estimated by 800 – 100 = 700 people still at the game; interval example: 700 is between 600 and 850.

BUILDING MAT 2-6a

ONES		
TENS		
HUNDREDS		

154

WORKSHEET 2-6a   Name _____
Subtraction by Estimation   Date _____

Use counters on the estimation building mat to solve the given problems. For each problem, write a word sentence that describes the estimation used and describe a numerical interval that contains the answer found.

1. Juan had 375 tickets to sell for the school play. He sold 241 of the tickets. Find a reasonable estimate for the number of tickets remaining to be sold.

2. Kayrin had 535 ounces of fudge for sale at her candy store on Monday morning. By Thursday afternoon she had sold 360 ounces. Estimate the number of ounces of fudge still available for sale on Friday.

3. Lori has saved $326 for a new bicycle. This amount is $139 more than her brother Jonathan has saved. Find the best estimate of the amount of money that Jonathan has saved.

4. Jerry wants to have 144 baseball cards in his collection. He only has 87 cards at this time. About how many more cards does he need to reach his goal? Estimate to the nearest ten.

5. On Saturday 815 people attended the soccer game. 134 people had to leave the game early. Approximately how many people were still at the game when it ended?

Copyright © 2003 by John Wiley & Sons, Inc.

Activity 2: Pictorial Stage

Materials

Worksheet 2-6b (frames)
Worksheet 2-6c (word problems)
Regular pencils

Procedure

1. Provide each student with two copies of Worksheet 2-6b, each sheet containing small frames that look like the earlier building mat, but each frame now includes a thousands column. Above each frame is a small box and a blank writing space. The small box is for recording the number of the word problem being solved on the frame, and the blank is for recording the initial numerical setup obtained from the problem, for example, $4,365 - 1,048 = ?$

2. Each student will solve problems by completing the frames on her or his own worksheet but might share results with a partner. Instead of placing counters on the mat to show numbers, students will now draw circles in the columns of the frames. If a number must round up to the next thousand, students should mark out the extra hundreds, tens, and ones and draw a new circle in the thousands column. If a number must round down to the nearest thousand, the extra hundreds, tens, and ones should just be marked out.

3. Give each student a copy of Worksheet 2-6c, which contains several word problems involving three- and four-digit numbers. Below each word problem, students will record the equation used to estimate the difference and will describe an interval that contains the estimate found. Interval descriptions will vary.

4. Guide students through Exercise 1 before allowing them to proceed to others independently.

Here is Exercise 1 to discuss with students as an example: "There were 2,780 tickets available for a weekend play, and 1,425 tickets had been sold by Wednesday. Estimate the number of play tickets still available to sell."

Students need to round to the nearest thousand to estimate the number of tickets left to sell, since both numbers are in the thousands. By rounding both numbers to thousands, only one subtraction fact will be needed to find an estimate. (If the smaller number were in the hundreds, both numbers might need to be rounded to the nearest hundreds in order to use a subtraction fact.) In 2,780, 780 is closer to a new thousand than to 0, so 2,780 rounds up to 3,000. In 1,425, 425 is closer to 0 than to a new thousand, so 1,425 rounds down to 1,000. The rounding will appear on the pictorial frame, along with its final subtraction equation, as follows:

THOUSANDS	HUNDREDS	TENS	ONES
○ ○ ○	⊖⊖⊖⊖⊖ ⊖⊖	⊖⊖⊖⊖⊖ ⊖⊖⊖	
○	⊖⊖⊖⊖	⊖⊖	⊖⊖⊖⊖⊖

Estimate: 3,000 − 1,000 = 2,000 estimated tickets left to sell

The subtraction fact used was 3 − 1 = 2. Also ask students to describe an interval that contains their estimate of 2,000; for example, "2,000 is between 1,800 and 2,400." Intervals will vary, but endpoints should be at most 1,000 points from the estimate (2,000), since rounding was to thousands.

Answer Key for Worksheet 2-6c

1. 2,780 − 1,425 = ?; 3,000 − 1,000 = 2,000 estimated tickets to sell; interval example: 2,000 is between 1,500 and 2,500.

2. 8,410 − 2,685 = ?; 8,000 − 3,000 = 5,000 estimated bushels sold; interval example: 5,000 is between 4,000 and 7,000.

3. 1,340 − 635 = ?; 1,300 − 600 = 700 estimated people on the grass; interval example: 700 is between 550 and 800.

4. 1,278 − 842 = ?; 1,300 − 800 = 500 estimated tickets to sell; interval example: 500 is between 450 and 550.

5. 4,508 − 3,725 = ?; 5,000 − 4,000 = 1,000 more estimated trout; interval example: 1,000 is between 500 and 1,500.

WORKSHEET 2-6b
Estimating to Subtract

Name _____

Date _____

Base 10 Drawing Frames

☐ _____

THOUSANDS	HUNDREDS	TENS	ONES

☐ _____

THOUSANDS	HUNDREDS	TENS	ONES

☐ _____

THOUSANDS	HUNDREDS	TENS	ONES

158

Name _____

Date _____

Base 10 Drawing Frames

THOUSANDS	HUNDREDS	TENS	ONES

THOUSANDS	HUNDREDS	TENS	ONES

WORSHEET 2-6c   Name _____

Estimating to Subtract   Date _____

To solve each word problem, draw circles on a frame on Worksheet 2-6b to show each number, then round as needed in order to subtract. Below the word problem on this worksheet, record the final estimating equation and an interval that contains the answer.

1. There were 2,780 tickets available for a weekend play, and 1,425 tickets had been sold by Wednesday. Estimate the number of play tickets still available to sell.

2. In 1998, Southeast Fruit Company picked 8,410 bushels of apples. 2,685 bushels were shipped to individuals, and the rest were sold to grocery stores. Estimate how many bushels were sold to the stores.

3. 1,340 people attended the rock concert at the park on Saturday. 635 people had reserved seats, while the rest of the people sat on the grass. About how many people sat on the grass? (Hint: Round to nearest hundreds.)

4. Students had 1,278 tickets to sell for the school raffle. On Tuesday, they had sold 842 of the tickets. Find a reasonable total for the number of tickets remaining to be sold.

5. The Gomez Fish Farm has 4,508 rainbow trout and 3,725 speckled trout. Estimate how many more rainbow trout than speckled trout are presently at the fish farm.

Activity 3: Independent Practice

Materials
 Worksheet 2-6d (word problems)
 Regular pencils

Procedure
Students work independently to complete Worksheet 2-6d. When all are finished, discuss the results.

Answer Key for Worksheet 2-6d
 1. A
 2. A
 3. D
 4. C
 5. D

Possible Testing Errors That May Occur for This Objective
- One or both numbers are rounded incorrectly; for example, 7,740 might be rounded to 7,000 instead of to 8,000.
- A subtraction fact error is made, such as in 1,500 − 800 = 600.
- A number that is an extraneous value in the problem, such as the year 1998, is used in the subtraction instead of an intended number.

WORKSHEET 2-6d

Estimating to Subtract

Name _____

Date _____

Show your work on another sheet of paper. Circle the best answer choice for each problem on this worksheet. Be ready to discuss how you solved each problem with the other students in your class.

1. Amisha had 321 school-spirit buttons to sell. She sold 178 of the buttons. She also sold 65 of the school pennants. Find the best estimate of the number of spirit buttons remaining to be sold.

   A. 100   B. 200   C. 300   D. 400   E. 500

2. Mrs. Wong bought a digital camera on sale for $194. The regular price of the camera was $403. Which is the best estimate of the amount of money she saved?

   A. $200   B. $300   C. $400   D. $500   E. $600

3. Kerri's two highest scores on her favorite computer game are 8,950 and 7,050. Which is the best estimate for the difference between her two scores?

   A. Less than 500

   B. Between 500 and 1,000

   C. Between 1,000 and 1,500

   D. Between 1,500 and 2,500

   E. More than 2,500

4. Jones Farm grew 1,450 pumpkins last year. That same year, Gross Farm grew 680 pumpkins and Shorty's Farm grew 941 pumpkins. Estimate how many fewer pumpkins Gross Farm grew than Jones Farm did.

   A. 600   B. 700   C. 800   D. 900   E. 1,000

5. Brown Conference Center has a total of 9,685 seats in its auditorium. On Friday 6,428 people attended a band concert in the auditorium, and on Saturday 7,740 people attended a stage musical there. What is a reasonable estimate for the total number of empty seats in the auditorium on Saturday?

   A. More than 6,000

   B. Between 4,500 and 6,000

   C. Between 3,000 and 4,500

   D. Between 1,500 and 3,000

   E. Less than 1,500

Objective 7
Estimate a solution to a word problem using rounding and multiplication of whole numbers.

Discussion
In the lessons described next, the focus will be on rounding the original two-digit or three-digit factors in the problems, then applying multiplication facts to find the estimated products. Students will have the opportunity to express the estimate of a product as a single number and also to find an interval that will contain that estimate. Both formats are used for the responses of test items involving estimation. It is assumed that students have already mastered the multiplication algorithm for at least two-digit factors. This complex algorithm is developed in detail in the lessons described in Objective 2 of this section.

Activity 1: Manipulative Stage

Materials
Set of base 10 blocks per pair of students (30 rods or tens per set)
Worksheet 2-7a
Regular pencil

Procedure
1. After students are comfortable with rounding individual whole numbers, they need to practice the method with story problems involving multiplication. This activity will introduce them to the idea by using a one-digit factor with a two-digit factor. Then only one factor must be rounded before multiplying.

2. Give each pair of students 30 rods or "longs" from the base 10 blocks, and give each student a copy of Worksheet 2-7a.

3. For each exercise on the worksheet, students should round the two-digit number to the nearest ten, then place this amount of tens or rods in one long row (left to right) on the desktop. The one-digit number will indicate how many rows of this rounded set of rods to make in order to find the estimated product.

4. After the total rods or tens are counted, a word sentence should be recorded below the exercise on the worksheet, stating the original factors and the final product used for the estimate. An interval containing the estimate should also be stated on the worksheet.

5. Discuss Exercise 1 with the students before allowing them to work the others independently.

Consider the story problem in Exercise 1: "There are 4 boxes of candy bars in the school store. Each box holds 24 candy bars. Estimate the total number of candy bars in the 4 boxes."

Students should round the number 24 to 20 as the nearest tens number, then place 2 tens rods in a row on the desktop to represent the estimate of the amount of candy bars. Because there are 4 boxes, students should continue placing tens rods on the desktop until there are 4 rows of 2 tens rods each. They should finally count the 8 tens rods, counting up by tens, to find the estimated total of 80 candy bars.

Have students record their results on Worksheet 2-7a below Exercise 1 in the following way: "4 of 24 is estimated as $\underline{4} \times \underline{2}0 = \underline{8}0$ candy bars." Note that the multiplication fact $4 \times 2 = 8$ is underlined in the equation. Also have students state and record below the exercise a possible interval that will contain their estimates; for example, the estimate of 80 lies in the interval between 50 and 100. (Intervals will vary.)

Answer Key for Worksheet 2-7a

1. 4 of 24 is estimated as $\underline{4} \times \underline{2}0 = \underline{8}0$ candy bars; possible interval: between 50 and 100

2. 5 of 25 is estimated as $\underline{5} \times \underline{3}0 = \underline{15}0$ flowers total; possible interval: between 100 and 200

3. 3 of 58 is estimated as $\underline{3} \times \underline{6}0 = \underline{18}0$ students; possible interval: between 150 and 200

4. 8 of 12 is estimated as $\underline{8} \times \underline{1}0 = \underline{8}0$ people; possible interval: between 75 and 100

5. 7 of 26 is estimated as $\underline{7} \times \underline{3}0 = \underline{21}0$ chairs; possible interval: between 180 and 250

164

Build with base 10 blocks to estimate the products of the given word problems. For each exercise, write a word sentence about the product found and state an interval that will contain the estimate.

1. There are 4 boxes of candy bars in the school store. Each box holds 24 candy bars. Estimate the total number of candy bars in the 4 boxes.

2. Each of 5 flower pots at the florist's shop contains 25 flowers. About how many flowers in all are in the 5 flower pots?

3. At 10 A.M., 3 buses will take students to a museum for a field trip. Each bus will carry 58 students. Estimate the total number of students going on the field trip.

4. There are 8 wagons in the parade. Each wagon holds 12 people. About how many people total are riding in the wagons?

5. At the puppet show, Jimmy saw 7 rows of chairs. Each row had 26 chairs. Estimate the total number of chairs Jimmy saw at the puppet show.

Activity 2: Pictorial Stage

Materials

Worksheet 2-7b
Red pencil and regular pencil

Procedure

1. Give each student a red pencil and a copy of Worksheet 2-7b. Remind students that 10 of 10 ones equal 1 ten and 10 of 10 tens make 1 hundred. These ideas were used in the development of the multiplication algorithm in Objective 2 of this section. This activity will involve two-digit factors.

2. For each exercise on the worksheet, students should round each two-digit factor to the nearest ten, then draw rectangles on the L-frame to represent the tens for the two factors. The multiplier should be drawn along the right vertical bar of the L-frame, and the multiplicand (or given set) should be drawn along the bottom bar of the frame.

3. Students should then complete the product by drawing large squares for hundreds inside the L-frame. The hundreds in the product region may then be counted to find the total or result.

4. A word sentence should be recorded below the completed L-frame to describe the estimated product, and the multiplication fact within the estimation equation should be underlined in red pencil. An interval containing the estimate should also be stated. Intervals will vary.

5. Guide students through Exercise 1 before allowing them to work the other exercises independently. Discuss the pattern found where tens multiplied by tens produce hundreds as the answer. For example, 2 tens × 3 tens (20 × 30) will equal 6 hundreds, or 600.

Consider the following word problem from Exercise 1: "Geni emptied 15 boxes of rubber bands into a large container. Each box held 38 rubber bands. Estimate the number of rubber bands in the container."

Students should round 38 to the nearest ten to get 40. Then they should draw 4 rectangles along the bottom of the L-frame under Exercise 1 to represent the set of 40 rubber bands estimated for 1 box. Because there were 15 boxes, round to 20 boxes. Students should draw 2 rectangles along the right vertical bar of the L-frame to represent the multiplier, or 20 boxes. They should now draw the product inside the L-frame. Because 10 of 1 ten equals a hundred, students should draw a large square to show each hundred. For the finished product, there will be 2 rows of 4 large squares each.

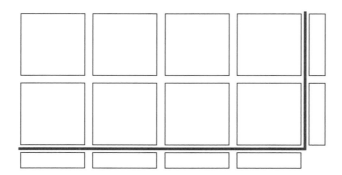

Students can now count the total squares, counting up by hundreds, to find the estimated total, 8 hundreds or 800 rubber bands. Below the drawing of the squares, students should record their results as follows: "15 × 38 was estimated as 20 × 40 = 800 rubber bands." Be sure to have them underline in red pencil the *fact* within the estimation equation. Also have students state an interval for their estimate; for example, the estimate of 800 lies in the interval between 750 and 900.

Answer Key for Worksheet 2-7b

1. 15 × 38 was estimated as 20 × 40 = 800 rubber bands; possible interval: between 750 and 900

2. 32 × 12 was estimated as 30 × 10 = 300 eggs; possible interval: between 200 and 400

3. 16 × 34 was estimated as 20 × 30 = 600 shells; possible interval: between 575 and 640

4. 32 × 35 was estimated as 30 × 40 = 1,200 seats; possible interval: between 1,100 and 1,300

WORKSHEET 2-7b

Drawing to Estimate Products

Name _____

Date _____

Draw diagrams to estimate the products of the given word problems. For each exercise, write a word sentence below the frame to describe the estimated product found and state an interval that will contain the estimate. Underline multiplication facts used with red pencil.

1. Geni emptied 15 boxes of rubber bands into a large container. Each box held 38 rubber bands. Estimate the number of rubber bands in the container.

2. Charlie bought 32 dozen eggs for the school's egg hunt. Estimate how many eggs he bought in all.

168

Name _____

Date _____

3. There are 16 buckets of seashells. Each bucket holds 34 seashells to be made into necklaces. About how many shells in all are available for making jewelry?

4. The auditorium has 32 rows of seats. Each row contains 35 seats. About how many seats total are in the auditorium?

Activity 3: Independent Practice

Materials
Worksheet 2-7c
Regular pencil

Procedure
Give each student a copy of Worksheet 2-7c. Each exercise requires a product to be estimated. Students should round to the nearest ten when they have two-digit factors. Remind them that the goal is to be able to apply a multiplication fact instead of computing partial products for the general multiplication algorithm.

Answer Key for Worksheet 2-7c
1. C

2. B

3. B

4. A

5. C

Possible Testing Errors That May Occur for This Objective
- The original factors in the problem are multiplied to find the product rather than their rounded amounts multiplied. Then the actual product found may or may not be rounded off. For example, 14×25 is computed to get 350 instead of 10×30 being used to get 300 as the estimate. Students may round their 350 to 400 and try to match to that response.

- Factors are rounded incorrectly, causing the wrong multiplication fact to be used. For example, for 85×43, students might round both numbers down and use 80×40 to find their estimate, instead of 90×40.

- Original factors may be correctly rounded, but then an incorrect product is found for the new multiplication fact. For example, for 57×82, 60×80 is used, but the product is incorrectly found to be 4,200.

WORSHEET 2-7c   Name _____

Estimating with Multiplication Date _____

Solve the following word problems by using multiplication facts and estimation. Show your work on another sheet of paper. Circle the best answer for each problem on this worksheet.

1. There are 8 display trays at the cooking contest. Each tray holds 24 cookies. About how many cookies total are on display at the contest?

  A. 140   B. 150   C. 160   D. 170

2. Ramon has 3 boxes of toy cars in his collection. Each box contains 15 cars. Estimate the total number of toy cars he has in his collection.

  A. Less than 50

  B. Between 55 and 70

  C. Between 75 and 85

  D. Between 90 and 100

3. A train has 17 boxcars. Each boxcar contains 40 shipping crates being delivered to a nearby warehouse. What is a reasonable estimate of the number of crates to be unloaded from the train at the warehouse?

  A. 900   B. 800   C. 600   D. 500

4. There are 36 boxes of paper clips on the store shelf. Each box contains 64 paper clips. About how many paper clips in all are on the store shelf?

  A. 2,400   B. 2,200   C. 2,000   D. Not here

5. Sam usually makes 18- to 22-minute phone calls. If he made 23 such phone calls of different time lengths during October, what would be a reasonable interval for the total minutes of all his calls?

  A. Less than 200

  B. Between 250 and 325

  C. Between 385 and 450

  D. Not here

Objective 8
Add or subtract four-digit decimals (tens to hundredths).

Discussion
Addition or subtraction with decimal numbers involving tenths or hundredths should not be difficult for students at this grade level if they understand the relationship of tenths and hundredths to ones and if their regrouping skills are strong. In particular, students need much experience with the "backward trading" aspect of place value in order to perform subtraction effectively. The activities described next will provide experience with both addition and subtraction.

Activity 1: Manipulative Stage

Materials
Building Mat 2-8a for each pair of students
100 small counters for each pair of students (same color or same style)
Worksheet 2-8a
Regular pencil

Procedure
1. Give each pair of students a copy of Building Mat 2-8a and 100 small counters. The counters may look alike or be the same color and size. Give each student a copy of Worksheet 2-8a.

2. It is assumed that students have had at least minimal experience in trading 10 ones for 1 ten, 10 tenths for 1 one, and 10 hundredths for 1 tenth with base 10 blocks or similar materials.

3. Have students use the counters on the building mats to model the word problems on Worksheet 2-8a.

4. For *addition*, only two decimal numbers will be involved at this stage. The two needed numbers given in the problem should both be shown on the mat. Students should form groups of 10 counters in each column where possible, beginning with the rightmost column, then trade each group of counters for a new counter in the next column to the left.

5. For *subtraction*, students should show only the larger amount (called the *minuend*) with counters on the building mat. They will begin with the hundredths column on the mat and remove the amount of hundredths counters indicated in the smaller amount (called the *subtrahend*). If there are not enough hundredths counters there to match what needs to be removed, a counter from the tenths column must be removed from the mat and 10 new hundredths counters placed in the hundredths column. The removal is then carried out. A similar process is followed to remove tenths, ones, and tens counters from the mat, as indicated in the subtrahend.

6. Answers should be recorded on Worksheet 2-8a as complete word sentences below the corresponding exercises.

7. Guide students through each exercise before proceeding to the next one.

Consider Exercise 1 on Worksheet 2-8a, which is an example of an *addition* word problem: "At the candy store, Kate sold 15.42 ounces of rocky road fudge and 27.84 ounces of peanut brittle. How many ounces total did Kate sell of both candies?"

Students should place counters on the mat to show the two numbers as follows:

TENS	ONES	TENTHS	HUNDREDTHS
○	○ ○ ○ ○ ○	○ ○ ○ ○	○ ○
○ ○	○ ○ ○ ○ ○ ○ ○	○ ○ ○ ○ ○ ○ ○ ○	○ ○ ○ ○

Ask students to join all the hundredths counters together and, if possible, remove and trade 10 hundredths for a new counter in the tenths column (hundredths trade not needed in this case). Then they should join all the tenths counters together to get 12 tenths. Ten of these 12 tenths should be traded for a new counter in the ones column. All the ones counters are combined for a total of 13 ones. Ten of these 13 ones should be traded for a new counter in the tens column.

Finally, there will be 4 counters in the tens column; no other trades are needed. Three counters remain in the ones column, 2 counters remain in the tenths column, and 6 counters remain in the hundredths column. Have various students tell how many counters remain in each column in the following way: 4 tens, 3 ones, 2 tenths, and 6 hundredths. The number name for the sum is 43.26, which students should read as "forty-three and twenty-six hundredths."

The answer should be recorded under Exercise 1 on Worksheet 2-8a as follows: "15.42 ounces and 27.84 ounces equal 43.26 total ounces sold." The final mat and counters will appear as shown.

TENS	ONES	TENTHS	HUNDREDTHS
○ ○	○ ○ ○	○ ○	○ ○
○ ○			○ ○ ○ ○

After Exercises 1 through 3 have been worked as examples of addition, discuss Exercise 4 as an example of *subtraction*, followed by the other subtraction word problems. Here is Exercise 4: "Josh bought 34.06 pounds of fertilizer for his grass. On Saturday, he spread 8.45 pounds on his side yard. How many pounds of fertilizer does Josh have left for the rest of his yard?"

Students should place counters on the building mat to show 34.06. The initial counters are shown on the mat.

TENS	ONES	TENTHS	HUNDREDTHS
○ ○ ○	○ ○ ○ ○		○ ○ ○ ○ ○ ○

Because 8.45 needs to be removed, have students begin with the hundredths column and remove 5 counters from the 6 counters, leaving 1 counter in the hundredths column. Next, 4 tenths need to be removed, but there are 0 tenths on the mat initially. So 1 counter needs to be removed from the ones column and traded for 10 new counters in the tenths column. Now 4 tenths counters may be removed from the (10 + 0) or 10 counters in the tenths column, leaving 6 tenths counters on the mat.

There are 3 ones currently on the building mat, but 8 ones need to be removed. Students must remove 1 counter from the tens column and trade it for 10 new counters in the ones column. There will then be (10 + 3) or 13 ones counters, so 8 ones counters may be removed from the mat, leaving 5 counters in the ones column. No counters need to be removed from the tens column, so 2 counters remain there.

Finally, the building mat shows 2 tens, 5 ones, 6 tenths, and 1 hundredth in counters after all removals have been made. Have various students tell how many counters remain in each column in the following way: 2 tens, 5 ones, 6 tenths, and 1 hundredth. The number name for the difference is 25.61, which students should read as "twenty-five and sixty-one hundredths."

The answer should be recorded under Exercise 4 on Worksheet 2-8a as follows: "34.06 pounds take away 8.45 pounds equals 25.61 pounds left." The final mat and counters will appear as shown.

TENS	ONES	TENTHS	HUNDREDTHS
○ ○	○ ○ ○ ○ ○	○ ○ ○ ○ ○ ○	○

Now guide students through the remaining subtraction exercises on Worksheet 2-8a.

Answer Key for Worksheet 2-8a (possible sentences to use)

1. 15.42 ounces and 27.84 ounces equal 43.26 total ounces sold.

2. 54.7 miles and 47.6 miles equal 102.3 miles driven in all.

3. 25.68 pounds and 6.40 pounds equal 32.08 pounds of fish caught in all.

4. 34.06 pounds take away 8.45 pounds equals 25.61 pounds left.

5. $27.50 take away $14.80 equals $12.70 he still had to pay for tickets.

6. 53.50 minutes take away 28.46 minutes equals 25.04 minutes left to pick up other students.

BUILDING MAT 2-8a

HUNDREDTHS	TENTHS	ONES	TENS

176

Building with Counters to Add or Subtract

Solve the following word problems by placing counters on Building Mat 2-8a. Below each exercise, write a word sentence that states the answer found for that exercise.

1. At the candy store, Kate sold 15.42 ounces of rocky road fudge and 27.84 ounces of peanut brittle. How many ounces total did Kate sell of both candies?

2. On a weekend trip, Tim's family drove 54.7 miles on the first day and 47.6 miles on the second day. How many miles in all did they drive on the two days?

3. On July 4, 25.68 pounds of fish were caught at the public fishing pond. Five hours later, 6.40 more pounds of fish were caught. How many pounds of fish total were caught at the pond that day?

4. Josh bought 34.06 pounds of fertilizer for his grass. On Saturday, he spread 8.45 pounds on his side yard. How many pounds of fertilizer does Josh have left for the rest of his yard?

5. Sean bought $27.50 worth of tickets for the soccer game. He then resold $14.80 worth of those tickets to his friends. How much of his own money did he finally spend on tickets?

6. The school bus took 53.50 minutes to pick up all its students. 28.46 minutes of its schedule was for picking up preschool students. How many minutes were left for picking up the other students?

Activity 2: Pictorial Stage

Materials

Worksheet 2-8b
Red pencil and regular pencil

Procedure

1. After students are comfortable using the mat and counters to add or subtract, have them work similar word problems with diagrams. Provide each student with a copy of Worksheet 2-8b and a red pencil. Each student should complete the frames on her or his own worksheet but might share results with a partner. Instead of placing counters on the mat to show numbers, students will now draw small circles in the columns of the frames.

2. For *addition*, groups of 10 circles will be formed in each column by drawing a red path around the group. The group of 10 circles will be marked out and a new circle drawn in the next column to the left to show a trade or regrouping. Circles remaining unmarked in the columns after all trades are completed will show the sum. Only two addends will be used in each addition problem.

3. For *subtraction*, to show a backward trade between columns, one circle in a column will be marked out with a red X and 10 new circles drawn in regular pencil in the next column to the right; a red arrow will be drawn from the old circle to the 10 new circles to indicate the trade. Except for trades, circles will be marked out in regular pencil to show their removal or subtraction from a column. Circles remaining unmarked in the columns after all trades and removals have been made will represent the difference.

4. Students should write an equation for the sum or difference below the completed frame.

5. Guide students through drawing the diagram for each word problem on Worksheet 2-8b. Examples will be discussed.

6. Finally, help students connect their drawing already shown on each frame to the vertical algorithm for addition or subtraction. Record the notation for each column as you review the combining and trading for addition (or the trading and removal for subtraction) that occurred in that column *on the frame*. The vertical notation might be recorded in the worksheet margin to the right of the corresponding frame, or may be recorded on a separate sheet of paper if more writing space is needed. The methods for such recordings will be discussed in specific examples provided next.

Consider Exercise 1 on Worksheet 2-8b as an example of *addition:* "Susan bought 14.08 ounces of taffy at the ballgame. Robin bought 16.73 ounces of taffy. How much taffy in all did the two girls buy?"

The two numbers from the word problem should be shown initially with circles on the frame as follows:

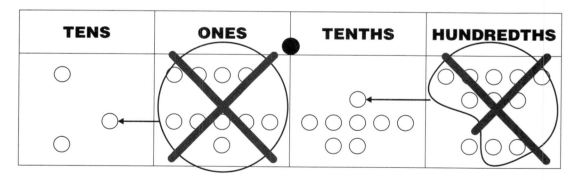

TENS	ONES	TENTHS	HUNDREDTHS

In the hundredths column, 10 circles will be grouped together with a red pencil and traded for one new circle in the tenths column. There will then be (0 + 7 + 1) or 8 tenths. No grouping of tenths is needed, because there are fewer than 10 tenths in the tenths column. One individual or ungrouped circle remains in the hundredths column.

In the ones column, 10 circles may be grouped with a red pencil and traded for one new circle in the tens column. No individual or ungrouped circles remain in the ones column.

There are now (1 + 1 + 1) or 3 circles in the tens column, which is not enough to make another trade. Have students state how many circles remain ungrouped in each column of the frame: 3 tens, 0 ones, 8 tenths, and 1 hundredth. The final sum is 30.81, which students should read aloud as "thirty and eighty-one hundredths." Students should record an equation below the frame to show the results: "14.08 + 16.73 = 30.81 ounces bought in all." The completed frame with all the groupings or trades marked in red pencil is shown here.

After the frames for Exercises 1 and 2 are completed, help students connect their trading on the two frames to the vertical algorithm for addition. Write the numerical algorithm to the right of each completed frame on Worksheet 2-8b or on a separate sheet of paper. Record the notation for each column as you review the combining and trading that occurred in that column *on the frame*. For example, for Exercise 1, students should notice that a trade was needed in the hundredths column, so 1 hundredth total should be recorded below the right column of the vertical format and a new 1 tenth should be recorded above the tenths column. Then 7 tenths with 1 new tenth make 8 tenths total in the tenths column with no trading needed. These two actions would be recorded in the vertical format as follows:

```
        1
     14.08
   + 16.73
       .81
```

Next, in the ones column, the 4 ones and 6 ones combined to make 10 ones. The 10 ones traded for a new ten in the tens column, leaving 0 ones in the ones column. This action would then be recorded in the vertical format:

```
     1  1
     14.08
   + 16.73
      0.81
```

Finally, in the tens column, the new ten, 1 ten, and the other 1 ten combined to make 3 tens. No trade was needed, so the 3 tens would be recorded this way:

```
     1  1
     14.08
   + 16.73
     30.81
```

Repeat the process with Exercise 2. Work through the steps slowly, using place value language as shown in the previous narrative. Do *not* allow students to omit place value references in their explanations, as is done in the following example: "1 plus 7 plus 5 equals 13; record the 3 and carry the 1." A correct way to say this might be: "1 new tenth plus 7 tenths plus 5 tenths equals 13 tenths; 10 tenths trade for 1 new one; 3 tenths remain."

Now consider Exercise 3 on Worksheet 2-8b as an example of *subtraction:* "The bird store had 36.2 pounds of bird seed in the storeroom. 18.9 pounds of seed were sold in 5 days. How many pounds of seed did the bird store still have after the 5 days?"

Have students draw small circles on the frame to show 36.2 as follows:

TENS	ONES	TENTHS	HUNDREDTHS
○ ○ ○	○ ○ ○ ○ ○ ○	○ ○	

Because 18.9 needs to be removed from the frame, have students begin with the tenths column. Neither amount has any hundredths. Nine tenths need to be removed, but there are only 2 tenths present in the tenths column. Therefore, a circle from the ones column must be marked out (X) in red pencil to show a trade is occurring; 10 new

circles should be drawn in the tenths column to show that 10 new tenths have been obtained from the trade. There are now 12 circles in the tenths column, so 9 circles should be marked out (/) with regular pencil to show the removal of 9 tenths. Three circles remain unmarked in the tenths column of the frame.

Five circles remain unmarked in the ones column, but 8 circles need to be removed from the ones column. One circle in the tens column must be marked out (X) in red pencil and traded for 10 new circles in the ones column. There are now 15 circles unmarked in the ones column, so 8 of them may be marked out (/) in regular pencil to show removal. Seven circles remain unmarked in the ones column.

Finally, one circle should be marked out (/) in regular pencil from the tens column to show removal of 1 ten, leaving 1 circle unmarked in the tens column. The circles remaining unmarked on the frame will be 1 ten, 7 ones, and 3 tenths. The number name is 17.3, which students should read aloud as "seventeen and three tenths." Below the completed frame, students should record the result as a number sentence or equation: "36.2 − 18.9 = 17.3 pounds of seed remaining at the bird store." The completed frame should appear as follows:

After students have completed their frames for Exercises 3 and 4, help them connect their tradings on the frames to the vertical algorithm for subtraction. Write the numerical algorithm to the right of each completed frame on Worksheet 2-8b or on a separate sheet of paper. For each subtraction exercise, record the notation for each column as you *review* the trading and removal that occurred in that column *on the frame*. For example, for Exercise 3, students should notice that 1 one was traded for 10 new tenths, leaving 5 ones in the ones column and 12 tenths in the tenths column. This action, along with the removal or marking out of 9 tenths, which left 3 tenths, would be recorded in the vertical format as follows:

$$
\begin{array}{r}
5\ 12 \\
3\cancel{6}.\cancel{2} \\
-18.9 \\
\hline
.3
\end{array}
$$

Next, in the ones column, only 5 ones remained, but 8 ones needed to be removed. Another trade from the tens column was needed to get 10 new ones. So (10 + 5) or 15 ones became available in the ones column, leaving 2 tens in the tens column; 8 ones were marked out, leaving 7 ones. This action would then be recorded in the vertical format, as shown here.

```
  2  15
    5̶ 12
  8̶ 6̶.2̶
 −1 8.9
 ──────
    7.3
```

Finally, in the tens column, 1 ten was marked out, leaving 1 ten in the column. No trade was needed, so the 1 ten would be recorded as shown:

```
  2  15
    5̶ 12
  8̶ 6̶.2̶
 −1 8.9
 ──────
 1 7.3
```

Work through these steps slowly, using place value language as shown in the previous narrative. Do *not* allow students to omit place value references in their explanations, as done in the following example: "Borrow 1 from 7 to make 15; 15 minus 8 equals 7; then 6 minus 4 equals 2, and 2 minus 1 equals 1." A possible *correct* way to say this would be: "1 tenth becomes 10 new hundredths, and these 10 hundredths plus 5 hundredths make 15 hundredths; 15 hundredths take away [minus] 8 hundredths leaves 7 hundredths; then the remaining 6 tenths take away 4 tenths leaves 2 tenths, and 2 ones take away 1 one leaves 1 one."

Answer Key for Worksheet 2-8b

1. $14.08 + 16.73 = 30.81$ ounces of taffy bought in all

2. $25.18 + 8.76 = 33.94$ minutes total in the air

3. $36.2 - 18.9 = 17.3$ pounds of seed left

4. $25.40 - 19.53 = 5.87$ feet farther

182

WORKSHEET 2-8b

Name _____

Drawing Diagrams to Add or Subtract   Date _____

Solve the following word problems by drawing small circles on the given base 10 frames. Use a red pencil to show any trades needed. Below each frame, write the number sentence that states the answer found for that exercise.

1. Susan bought 14.08 ounces of taffy at the ballgame. Robin bought 16.73 ounces of taffy. How much taffy in all did the two girls buy?

TENS	ONES	TENTHS	HUNDREDTHS

2. George's kite flew in the air for 25.18 minutes, then later flew for 8.76 more minutes. What was the total time the kite flew in the air?

TENS	ONES	TENTHS	HUNDREDTHS

WORSHEET 2-8b Continued

Name _____

Date _____

3. The bird store had 36.2 pounds of bird seed in the storeroom. 18.9 pounds of seed were sold in 5 days. How many pounds of seed did the bird store still have after the 5 days?

TENS	ONES	TENTHS	HUNDREDTHS

4. In pole-climbing class, Juan climbed 25.40 feet on his first day. He then climbed 19.53 feet the following day. How much farther did he climb on the first day than on the second day?

TENS	ONES	TENTHS	HUNDREDTHS

Activity 3: Independent Practice

Materials
Worksheet 2-8c
Regular pencil

Procedure
Have students apply the addition and subtraction algorithms to solve the word problems on Worksheet 2-8c. Exercise 3 will involve three addends. Discuss the idea that the trading process still holds; just more quantities have to be combined within each place value column before one or more trades occur. (Consider a trade as always 10 smaller units for 1 larger unit, so 20 smaller units require two trades.) When all have finished the worksheet, have various students share their answers with the class. Encourage them to use the correct place value language as they describe the computational steps they used to solve the problems.

Answer Key for Worksheet 2-8c
1. $38.5 - 9.4 = 29.1$ inches of ribbon left

2. $43.80 + 21.34 = 65.14$ miles from city A to city C

3. $8.5 + 12.7 + 15.9 = 37.1$ ounces of cola in all

4. $\$76.30 - \$58.80 = \$17.50$ more earned on Friday

5. $19.8 + 20.75 = 40.55$ feet jumped in all

6. $60 - 32.38 = 27.62$ more miles left in trip

Possible Testing Errors That May Occur for This Objective

Addition

- When three or more addends are involved in a word problem, students will add only the first two numbers given in the problem and ignore the other addends.

- Students fail to regroup their ones, tenths, or hundredths when adding two numbers. For example, in $1.28 + 3.95$, the 13 hundredths are recorded as 3 hundredths only; the other 10 hundredths are not traded for a new tenth. Similarly, the 12 tenths (after the hundredths trade) may be recorded as 2 tenths and the other 10 tenths ignored.

- Addition fact errors may occur when the sum of two or three numbers is computed, even though regrouping is used correctly. For example, in $4.9 + 12.7$, students will use 9 tenths + 7 tenths incorrectly as 15 tenths, recording the 5 tenths and trading the other 10 tenths correctly for a new one.

Subtraction

- Students use the correct numbers, but they reverse the digits in order to subtract without regrouping. For example, in 6.4 – 4.7, they will use 7 tenths – 4 tenths, instead of 14 tenths – 7 tenths.

- Students use the correct numbers, but they fail to decrease the number of ones after they regroup, say, 1 one to 10 tenths in order to subtract in the tenths column. As an example, in 6.4 – 4.7, along with finding 14 tenths – 7 tenths = 7 tenths, students will use 6 ones – 4 ones = 2 ones, instead of 5 ones – 4 ones.

186

WORKSHEET 2-8c

Name _____

Solving Word Problems with
Decimal Addition or Subtraction

Date _____

Solve the following word problems by using addition or subtraction. For each exercise, show all computational steps, then write a number sentence that states the answer. Write on another sheet of paper if more work space is needed.

1. Louise had a piece of ribbon that was 38.5 inches long. She cut off 9.4 inches to use for an art project. How many inches of ribbon does she still have?

2. A map shows that it is 43.80 miles from city A to city B. Then from city B to city C it is 21.34 miles. How many miles is city A from city C if you go through city B on the way to city C?

3. On Monday Liu drank 8.5 ounces of cola for lunch. On Tuesday she drank 12.7 ounces of cola, and on Wednesday she drank 15.9 ounces. How many ounces of cola did she drink in all for the three days?

4. A concession stand earned $76.30 on hot dog sales at the Friday night game but earned only $58.80 on hot dogs at the Saturday game. How much more was earned on hot dog sales on Friday than on Saturday?

5. Bill jumped 19.8 feet in his first attempt at the long jump at the high school track meet on Monday. In his second attempt, he jumped 20.75 feet. How many feet in all did he jump that day?

6. George has to make a 60-mile trip. He has already driven 32.38 miles. How many more miles must he drive to finish the trip?

Name _____

Date _____

COMPUTATIONAL ALGORITHMS AND ESTIMATION IN PROBLEM SOLVING: PRACTICE TEST ANSWER SHEET

Directions: Use the Answer Sheet to darken the letter of the choice that best answers each question.

1. ◯ A ◯ B ◯ C ◯ D   9. ◯ A ◯ B ◯ C ◯ D

2. ◯ A ◯ B ◯ C ◯ D   10. ◯ A ◯ B ◯ C ◯ D

3. ◯ A ◯ B ◯ C ◯ D   11. ◯ A ◯ B ◯ C ◯ D

4. ◯ A ◯ B ◯ C ◯ D   12. ◯ A ◯ B ◯ C ◯ D

5. ◯ A ◯ B ◯ C ◯ D   13. ◯ A ◯ B ◯ C ◯ D

6. ◯ A ◯ B ◯ C ◯ D   14. ◯ A ◯ B ◯ C ◯ D

7. ◯ A ◯ B ◯ C ◯ D   15. ◯ A ◯ B ◯ C ◯ D

8. ◯ A ◯ B ◯ C ◯ D   16. ◯ A ◯ B ◯ C ◯ D

SECTION 2: COMPUTATIONAL ALGORITHMS AND ESTIMATION: PRACTICE TEST

1. On Thursday Ann made 75 friendship bracelets. On Friday she made 147, and on Saturday she made 204 of the bracelets. How many bracelets did she make total for the three days?

   A. 279   B. 222   C. 316   D. 426

2. A concession stand sold 653 hot dogs at the Friday night game but only 568 hot dogs at the Saturday game. How many more hot dogs were sold on Friday than on Saturday?

   A. 85   B. 115   C. 174   D. 195

3. Ronnie has 5 boxes of toy cars in his collection. Each box contains 27 cars. How many toy cars does he have in all in his collection?

   A. 125   B. 135   C. 150   D. 164

4. A train has 16 boxcars. Each boxcar contains 80 shipping crates being delivered to a nearby warehouse. How many crates will have to be unloaded from the train at the warehouse?

   A. 196   B. 480   C. 870   D. 1,280

5. Luis has 56 toy cars in his collection. The cars are stored in equal amounts in 4 boxes. How many toy cars does Luis have in each box?

   A. 16   B. 60   C. 14   D. 224

6. 207 children have applied to attend a summer camp. At the camp, the children are to be equally assigned to 8 groups. Any children not assigned to a group will be put on a waiting list. How many children will be assigned to each group and not put on the waiting list?

   A. 215   B. 37   C. 25   D. 199

7. A bakery had 40 brownies for sale. Five sacks were already prepared, with 3 brownies per sack. The sacks were sold first. How many brownies then remained to be sold?

   A. 25   B. 15   C. 35   D. 48

SECTION 2: COMPUTATIONAL ALGORITHMS AND ESTIMATION: PRACTICE TEST

8. Twenty-eight school desks were in storage. Fifteen of the desks were small desks. The rest were large desks. Six of the large desks were broken, so they were thrown away. How many large desks still remain in storage?

   A. 13   B. 7   C. 9   D. 49

9. Mr. Lopez used 359 bricks to build his porch steps and 588 bricks to build the sidewalk. About how many bricks were needed for the sidewalk and the steps together?

   A. Between 200 and 350

   B. Between 500 and 700

   C. Between 850 and 960

   D. Between 980 and 1,050

10. Juanita bought a used car. She paid $1,200 more than her friend Sasha paid for a used car. Sasha paid $5,480 for her car. Estimate how much Juanita paid for her car.

    A. $8,000   B. $7,000   C. $6,000   D. $5,000

11. Lee had 258 tickets to sell for the school play. He sold 127 of the tickets. Find a reasonable estimate of the number of tickets remaining to be sold.

    A. 100   B. 200   C. 300   D. 400

12. At a local factory, 8,700 school-spirit buttons and 3,275 school pennants were produced last year. 1,927 of the buttons were defective. Find the best estimate of the number of spirit buttons that were not defective.

    A. Less than 5,600

    B. Between 6,000 and 6,800

    C. Between 6,900 and 7,500

    D. More than 8,000

190

SECTION 2: COMPUTATIONAL ALGORITHMS AND ESTIMATION: PRACTICE TEST

13. Sandra has 3 books of stamps in her collection. Each book contains 45 stamps. Estimate the total number of stamps she has in her collection.

    A. Less than 70

    B. Between 70 and 105

    C. Between 105 and 145

    D. Between 145 and 180

14. A train has 24 boxcars. Each boxcar contains 30 shipping crates being delivered to a nearby warehouse. What is a reasonable estimate of the number of crates to be unloaded from the train at the warehouse?

    A. 500   B. 600   C. 800   D. 900

15. On Monday Linnie drank 10.5 ounces of cola for lunch. On Tuesday she drank 12.7 ounces of cola, and on Wednesday she drank 8.9 ounces. How many ounces of cola did she drink in all for the three days?

    A. 32.1   B. 20.1   C. 23.2   D. 21.6

16. A concession stand earned $86.50 on drink sales at the Friday night game but earned only $59.80 on drinks at the Saturday game. How much more was earned on drink sales on Friday than on Saturday?

    A. $27.30   B. $135.30   C. $26.70   D. $146.30

Section 2: Computational Algorithms and Estimation in Problem Solving: Answer Key for Practice Test

The objective being tested is shown in brackets beside the answer.

1. D [1]
2. A [1]
3. B [2]
4. D [2]
5. C [3]
6. C [3]
7. A [4]
8. B [4]

9. D [5]
10. C [5]
11. B [6]
12. C [6]
13. D [7]
14. B [7]
15. A [8]
16. C [8]

GRAPHING, STATISTICS, AND PROBABILITY

Objective 1

Complete a two-column (or two-row) numerical table, using recognized patterns in the column (or row) entries, in order to solve word problems.

Discussion

To complete a table, students must be able to find a common addend or factor for any two adjacent entries in the same column (or row) in order to extend the column (or row) to new entries. Often they must be able to extend *both* columns (or rows) in order to complete the table. Students need much practice with finding and extending patterns in tables of values. They also need to be able to prepare their own tables. These skills are necessary for future studies in algebra. The following activities will provide such practice. More extensive practice with building or extending sequences may be found in Section 1, Objective 3.

Activity 1: Manipulative Stage

Materials

    100 square tiles per 4 students
    Paper and regular pencil

Procedure

1. Give each group of 4 students a set of 100 square tiles (1-inch paper squares or commercially available square tiles). Have each student prepare a two-column table. The left column heading should be "Number of Design," and the right column heading should be "Number of Tiles." There should be a minimum of six rows of entries in the table.

2. Have groups build a simple, flat design several times, increasing the tiles according to the same pattern each time to gradually enlarge the design. Students should complete their tables as they build, each time recording which design it is and how many tiles total are in the design.

3. After they have built the first three designs based on the same pattern, ask them to predict how the fourth design will look.

4. Then present a word problem to them that involves the designs. Students should continue to build their designs, checking and recording the total tiles each time, until they build the design required to answer the question in the problem.

5. Have students write a sentence below their tables that answers the question in the problem.

6. After students have built the necessary designs of an assigned pattern and/or completed the table, ask them how the numbers are changing in the left column and in the right column.

7. Repeat the process, using a new design pattern and a new table.

The first pattern to make is a four-wing design. The first three designs in the sequence are shown below. A possible prediction for the fourth design is "four wings with 4 square tiles per wing."

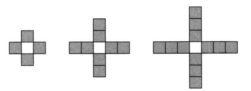

After students have built the first three designs and predicted the fourth design, present the following problem to them: "George wants to cover a table top with blue tiles arranged in a four-wing design. The background will be in white tiles. He plans to use 24 tiles for the design. Which design in your sequence will he be using?"

They should then continue to build their designs, checking and recording the total tiles each time, until they build the sixth design, which will use 24 tiles. Have students write a sentence below their tables that answers the question in the problem. For example, "George will use the sixth design or 24 tiles to make his table top."

The final table entries will be the following pairs: (1,4), (2,8), (3,12), (4,16), (5,20), (6,24). The numbers in the right column of the table will increase by 4 each time. The left column numbers will increase by 1 each time.

Here are the first three designs for a second pattern to build, making a tower-and-wall design. A possible prediction for the fourth design is "4 single tiles connecting pairs of towers with 5 towers total." Here's a word problem to use: "The Chiu family members are building a low concrete-block fence along one side of their backyard. It will have the tower-and-wall design. Each square tile represents a concrete block. If the fence is to have six towers, including a tower on each end, how many blocks will they need to build the fence?" Students will continue to build until they reach the fifth design, which requires 17 tiles. A possible sentence to record is this: "The Chius will need 17 concrete blocks for their fence." If building continues, table entries might be the following six pairs: (1,5), (2,8), (3,11), (4,14), (5,17), (6,20). Right column numbers increase by 3 each time, and the left column increases by 1.

Activity 2: Pictorial Stage

Materials
Worksheet 3-1a
Regular pencils

Procedure
1. Give each student a copy of Worksheet 3-1a. Have students work with partners to draw the sequences on Worksheet 3-1a. Tables will now be presented in row format.

2. Ask students to extend each sequence to the sixth design. They should complete the table given with each sequence.

3. They should then answer the question given with the fence designs, using the data from the completed table.

4. When students are finished with their diagrams and tables, ask about the changes between adjacent entries in the rows of each table.

Here are the first four designs and the completed table for the first sequence from Worksheet 3-1a. The top row numbers in the table change by 1 each time, and the bottom row numbers change by 2 each time. The fifth design will use 11 tiles.

Number of Design	1	2	3	4	5	6
Total Tiles	3	5	7	9	11	13

After students have completed Exercises 1 through 3 on Worksheet 3-1a, assign the following word problem for them to draw and solve on the back of the worksheet: "The Handyman Shop repairs 1 tricycle and 1 bicycle per day by replacing all wheels. On the first day, 1 tricycle and 1 bicycle are repaired. After two days, 2 tricycles and 2 bicycles have been repaired. If this pattern continues, how many wheels will have been used for repair work at the end of the fourth day?"

Have students draw simple diagrams to represent the objects and record the amounts in a two-row table. The first "set" will consist of 1 bicycle and 1 tricycle. Each new set must increase by 1 bicycle and 1 tricycle over the previous set. The top row of the table will show "Number of Vehicles," so 2 will be the first entry and 4 the second entry. The bottom row will show "Number of Wheels," so 5 will be the first entry there and 10 the second entry. The numbers in the top row will increase by 2 each time, and the numbers in the bottom row will increase by 5 each time. The first 3 "sets" are shown here as diagrams ordered from left to right. The fourth pair of entries must be found for the table in order to find the answer: "After the fourth day, 20 wheels were used in repairs."

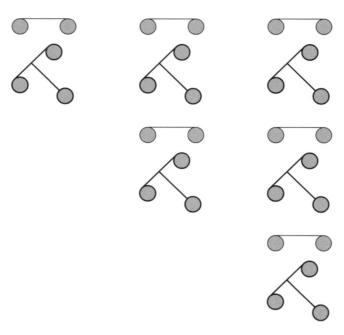

Answer Key for Worksheet 3-1a (answers and table entries only)

1. 5th design uses 11 tiles; (1,3), (2,5), (3,7), (4,9), (5,11), (6,13)

2. 8th design uses 12 tiles; (1,5), (2,6), (3,7), (4,8), (5,9), (6,10)

3. 6th design uses 18 tiles; (1,3), (2,6), (3,9), (4,12), (5,15), (6,18)

4. By 4th day, 20 wheels were used; (2, 5), (4,10), (6,15), (8,20)

WORKSHEET 3-1a

Using Tables to Solve Problems

Name _____

Date _____

Draw the next three terms or fence designs for each sequence given below. Complete the table for each sequence. Answer each question.

1. Which fence design will use 11 tiles?

_____   _____   _____

Number of Design	1	2	3			
Total Tiles	3			9		13

2. How many tiles will the eighth fence design use?

_____   _____   _____

Number of Design	1	2	3			
Total Tiles	5					

3. Which fence design will use 18 tiles?

_____   _____   _____

Number of Design	1	2	3			
Total Tiles						

Activity 3: Independent Practice

Materials
Worksheet 3-1b
Regular pencils

Procedure
Give each student a copy of Worksheet 3-1b. Have students work independently to complete the worksheet, then discuss their results. Ask various students to explain the numerical patterns found in each table.

Answer Key for Worksheet 3-1b (possible sentences given for items 1 and 2)
1. 42 cookies will be in 7 packages.

2. Ms. Gomez can buy 18 bags for $24.

3. B

Possible Testing Errors That May Occur for This Objective
- The number given is the next one for the *other* column (or row) in the table, not the column that is requested. For example, for the pairs of data for (boxes, cookies): (1,4), (2,8), (3,12), if the next amount of cookies is requested, students might respond with 4 (which follows 1, 2, 3 boxes) instead of with 16 (which follows 4, 8, 12 cookies).

- The first missing number in a column (or row) is found for the answer, but the test item actually requires the second or third missing number for the answer. Further extension of the sequence is needed.

- One of the numbers actually shown in the table is selected to answer the test question, rather than a number resulting from extending the listed values based on an observed pattern.

WORKSHEET 3-1b

Using Patterns in Tables

Name _____

Date _____

Apply patterns to complete or extend the tables provided next, and use the information to answer the given questions. For Exercises 1 and 2, write a sentence to describe the answer.

1. If the number of packages and number of cookies continue in the pattern shown, how many cookies will there be in 7 packages?

Number of Packages	1	2	3	4			
Number of Cookies	6	12	18	24			

_____

_____

_____

2. Large bags of chips are on sale at the grocery store this week. The chart shows the cost of the chips, including tax. If the pattern continues, how many bags of chips can Ms. Gomez buy for her party with $24?

Number of Bags	Total Cost
3	$4
6	$8
9	$12
12	$16

_____

_____

_____

3. Make your own two-column table (on the back of this worksheet) with appropriate headings and record the following data in the table: 4 pens for $2, 8 pens for $4, and 12 pens for $6. If you buy 24 pens at this same rate, how much will you pay for the pens? Circle the letter of your answer.

A. $8   B. $12   C. $16   D. $24

Objective 2

Identify a set of points on a number line, using *greater than* and *less than*.

Discussion

The language of "greater than" and "less than" is difficult for young students. They need much practice applying these expressions. In particular, they need to use them in their spoken language as well as their written language when describing numerical situations.

Activity 1: Manipulative Stage

Materials

    Building Mat 3-2a (1 mat per pair of students)

    Packets of small counters (1 packet per pair of students, 10 small counters per packet)

    Worksheet 3-2a

    Regular pencils

Procedure

1. Give each pair of students a copy of Building Mat 3-2a, which contains a large number line marked from 90 to 100, and a packet of 10 small counters.

2. Give each student a copy of Worksheet 3-2a. The worksheet contains expressions that describe different sets of numbers on the number line, using the "greater than" and "less than" language. The conjunctions "but" and "and" will be interchanged in some of the expressions as well.

3. Partners should work together to place counters on the marks of numbers that satisfy each expression. Call on various students to describe the set of numbers they have marked on their mats. Encourage them to use complete sentences that list the numbers marked and include the expressions.

4. After several students have practiced stating their results aloud, all students should record a similar written statement below each exercise on the worksheet.

5. Work through each exercise with the entire class before progressing to the next one on the worksheet. A discussion of Exercise 1 is presented next.

      For an example, consider this expression for Exercise 1 on Worksheet 3-2a: "greater than 95 but less than or equal to 100." Students should place counters on the number line marks of 96, 97, 98, 99, and 100. They should think of 95 as the lower bound, so they would place counters at 96 and higher. Similarly, they should think of 100 as the upper bound, so they would place counters at 99 and lower, at least until they reach 96. Also, a counter should be placed on 100 itself, because 100 is included in the set being described. A possible oral response that a student might give is as follows: "The numbers that are greater than 95 but less than or equal to 100 are the numbers 96, 97, 98, 99, and 100." A similar written statement should be recorded below the original expression on Worksheet 3-2a.

Answer Key for Worksheet 3-2a (possible sentences to record)

1. The numbers 96, 97, 98, 99, and 100 are greater than 95 but less than or equal to 100.

2. The numbers 91, 92, 93, 94, and 95 are greater than 90 and less than 96.

3. The numbers 92, 93, 94, 95, 96, and 97 are less than 98 but equal to or greater than 92.

4. The numbers 93, 94, and 95 are less than or equal to 95 and greater than or equal to 93.

5. The number 98 is greater than 97 but less than 99.

202

BUILDING MAT 3-2a

WORKSHEET 3-2a   Name _____

Building Intervals of Whole Numbers   Date _____

Place small counters on Building Mat 3-2a to represent each set of numbers described below. Write a sentence about each set under the appropriate exercise.

1. greater than 95, but less than or equal to 100

_____

_____

_____

2. greater than 90, and less than 96

_____

_____

_____

3. less than 98, but equal to or greater than 92

_____

_____

_____

4. less than or equal to 95, and greater than or equal to 93

_____

_____

_____

5. greater than 97, but less than 99

_____

_____

_____

Activity 2: Pictorial Stage

Materials
>   Worksheet 3-2b
>   Regular pencils

Procedure

1. Give each student a copy of Worksheet 3-2b, which contains several number lines with sets of points already marked or expressions that need to be marked on blank number lines.

2. Below each marked number line, have students write a word sentence that describes the set of numbers already marked on that line.

3. For each blank number line, after students have marked the appropriate numbers for the given expression, ask various students to verbally state their result. Again, they should use complete sentences to describe the set of numbers marked, as shown in step 2.

4. After students complete Worksheet 3-2b, introduce them to the notation that uses < and >. Have them write the symbolic statement that corresponds to the word sentence they used to describe each number line on the worksheet. Because word sentences will vary, so will the symbolic forms used. Emphasis should be on direct translations from words to symbols, since this is merely an introduction to the special notation. Do not strive for mastery of the symbols at this time.

5. Discuss Exercise 1 before allowing students to continue independently with the other exercises. Have them share their sentences with the entire class after all have finished the worksheet.

For Exercise 1, the number line shows the marked numbers 4, 5, 6, and 7. For a possible sentence, a student might write the following: "The numbers 4, 5, 6, and 7 are equal to or greater than 4, and less than 8." When "equal to" is included, the extra conjunction "or" may confuse students. Adding a comma helps separate the two main ideas of the phrase. Other descriptions are possible for the same number line, such as "numbers greater than 3 and less than 8" and "numbers greater than 3, but less than or equal to 7." Students need this experience with words before they try to write with the symbols < and >.

Later, when students practice writing the symbolic notation for their sentences, the initial word sentence given for Exercise 1 will translate to the following: $4 \leq N < 8$, to be read as "the numbers greater than or equal to 4, and less than 8," using the phrases of the original sentence. N represents all the whole numbers in the given list. Since this is only an introduction, have students order their numbers in the statement in increasing order, left to right, to correspond with the number line used. Be sure that the two symbols within the symbolic statement point in the same direction. The statement "$3 < N > 8$" is not correct because < and > point in opposite directions within the same statement.

Answer Key for Worksheet 3-2b (possible sentences to use, along with their direct translations to symbols)

1. The numbers 4, 5, 6, and 7 are equal to or greater than 4, and less than 8; $4 \le N < 8$

2. The whole numbers 14, 15, and 16 are greater than 13 and less than 17; $13 < N < 17$

3. The decimal numbers 2.0, 2.1, 2.2, and 2.3 are less than or equal to 2.3, but greater than or equal to 2.0; $2.0 \le N \le 2.3$

4. The numbers 1, 2, 3, 4, 5, and 6 are less than or equal to 6, but greater than 0; $0 < N \le 6$

5. The whole numbers 6, 7, 8, and 9 are greater than 5 and less than 10; $5 < N < 10$

206

WORSHEET 3-2b   Name _____

Naming Intervals of Numbers   Date _____

Write a sentence about each marked set of numbers under the appropriate number line. If an expression is given with a blank number line, mark numbers on the number line to match the expression, then write a sentence about the set marked.

1.

_____

_____

2.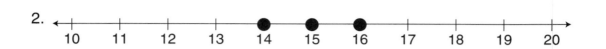

_____

_____

3.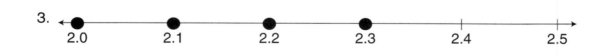

_____

_____

4. less than or equal to 6, but greater than 0

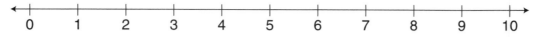

_____

_____

5. greater than 5 and less than 10

_____

_____

Activity 3: Independent Practice

Materials
    Worksheet 3-2c
    Regular pencils

Procedure
Give each student a copy of Worksheet 3-2c to complete independently. After all have finished, have them share their answers with the class.

Answer Key for Worksheet 3-2c
1. 51 through 58 in list

2. 2.9, 3.0, 3.1, 3.2, 3.3

3. C

4. B

5. C

6. A

Possible Testing Errors That May Occur for This Objective
- The lower endpoint is included when the test item asks for the numbers in an open interval that excludes the lower endpoint of the interval. For example, for numbers "greater than 5," students will include 5 in the set of numbers listed.

- The upper endpoint is included when the test item asks for the numbers in an open interval that excludes the upper endpoint of the interval. For example, for numbers "less than 8," students will include 8 in the set of numbers listed.

- Students will list only the two numbers given in the interval description and omit the numbers that are between the two endpoints. For example, for "greater than 1.2, and less than or equal to 1.5," students will list only 1.2 and 1.5, omitting 1.3 and 1.4.

WORKSHEET 3-2c   Name _____

Naming Intervals of Numbers   Date _____

Complete each exercise. Be ready to share your answers with the class.

1. List the whole numbers that are greater than 50, but less than or equal to 58.

2. List the decimal numbers in tenths that are less than 3.4 and greater than 2.8.

3. Which set contains whole numbers greater than 0 but less than 6? Circle
    your answer.

    A. 0, 1, 2, 3, 4, 5   C. 1, 2, 3, 4, 5

    B. 1, 2, 3, 4, 5, 6   D. 0, 1, 2, 3, 4, 5, 6

4. Which set contains decimal numbers in tenths that are greater than or equal to
    1.9, and less than 2.3? Circle your answer.

    A. 1.9, 2.0, 2.1, 2.2, 2.3   C. 1.8, 1.9, 2.0, 2.1, 2.2

    B. 1.9, 2.0, 2.1, 2.2   D. 2.0, 2.1, 2.2, 2.3

In Exercises 5 and 6, which notation correctly represents the given set of numbers?
Circle your answer.

5. Set: 12, 13, 14, 15 (whole numbers only)

    A. $12 < N \le 15$ C. $11 < N < 16$

    B. $12 \le N < 15$ D. $13 \le N \le 15$

6. Set: 5.6, 5.7, 5.8 (tenths only)

    A. $5.6 \le N < 5.9$ C. $5.5 \le N \le 5.8$

    B. $5.6 < N < 5.8$ D. $5.5 < N < 5.8$

Objective 3
Find the mean of a set of data.

Discussion
Often students can carry out the procedure of "adding all quantities given, then dividing their sum by the number of quantities used as addends." If asked, they define the mean in this way. Students do not, however, realize that finding the mean is equivalent to finding what the equal share will be when an existing distribution of unequal quantities is redistributed equally. In other words, if three children had different amounts of baseball cards and they were to redistribute what they had so that each person had the same amount of cards, then each person's "fair share" would be the mean of the original three amounts. Students need to understand the "equal distribution" idea of the mean.

Activity 1: Manipulative Stage

Materials
Sets of base 10 blocks (1 set per 4 students; 8 hundreds, 30 tens, and 30 ones per set)
Worksheet 3-3a
Regular pencils

Procedure
1. Give each group of 4 students a set of base 10 blocks (8 hundreds, 30 tens, and 30 ones). Give each student a copy of Worksheet 3-3a.

2. For each exercise on Worksheet 3-3a, each group is to separate the given amounts into the stated number of equal shares. They should then write a word sentence about their results and record the sentence below the exercise.

3. Discuss Exercise 1 before allowing the groups to continue working the other exercises independently on the worksheet. Have various groups share their results after all have finished the worksheet.

For Exercise 1, the amounts 141, 224, and 103 need to be separated into 3 equal shares. Students should place base 10 blocks on the table to show each amount. The amounts will be as follows: 1 hundred, 4 tens, and 1 one; 2 hundreds, 2 tens, and 4 ones; and 1 hundred and 3 ones. When the blocks are combined, there will be a total of 4 hundreds (flats), 6 tens (rods), and 8 ones (cubes).

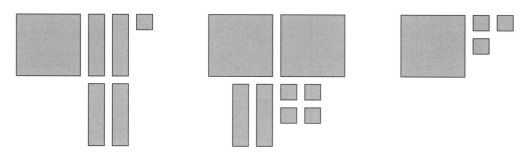

Ask the students to redistribute the blocks into 3 equal shares. Students should begin by separating 3 of the 4 hundreds into 3 separate piles, with 1 hundred per pile. The extra hundred must be traded for 10 new tens. Combining these with the original 6 tens, students are able to separate 15 of the 16 tens into the 3 piles with 5 tens per pile. The extra 10 must be traded for 10 new ones. These ones, combined with the original 8 ones, may now be separated into the 3 piles with 6 ones per pile. No blocks remain to be shared.

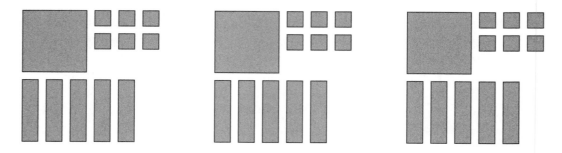

Each pile now contains 1 hundred, 5 tens, and 6 ones. Therefore the *mean* or "equal share" of 141, 224, and 103 shared 3 ways is 156. Students should record their result as a word sentence on their own worksheets. For this exercise, they might record the following: "The mean or equal share of 141, 224, and 103 is 156."

Answer Key for Worksheet 3-3a (possible sentences to use)
1. The mean or equal share of 141, 224, and 103 is 156.

2. The mean or equal share of 234 and 562 is 398.

3. The mean or equal share of 143, 231, and 115 is 163.

4. The mean or equal share of 42, 29, 45, 26, and 18 is 32.

5. The mean or equal share of 205, 164, 84, and 127 is 145.

WORKSHEET 3-3a

Building Equal Shares

Name _____

Date _____

For each exercise, show the given amounts with base 10 blocks. Separate the total blocks into the stated number of equal shares. The new share found will be the *mean* of the given amounts. Write a word sentence about the mean below the exercise.

1. Amounts: 141, 224, and 103 in 3 equal shares

_____

_____

_____

2. Amounts: 234 and 562 in 2 equal shares

_____

_____

_____

3. Amounts: 143, 231, and 115 in 3 equal shares

_____

_____

_____

4. Amounts: 42, 29, 45, 26, and 18 in 5 equal shares

_____

_____

_____

5. Amounts: 205, 164, 84, and 127 in 4 equal shares

_____

_____

_____

Activity 2: Pictorial Stage

Materials
  Worksheet 3-3b
  Regular pencils and red pencils

Procedure
1. Give each student a copy of Worksheet 3-3b and a red pencil.

2. Have students work in pairs, but each person should complete her or his own worksheet. In this activity, students will draw diagrams of base 10 blocks to find equal shares, as well as connect their steps to the symbolic notation for finding the mean.

3. For each problem, students should draw the appropriate sets of base 10 blocks to represent the amounts stated in the problem, count up their total to record as the dividend, and write the number of sets involved as the divisor. They should perform the symbolic division to get a quotient.

4. Then they should subdivide their drawn blocks into equal groups to see if the new group size found has the value of the quotient that was computed. For trades, mark out the block that needs to be traded with red pencil, then draw the 10 new blocks. Draw rings around blocks with regular pencil to form the groups.

5. Work each problem on Worksheet 3-3b completely with the class before continuing to the next problem. The first problem will be discussed next.

    Consider Exercise 1: "Charlie has 143 sports cards, Juanita has 231 sports cards, and Sean has 115 sports cards. What would be the mean (average) number of cards they have?"
    Students should draw shapes to represent the base 10 blocks for each of the three amounts, count up their total value, then do the division computation and the equal sharing or forming of equal groups as shown.

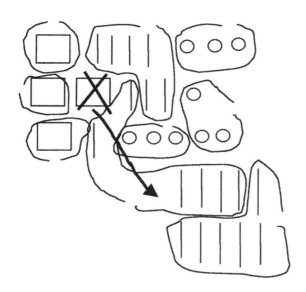

Counted total: 4 H, 8 T, 9 O

$$\begin{array}{r} 1\,6\,3 \\ 3\overline{)4\,8\,9} \end{array}$$ equal share
or mean

From drawn sharing:
3 groups of 3 ones
3 groups of 6 tens
3 groups of 1 hundred

Combine 1 group of
each block type: 163

Answer Key for Worksheet 3-3b

1. 163 sports cards per person

2. 263 ribbons per person

3. 159 marbles per person

4. 23 desks per classroom

WORSHEET 3-3b   Name _____
Forming Equal Shares   Date _____

For each exercise, show the given amounts by drawing diagrams of base 10 blocks on a separate sheet of paper. Separate the total blocks into the stated number of equal shares or groups. The new share found will be the *mean* of the given amounts. Below the exercise, compute to find the mean and compare the quotient to the share of blocks found.

1. Charlie has 143 sports cards, Juanita has 231 sports cards, and Sean has 115 sports cards. What would be the mean (average) number of cards they have?

2. Marian sold 321 school booster ribbons, and Charlie sold 205 ribbons. What was the average number of ribbons sold per person?

3. Luis has 130 marbles, Nick has 192 marbles, and Rachel has 155 marbles. What is the mean number of marbles they have?

4. Ms. Lopez has 24 desks in her classroom. Mr. Davis has 21 desks, Ms. Wong has 22 desks, and Mr. Thomas has 25 desks in their respective classrooms. What is the mean number of desks per classroom?

Activity 3: Independent Practice

Materials
Worksheet 3-3c
Regular pencils

Procedure
Give each student a copy of Worksheet 3-3c to complete independently. After all have finished, have various students share their results with the entire class. Exercise 5 will require them to do some backward thinking in order to solve it.

Answer Key for Worksheet 3-3c
1. B

2. C

3. A

4. B

5. D

Possible Testing Errors That May Occur for This Objective
- Students use the correct process to compute the mean but make an addition or division error.

- One of the original numbers stated in the test item is selected as the mean, and no attempt is made to compute the mean as requested.

- Students find the mean of only two numbers stated in the test item, ignoring other numbers that are also needed to find the mean.

WORSHEET 3-3c   Name _____

Computing the Mean   Date _____

Compute to solve each problem. Circle your answer.

1. Susan has 120 baseball cards, John has 182 baseball cards, and Anna has 175 baseball cards. What is the mean (average) number of cards they have?

    A. 151   B. 159   C. 75   D. 120

2. On Monday, Georgio sold 42 pens at the school store. On the next four days, he sold the following amounts: 28, 46, 28, and 16 pens. Over the five days, how many pens did he average selling per day?

    A. 46   B. 28   C. 32   D. 30

3. The Booster Club sold 225 cold drinks at Friday's ballgame and 301 cold drinks at Saturday's ballgame. What was the average number of cold drinks sold per game?

    A. 263   B. 225   C. 260   D. 301

4. In October, 151 students went on a field trip. 214 students went in November, and 106 students went in December. What is the mean number of students who went each month?

    A. 214   B. 157   C. 120   D. 106

5. Jim has test scores of 80, 86, and 91. What does he need to make on the fourth test in order to have a mean score of 85 on the four tests?

    A. 95   B. 88   C. 85   D. 83

Objective 4
Construct, interpret, and apply pictographs.

Discussion
Students have great difficulty learning to look for and apply legends for pictographs. Graphs, where each symbol represents a unit value, are much easier for them to read. The following activities provide practice in using a single symbol as multiple units.

Activity 1: Manipulative Stage

Materials
Bag of small counters per 2 students (2 colors, 12 counters per color)
Building Mat 3-4a (1 mat per 2 students)

Procedure
1. Give each pair of students a bag of small counters (2 colors, 12 counters per color) and a copy of Building Mat 3-4a. This activity will provide practice with equating several of one object with only one of another object, a prerequisite skill for ratio.

2. Ask students to make a row of 8 counters in the same color (for example, red counters) in the top row of Building Mat 3-4a. Then have them form a row of counters on the bottom row of the mat, using the second color (for example, blue) and putting a counter down for each 2 red counters in the row above. Have students adjust the red counters to form pairs. When they finish, they should have 8 red counters in the top row and 4 blue counters in the bottom row.

3. Discuss the idea that if each blue counter equals 2 red counters, then 4 blue counters must equal the sum: 2 + 2 + 2 + 2, or the product: 4 sets of 2 red counters, which makes 8 red counters. Here is an example of the two rows on the building mat:

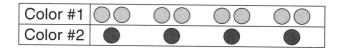

4. Repeat this process, (1) using 9 red counters in the top row of the mat and putting down 1 blue counter in the bottom row for every 3 red counters in the top row; and (2) using 10 red counters on the top and 1 blue counter on the bottom for every 5 red counters. In each case, have students use the sum and product language demonstrated in step 3.

5. Now have students make a top row of 10 red counters again, but this time use 1 blue counter in the bottom row for every 4 red counters. Students will be able to put down 2 blue counters but will find only 2 red counters still remaining to be matched instead of 4 red counters. Ask students what they might do in the bottom row to represent the 2 red counters. Ideally, they will see that if a whole blue counter is equal to 4 red counters, then 2 red counters will match to half of a whole blue counter. Tell students to put a third blue counter in the bottom row but to cover up half of that counter with their finger so that their bottom row just shows 2 and a half blue counters.

6. Now reverse the process. Tell students how many blue counters to place in the bottom row and how many red counters each blue counter equals. Students will then build the top row of red counters, based on the given ratio of blue to red.

7. For example, if students have 2 blue counters in the bottom row and they are matching each blue counter to 4 red counters, they should put 4 red counters in the top row, followed by another 4 red counters, making a total of 8 red counters in the top row. Notice how the red counters are placed in the top row *in groups of 4*, not just as a total set of 8. This reflects the ratio used: 1 blue to 4 reds.

8. Repeat the process, (1) using 3 blue counters on the bottom row, followed by placing on the top row 2 red counters per blue counter; and (2) using 4 blue counters on the bottom row, followed by placing on the top row 3 red counters per blue counter.

9. Finally, ask students what they might expect to see in the top row if they have 4 and a half blue counters in the bottom row and each blue counter equals 2 red counters. Ideally, they will suggest that the 4 whole blue counters will yield 4 groups of 2 red counters each and that the half of a blue counter will equal half of the 2 red counters, or 1 red counter, making a total of 9 red counters on the top row.

BUILDING MAT 3-4a

Color
#1

Color
#2

Activity 2: Pictorial Stage

Materials
   Worksheet 3-4a
   Regular pencils

Procedure

1. Give each student a copy of Worksheet 3-4a. Have students work together in pairs, but each person will complete her or his own individual worksheet.

2. Worksheet 3-4a contains two pairs of graphing frames. In each pair of frames, the headings are the same, but the first frame will contain a completed picture graph, whereas the symbol represents a *single unit*. The second frame of the pair will not have any symbols drawn yet but will have a legend that tells how many single units one symbol will equal.

3. Students are to work together to complete each blank frame, applying its legend to convert the data from its "partner" completed graph. They will use the grouping skills developed in the Manipulative Stage.

4. The first pair of graphs will require students to change from a single-unit symbol to a multiple-unit symbol. The second pair of graphs will reverse this process.

5. Below each pair of completed graphs, have students write two word sentences about the data. For Exercise 1, one sentence might be: "There are 8 Snickers candies in the School Store." Encourage students to write sentences that *compare* two quantities on the graph; for example, "There are 6 more Snickers than Kit Kats at the school store."

6. After students have completed the worksheet, have various students explain how they formed their groups and exchanged symbols. Have students read their sentences aloud to the class.

7. The first *pair* of graphs in Exercise 1 will be shown completed.

In Exercise 1, students must exchange every 4 candies (smiley faces) for 1 triangle. Thus, the row of only 2 candies must be exchanged for half a triangle. The rows of *shaded* triangles on the bottom graph represent what the students have *drawn*, but not necessarily colored, to complete the frame. Color may be added if you prefer. Sample sentences are also included.

NUMBER OF CANDIES AT SCHOOL STORE

Snickers	☺ ☺ ☺ ☺ ☺ ☺ ☺ ☺
Jolly Rogers	☺ ☺
Peanut Butter Cups	☺ ☺ ☺ ☺
Kit Kat	☺ ☺

Each ☺ is 1 candy.

NUMBER OF CANDIES AT SCHOOL STORE

Snickers	△ △
Jolly Rogers	◿
Peanut Butter Cups	△
Kit Kat	◿

Each △ is 4 candies.

There are 2 Jolly Rogers candies at the school store.
Altogether there are 16 candies for sale at the school store.

Answer Key for Worksheet 3-4a

1. (Shown in the previous illustration.)

2. Top graph (in circles): Chevrolet—12; Nissan—6; Ford—9; Buick—15. Possible sentences: "3 more Fords were sold than Nissans."; "12 Chevrolets were sold this month."

222

WORKSHEET 3-4a

Name _____

Transforming Picture Graphs

Date _____

Follow the teacher's directions to draw new picture graphs below. Write two sentences about each pair of picture graphs.

1. NUMBER OF CANDIES AT SCHOOL STORE

Snickers	☺☺☺☺☺☺☺☺
Jolly Rogers	☺☺
Peanut Butter Cups	☺☺☺☺
Kit Kat	☺☺

Each ☺ is 1 candy.

NUMBER OF CANDIES AT SCHOOL STORE

Snickers	
Jolly Rogers	
Peanut Butter Cups	
Kit Kat	

Each △ is 4 candies.

_____

_____

2. NUMBER OF CARS SOLD THIS MONTH

Chevrolet	
Nissan	
Ford	
Buick	

Each ◯ is 1 car.

NUMBER OF CARS SOLD THIS MONTH

Chevrolet	☐☐
Nissan	☐
Ford	☐☐
Buick	☐☐☐

Each ☐ is 6 cars.

_____

_____

Copyright © 2003 by John Wiley & Sons, Inc.

Activity 3: Independent Practice

Materials
Worksheet 3-4b
Regular pencils

Procedure
Give each student a copy of Worksheet 3-4b to be completed independently. Ask students to be ready to share their answers after all have finished.

Answer Key for Worksheet 3-4b
1. D

2. A

3. C

4. A

Possible Testing Errors That May Occur for This Objective
- Students count the required amount of symbols shown without applying the legend value to the symbol. For example, they find 7 car symbols directly from the graph as the answer but fail to find 7 symbols × 3 cars per symbol = 21 cars for the actual amount of cars needed.

- Students incorrectly count the needed symbols appearing on the graph but correctly apply the legend. For example, they find 4 symbols × 2 hot dogs per symbol = 8 hot dogs, when they should have found 5 symbols × 2 hot dogs per symbol = 10 hot dogs.

- When only half of a symbol is shown in the graph, students either ignore it when counting or consider it as another whole symbol. For example, if a symbol equals 4 marbles, then half the symbol will equal 2 marbles. Students ignore the extra 2 marbles or count them as 4 marbles when finding a total.

224

WORKSHEET 3-4b

Interpreting Picture Graphs

Name _____

Date _____

Use the graph below to answer Exercises 1 and 2.

THE CAR WASH

Time	Number of Cars Washed
9:00 – 10:00	🚗 🚗 🚗
10:00 – 11:00	🚗 🚗
11:00 – 12:00	🚗 🚗 🚗 🚗
12:00 – 1:00	🚗 🚗 🚗

Each 🚗 means 6 cars.

1. How many cars were washed at the car wash from 11:00 to 1:00?

    A. 6   B. 18   C. 24   D. 39

2. If the car wash charges $5 to wash each car, how much money was earned from 9:00 to 10:00?

    A. $90   B. $30   C. $15   D. $5

Use the graph below to answer Exercises 3 and 4.

THE PICNIC

Names	Number of Hot Dogs Eaten
Jose	🌭
Ken	🌭 ◖
Miriam	🌭
Sonia	🌭 🌭

Each 🌭 equals 2 hot dogs.

3. How many hot dogs did Sonia eat at the picnic?

    A. 2   B. 3   C. 4   D. 5

4. How many hot dogs did Jose and Ken eat in all?

    A. 5   B. 4   C. 3   D. 2

Objective 5
Construct, interpret, and apply (single) bar graphs.

Discussion
Often students are asked to make comparisons between and among the bars of a bar graph. This is difficult for young students. They more easily find a single bar that is the longest or the shortest bar. Students also may have difficulty reading bar graphs in which each cell represents multiple units. They need experience reading this type of scale. The following activities will help students move from single-unit to multiple-unit scales.

Activity 1: Manipulative Stage

Materials
Sets of 30 1-inch square tiles per 4 students
Building Mat 3-5a (inch grid paper)
Regular pencils

Procedure
1. Give each group of 4 students a copy of Building Mat 3-5a (or inch grid paper) and 30 1-inch square tiles or paper squares (or enough for 1 tile per student in the class). If necessary, before copying, extend the grid lines of Building Mat 3-5a in order to add one more column.

2. Survey the class with the following question (or a similar question), which has four response choices: "Which of these four cartoon characters do you like best? Bart Simpson, Casper, Donald Duck, or Rugrats?"

3. Write the results of the survey on the board. Using the shorter edge of the building mat or grid paper as the bottom axis, students should label every other column with one of the cartoon names.

4. They should then place tiles in the column spaces above the names, placing 1 tile per space and 1 tile for each vote. The finished graph will look like a vertical bar graph made of tiles. Depending on the class data used, some columns of tiles may have to temporarily extend off the top of the grid. For discussion purposes here, suppose that the voting is as follows: Bart—4, Casper—10, Donald—4, and Rugrats—7. Above Bart's name, there is a bar 4 tiles long; Casper's bar is 10 tiles long; Donald's bar is 4 tiles long; Rugrats' bar is 7 tiles long.

5. Now ask students to stack the tiles in each column in *pairs* as much as possible. Bart's column and Donald's column will each become 2 stacks of 2 tiles each; Casper's column will be 5 stacks of 2; Rugrats' column will be 3 stacks of 2, then 1 single tile at the top.

6. Check each group's new "tile" bar graph for correctness. A graph of the sample data is shown here. Students' graphs will be used for the activity in the Pictorial Stage that follows.

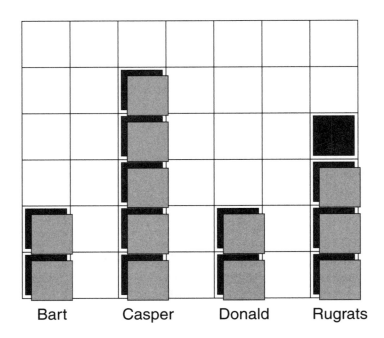

BUILDING MAT 3-5a

Activity 2: Pictorial Stage

Materials

    Building Mat 3-5a with tiles (completed graph from Activity 1)
    Regular pencils

Procedure

1. Each group of 4 students should have the tile graph they completed in Activity 1.

2. Ask students to number the left vertical edge of their grid paper without removing the tiles. Because each grid space in each column should hold a stack of 2 tiles, students should label the scale steps in multiples of 2: 2, 4, 6, 8, 10. The bottom mark of the scale should be 0.

3. If a grid space holds a complete stack of 2 tiles, the tiles should be removed and the entire space shaded in regular pencil. If a grid space holds only 1 tile, that is a half-stack. That single tile should be removed, and only the lower half of the grid space should be shaded.

4. Add titles for the graph and its two axes. A sample graph is shown here.

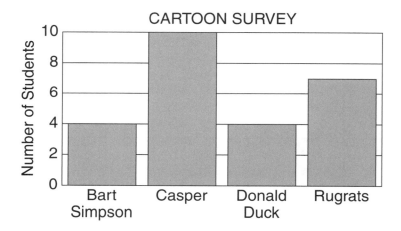

5. Use the finished bar graph to ask a variety of questions of the students. Try to use wording not often included in their textbooks. Here are some possibilities, based on the cartoon data given as an example.

Which cartoon characters had more than 8 votes? (only Casper)

How many students voted in this survey? (25)

Which cartoon characters had fewer than 6 votes? (Bart and Donald)

Which cartoon characters had between 5 and 8 votes? (Rugrats)

How many votes did Casper and Rugrats receive together? (10 + 7 =17)

How many more votes did Casper receive than Donald Duck? (10 – 4 = 6 more)

Which cartoon characters received the same number of votes? (Bart and Donald)

Activity 3: Independent Practice

Materials

Worksheet 3-5a

Regular pencils

Procedure

Give each student a copy of Worksheet 3-5a to complete independently. Ask students to be ready to share their answers with the entire class after all have finished.

Answer Key for Worksheet 3-5a

1. B

2. C

3. D

4. A

Possible Testing Errors That May Occur for This Objective

- When required to find two bars of *equal length* to determine an answer, students will focus on the two *tallest* bars (or the two *shortest* bars) of the graph that *differ* in length from each other.

- When asked to compare two bar lengths, students will simply select the tallest or the shortest of the two bars to determine the answer instead of making the comparison.

- Students will select the first or the last bar of the graph to determine an answer, ignoring the actual question.

WORSHEET 3-5a

Name _____

Interpreting Bar Graphs

Date _____

Use the graph below to answer Exercises 1 and 2.

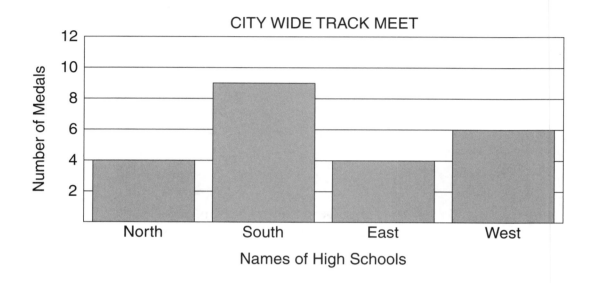

1. Which schools won the same number of medals at the track meet?

   A. North and South

   B. North and East

   C. East and West

   D. South and West

2. How many medals did South High School win at the track meet?

   A. 4   B. 8   C. 9   D. 10

WORSHEET 3-5a Continued   Name _____

Date _____

Use the graph below to answer Exercises 3 and 4.

3. How many more students liked chocolate than liked vanilla?

    A. 11   B. 6   C. 10   D. 5

4. How many students participated in the ice cream survey?

    A. 26   B. 20   C. 17   D. 15

Objective 6
Construct, interpret, and apply (broken) line graphs.

Discussion
Students at this grade level have had more experience with bar graphs and picture graphs than with broken line graphs. Even though they have had practice on the other types of graphs with scales numbered in multiples of two or more, they may still need experience with simply reading the line graph to answer higher-level questions.

Activity 1: Manipulative Stage

Materials
    30 square tiles (or enough for 1 tile per student)
    5 labeled index cards (1 numeral per card: 1, 2, 3, 4; 1 card with "More than 4")
    Piece of colored yarn (48 inches long)

Procedure
1. This activity will be done with the class as a whole.

2. Give each student a 1-inch square tile or paper square.

3. Draw a line segment near the lower edge of the chalkboard to represent the horizontal axis of the graph (or attach a piece of yarn to a large bulletin board in the classroom to show the same thing), and place the small numeral cards for 1, 2, 3, and 4, as well as the card for "More than 4," in the same order below this line segment to serve as the horizontal scale.

4. Survey the class with the following question: "How many children are in your immediate family? 1, 2, 3, 4, or more?" Other, similar questions might be used.

5. To show their votes, students will take turns taping their tiles edge to edge above the appropriate cards, placing 1 tile per student. At first, the finished graph will look like a vertical bar graph made of tiles.

6. Now draw a large dot at the center, just above the top edge of each column of tiles. Connecting from left to right, tape the long piece of colored yarn to the board at each of the large dots to create the appearance of a broken line.

7. Cut the excess yarn off at the first and last dots; do not connect from those two dots back down to the drawn horizontal line segment.

8. This class graph will be used for the activity in the Pictorial Stage that follows. A sample tile-and-yarn graph is shown. Ask students questions about the class graph, like the following:

   How many students have 3 children in their family?

   How many more students have 2 children in their family than have 4 children?

   What size of family is the most popular in our class?

   How many children were surveyed in our class today?

9. Also discuss the steepness of the yarn between any two adjacent columns of tiles. If the two columns differ only by one tile, the yarn section between the columns is not very steep. If the two columns differ by several tiles, the connecting yarn section is much steeper.

Here is a sample showing the attached yarn above the columns of tiles:

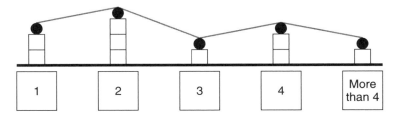

Activity 2: Pictorial Stage

Materials
Completed broken line graph from Activity 1
Worksheet 3-6a (or half-inch grid paper)
Red pencils and regular pencils

Procedure
1. The class line graph made with tiles in Activity 1 will be used for this activity.

2. Give each student a copy of Worksheet 3-6a (half-inch grid paper) and a red pencil.

3. Have students label the left vertical axis (longer edge) of the grid paper in unit intervals, but number only every other mark on the axis. The lower horizontal axis (shorter edge) should be labeled to show the numbers 1, 2, 3, and 4, followed by "more than 4." These lower labels should be written directly on vertical grid marks where they cross the horizontal axis, not between the marks. Proper titles should also be written for each axis and the total graph.

4. Now have students transfer the large dots shown on the Activity 1 line graph to their own grids and connect the dots by drawing a red path between adjacent dots. The dots on the grid should represent the same vertical distance as the top edges of the tile columns. That is, if 5 tiles were used to make a column on the board, then the column's corresponding dot should match to the 5-mark on the vertical axis of the grid paper. The dots should be marked on vertical grid bars, not within a space or between two vertical grid bars.

5. Here is a sample of the finished graph, using the example from Activity 1:

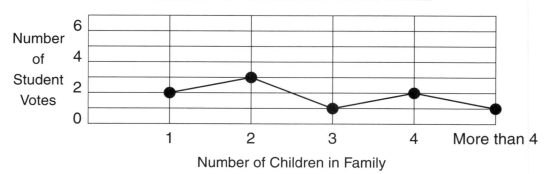

6. After students have completed their line graphs, ask them various questions about the graph. Here are examples of higher-level questions for the sample graph (that is, questions that require students to *compute* with vertical values from the graph):

    How many students have at most 3 children in their families? (2 + 3 + 1 = 6 students)

    How many more students have 2 children in the family than have more than 4 children? (3 – 1 = 2 more students)

    How many students have 3 or 4 children in their families? (1 + 2 = 3 students)

    Between which two horizontal values is the red line segment the steepest? (between "2 children" and "3 children," where the vertical difference or change is 3 – 1, or 2)

WORKSHEET 3-6a
(Half-Inch Grid)

Activity 3: Independent Practice

Materials
Worksheet 3-6b
Regular pencils

Procedure
Give each student a copy of Worksheet 3-6b to complete independently. Ask students to be ready to share their answers when all have finished the worksheet.

Answer Key for Worksheet 3-6b
1. C

2. A

3. D

4. D

Possible Testing Errors That May Occur for This Objective
- When the test item requires the sum (or difference) of several values shown on the line graph, students select the wrong set of values to add or subtract.

- Students select the greatest value (highest point) or the least value (lowest point) shown on the line graph, even though the question requires a different value or a combination of values. They ignore the information given in the test item.

- The correct point on the graph is selected for finding the answer, but the vertical scale is read incorrectly. Hence, the wrong value is selected for the response.

WORKSHEET 3-6b   Name _____

Interpreting Broken Line Graphs   Date _____

Use the graph below to answer Exercises 1 through 4.

SODA EXPERIMENT

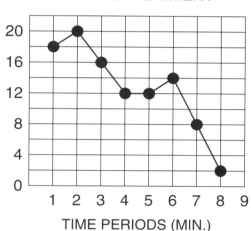

NUMBER OF BUBBLES POPPED ON TOP OF SODA

TIME PERIODS (MIN.)

1. How many bubbles popped on top of the soda during the sixth minute?

   A. 20   B. 18   C. 14   D. 12

2. Which time periods produced the same number of bubbles?

   A. 4 and 5   B. 1 and 8   C. 2 and 6   D. 7 and 8

3. How many more bubbles popped during the second minute than during the eighth minute?

   A. 12   B. 14   C. 16   D. 18

4. Of the given pairs of time periods, which pair showed the greatest change in number of bubbles between the two time periods?

   A. 1 and 2   B. 2 and 3   C. 4 and 5   D. 7 and 8

Objective 7

Use a pair of numbers to compare favorable outcomes to all possible outcomes of a single-staged experiment or situation, and identify which outcome has the greater chance of occurring.

Discussion

Prediction based on limited information is a major topic in probability. Because present relationships must be extrapolated to a future setting, young students have great difficulty with this topic. Experience is needed, as well as increased logical reasoning. The activities described next will provide such experience.

Activity 1: Manipulative Stage

Materials

    Large, cutout paper circles (8-inch diameter)
    Scissors
    Glue
    Colored markers (red, green, yellow)

Procedure

1. Give each pair of students two copies of a large, cutout paper circle (approximately 8 inches in diameter) that has already been subdivided into 16 equal sectors. Do not make the subdividing line segments on the circles bold; use a narrow-width pen when drawing them.

2. Each student pair should also have scissors, glue, and three colored markers (red, green, yellow).

3. Using 4 adjacent sectors on one copy of the circle, have students color 2 sectors red, 1 sector yellow, and 1 sector green. Discuss what they notice about the number of sectors for each color; for example, there are twice as many red sectors as there are yellow (or green), and the number of yellow sectors equals the number of green sectors.

4. Ask how the colors might be related on the whole circle or disk if the present color relationships are maintained as all the sectors are colored. Accept any ideas at this point; you are asking for predictions at this stage of the activity.

5. Now have students color the other sectors, using the same pattern: red, red, yellow, green, with each new group of 4 sectors of the circle. Monitor their work to be sure that they are maintaining the 2:1:1 coloring ratio in each quadrant of the circle. (The differently shaded interiors shown in the illustration represent the different colors.)

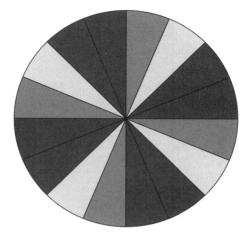

6. When students have finished coloring their circles, have them cut their colored sectors apart into 16 individual sectors. They should then separate the 16 sectors into 3 new groups by color. There will be 8 red sectors, 4 green sectors, and 4 yellow sectors.

7. Have students glue the cutout sectors onto the blank sectors of their second circle, keeping all sectors of the same color adjacent to each other.

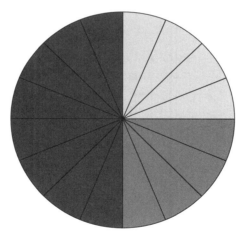

8. When all students are finished, ask them to look at their new circle to see how the different colors compare now. The red area of the circle should be twice as large as the area for either the yellow or the green; the green and yellow areas of the circle should be equal.

9. Earlier, at the time of predicting, students saw only individual sectors, so they could compare them at the "countable quantity" level. Now they see "continuous areas" of color. The purpose of this activity is to help students analyze the different colored areas of a circular spinner and connect those areas to specific quantities (a good readiness activity for ratios described in words rather than with ratio notation like 2:1).

10. Show students several other simple spinners and ask them to predict what the original color relationships might have been, using the colored sector approach. You might use the same 16-sector circle pattern but color different amounts of sectors so that areas are easy to visually compare. Sectors of the same color should be touching each other, but individual sectors should still be clearly marked or visible. Here are some possible sector combinations to use, with their simpler ratios in parentheses: 12 green, 4 yellow (3 green for each yellow); 4 red, 4 yellow, 4 green, 4 orange (1 R with 1 Y, 1 G, and 1 Or); 2 red, 2 yellow, 4 green, 4 orange, 4 blue (1 R with 1 Y, 2 G, 2 Or, and 2 B); and 8 blue, 8 yellow (1 B and 1 Y).

Activity 2: Pictorial Stage

Materials
Worksheet 3-7a (spinner patterns)
Jumbo paper clips (for spinner needles)
Regular paper and regular pencils

Procedure
1. In this activity, students will be presented with a spinner and asked to identify the numerical ratio of its colors, then actually spin the spinner many times, keeping a record of how many times each color is selected. The idea is to compare the new quantities for the colors to the initial numerical ratio identified for the spinner's colors.

2. Have students work in groups of 4 students each. For half the groups, assign each group the spinner divided into four equal sections with 3 sections colored red and 1 section colored yellow. For the other half of the groups, assign each group the spinner divided into five equal sections, with 1 section colored red, 1 colored blue, 1 colored yellow, and 2 colored green. See Worksheet 3-7a for the spinner patterns.

3. Give each group a jumbo paper clip. The paper clip, held at the center of a spinner by a pencil through the looped end, will serve as the spinner needle.

4. Hold up the 2-color spinner and ask the class to predict what the numerical ratio might be for the two colors (for example, 3 R and 1 Y, since the area for red appears to be 3 times as great as the area for yellow; think of the spinner as having 4 parts total).

5. Repeat the question for the 4-color spinner (for example, ratio should be 1 R with 1 B, 1 Y, and 2 G, since the area for green appears to be 2 times as great as the area for either red, blue, or yellow; think of the spinner as having 5 parts total).

6. Each group should spin its own spinner 20 times. Group members should take turns as the spinning person, and the group should keep a record of how many times group members spin each color on their particular spinner.

7. After all groups have finished, ask each group to compare its total spins for each color to the numerical ratio predicted for its spinner. Some groups' total will show distributions similar to that of the spinner's ratio; others may not. That's the way probability works!

8. Finally, compile all distributions from groups having the same spinner; that is, get a total for red, a total for yellow, and so on. Because the quantities are greater, the distribution of spins by color should be closer to that of the spinner's numerical ratio. For example, consider the 4-color spinner with the ratio 1R:1Y:1B:2G. If 3 groups were using that spinner, the combined group totals might be 13 reds, 11 yellows, 10 blues, and 26 greens, for a total of 60 spins in all.

9. Discuss how the number of green spins compares to the number of yellow spins, and so on. You want a general relationship here: the number of greens (26) is twice the number of reds and over twice that of the yellows (11); the number of reds (13) is close to the number of blues (10) and close to the number of yellows (11); and so forth. So even though this predicted situation may never actually occur, if group members make 20 spins with the 4-color spinner used in this activity, they could *expect* or *predict* that they might spin red about 4 times ($\frac{1}{5}$ of 20), green about 8 times ($\frac{2}{5}$ of 20), and so on.

WORKSHEET 3-7a
Spinner Patterns

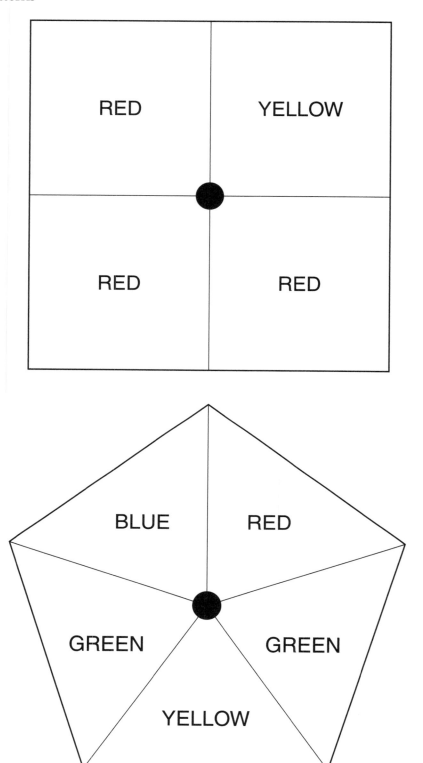

Activity 3: Independent Practice

Materials
Worksheet 3-7b
Regular pencil

Procedure
Give each student a copy of Worksheet 3-7b to complete independently. Ask students to be ready to share their results after all have completed the worksheet.

Answer Key for Worksheet 3-7b
1. B

2. D

3. A

4. C

5. A

Possible Testing Errors That May Occur for This Objective
- The total number of possible outcomes stated in the test item will be selected for the response instead of the number of ways predicted for the given event.

- If a spinner is shown in the test item, some students may be visually influenced by the spinner needle in the diagram and select the sector containing the needle rather than the sector required by the problem.

- Incorrect proportional reasoning is used. For example, if a certain color appears in 1 out of 4 equal sectors on a spinner and 20 spins total are made, students will not realize that 1 out of 4 is equivalent to 5 out of 20, so 5 spins might be predicted for that color.

244

Complete the exercises below and be ready to share your answers. Use this spinner to answer Exercises 1 through 3.

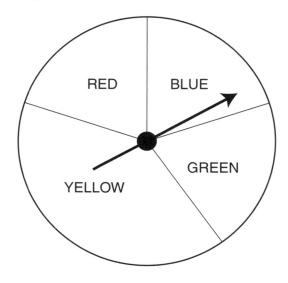

1. In a total of 20 spins, to which color will the spinner probably point the greatest number of times?

   A. Red   B. Yellow   C. Blue   D. Green

2. To which two colors will the spinner probably point about the same number of times out of 20 spins total?

   A. Red and yellow   B. Yellow and blue   C. Green and yellow   D. Blue and green

3. If the color red is selected 5 times out of 25 spins total, what would be a reasonable number of spins to expect for yellow out of the 25 spins?

   A. 12   B. 25   C. 5   D. 3

4. If you toss a coin 50 times, about how many times might you expect to get *heads*?

   A. 8   B. 15   C. 25   D. 40

5. If a spinner contains 4 equal sectors and each sector is colored, which color combination for the spinner will probably cause blue to be selected most often?

   A. 1 red, 3 blue   C. 3 green, 1 blue

   B. 2 blue, 2 green   D. 1 red, 1 blue, 2 yellow

Objective 8

Identify possible two-member or three-member outcomes of a situation (multistaged experiment without order).

Discussion

Students must connect possible outcomes to the original set of objects from which they come. When outcomes are single objects, it is easier for students to predict what choices are available. In some probability problems, however, an outcome may consist of 2 or 3 objects drawn from the original set of objects. The sample space then consists of all the possible pairs or triples that can be made with the total set of objects rather than the individual objects themselves. Students need more practice with such multistage experiments, that is, those in which more than one draw is made from a set of objects to create a single outcome.

Activity 1: Manipulative Stage

Materials

Sets of strips of colored construction paper (initially, 4 strips per set; 1 strip per color, using red, blue, green, and yellow; later, purple and orange)

Regular pencils and regular paper

Procedure

1. Give each group of 4 students a set of 4 colored strips cut from construction paper (1 strip each of red, blue, green, and yellow). Make strips approximately 1 inch by 3 or 4 inches in size. Measurements do not need to be exact. Later in the activity, a purple strip and an orange strip will be added to each set.

2. Have students place their set of 4 strips in a loose pile on the desktop in front of them, then draw out 2 strips at a time (a pair) from the set, record the 2 colors as a pair (for example, red-blue or RB) on a sheet of paper, and return the strips to the original pile.

3. Students should repeat this process, recording only the new pairs they find, until they think all possible pairs have been drawn. Because the strips are drawn out as a pair, there is no order to how they have been drawn out. Consequently, a red-blue pair is considered the same as a blue-red pair. Students need to record only one of two such pairs.

4. When each group is finished or thinks all possible pairs have been found, compare all the lists for completeness. There should be 6 pairs found: RB, RG, RY, BG, BY, and GY.

5. Ask students if there is a way to organize their list of pairs so that they know for certain that all possible 2-color combinations have been found. Ideas will vary. (Do you see a pattern in the way the checklist of pairs was made?)

6. Now give each group two more colored strips (1 purple and 1 orange) to add to the group's original set, making a total of 6 colored strips in the new set.

7. Have students repeat the drawing process, but this time have them draw out 3 strips at a time (a triple). Again, there will be no order to how the strips are drawn out of the pile. Each triple drawn should be recorded in word or letter format (for example, red-blue-purple or RBP).

8. When all groups are finished with their lists, compare them for completeness. There should be 20 possible outcomes listed for this new sample space of triples: RBG, RBY, RBP, RBO, RGY, RGP, RGO, RYP, RYO, RPO, BGY, BGP, BGO, BYP, BYO, BPO, GYP, GYO, GPO, YPO.

9. Again, ask students if there is a way to organize the list of triples they have made so that they know for certain that all possible 3-color combinations have been found. Ideas will vary. (The list was made using the set of colors: R, B, G, Y, P, and O. Do you see a pattern in the way the checklist of triples was made?)

Activity 2: Pictorial Stage

Materials

Worksheet 3-8a
Regular pencils

Procedure

1. Give each student a copy of Worksheet 3-8a, but have students work with partners. The worksheet contains 5 circles with a color name written inside each circle; 2 reds, 1 blue, 1 green, and 1 yellow will be used for the circles' colors.

2. Each pair of students should try to make a list on the worksheet of the different pairs of circles they can copy from the set of 5 circles. They may either draw and label two circles together to record a pair formed or simply list the color pair by the color names involved (for example, red-blue or RB), as done in the Manipulative Stage. A red-blue pair is the same as a blue-red pair, so only one should be recorded. Remind students that if there are 2 red circles in the original set, they can form the pair: red-red.

3. Compare lists when all partners are finished. The final list should have the following pairs as outcomes: RR, RB, RG, RY, BG, BY, GY. Because there are two circles that look alike (the two red circles), any pair formed with one of them will look like a pair formed with the other. For example, the first red paired with blue will look like the second red paired with the same blue. These copies diminish the number of distinct pairs found in the final sample space of pairs. If there had been 5 different colors of circles, 10 pairs would have been possible instead of the 7 pairs found in this activity.

4. Ask students to share how they knew they had found all possible distinct pairs for this activity.

248

WORKSHEET 3-8a   Name _____

Identifying Pairs in Probability   Date _____

List all possible distinct pairs of circles that can be made from this set of 5 circles. Be ready to tell the class why you think your list of pairs is complete.

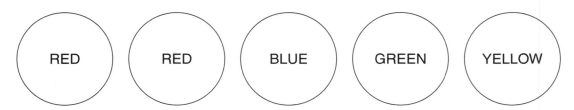

Activity 3: Independent Practice

Materials
Worksheet 3-8b
Regular pencils

Procedure
Give each student a copy of Worksheet 3-8b to complete independently. Ask students to be ready to share their answers when all have completed the worksheet.

Answer Key for Worksheet 3-8b
1. C

2. D (possible triples without order: TTH, TTC, HCT, HCC, TCC, where T = triangle, C = cross, and H = heart)

3. A

Possible Testing Errors That May Occur for This Objective
- When forming a pair or triple, students select a response that contains a repeated color when the color appears only once in the original set of colors. For example, yellow-blue-blue is selected, but blue appears only one time in the original set of colors; thus, blue would not be available for a second drawing.

- Students focus on only one color and select a response that lists that color two or three times (for example, green-green-green as a triple), even though the chosen color appears only once in the original set and can be drawn only one time as part of a pair or a triple.

- Students do not understand how to make combinations, so they select a response randomly, often the first or the last response in the list.

- Students select a pair or triple in which at least one of the objects is not a member of the original set of objects used for the drawing (for example, red-blue-purple is selected as a triple when purple is not included in the original list of colors).

250

WORKSHEET 3-8b   Name _____

Finding Possible Combinations   Date _____

Work the exercises below and be ready to share your answers with the entire class.

1. Six sticks of chalk are in a drawer, as shown below. They are the same size but
    are different colors. In the set, 1 stick is red, 2 are green, 2 are blue, and 1 is
    yellow. If you took 3 sticks from the drawer without looking, which could
    possibly be the 3 sticks you took?

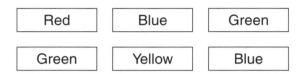

| Red | Blue | Green |
| Green | Yellow | Blue |

    A. Yellow, red, red   C. Blue, yellow, blue

    B. Green, red, purple   D. Green, green, green

2. Five counters are in a box and are the same size and shape. Each counter has a
    design on it, as shown below. How many distinct outcomes are possible if 3
    counters selected from the box at the same time represent an outcome?

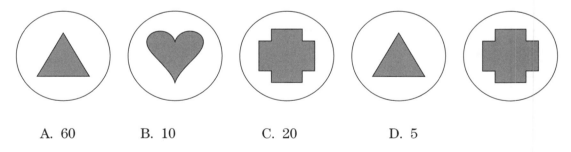

    A. 60   B. 10   C. 20   D. 5

3. A bowl contains 8 coins: 1 quarter, 2 dimes, 3 nickels, and 2 pennies. Which
    combination of coins has a total value of 47 cents and all coins can be drawn
    from the bowl at the same time?

    A. 1 quarter, 2 dimes, 2 pennies   C. 1 quarter, 4 nickels, 2 pennies

    B. 1 quarter, 3 nickels, 7 pennies   D. 4 dimes, 1 nickel, 2 pennies

Section 3

Name _____

Date _____

GRAPHING, STATISTICS, AND PROBABILITY: PRACTICE TEST ANSWER SHEET

Directions: Use the Answer Sheet to darken the letter of the choice that best answers each question.

1. ○ A ○ B ○ C ○ D
2. ○ A ○ B ○ C ○ D
3. ○ A ○ B ○ C ○ D
4. ○ A ○ B ○ C ○ D
5. ○ A ○ B ○ C ○ D
6. ○ A ○ B ○ C ○ D
7. ○ A ○ B ○ C ○ D
8. ○ A ○ B ○ C ○ D
9. ○ A ○ B ○ C ○ D
10. ○ A ○ B ○ C ○ D
11. ○ A ○ B ○ C ○ D
12. ○ A ○ B ○ C ○ D
13. ○ A ○ B ○ C ○ D
14. ○ A ○ B ○ C ○ D
15. ○ A ○ B ○ C ○ D
16. ○ A ○ B ○ C ○ D

251

SECTION 3: GRAPHING, STATISTICS, AND PROBABILITY: PRACTICE TEST

1. When a bicycle and a tricycle are counted together as 2 vehicles, 5 wheels are involved. When 2 more such vehicles are counted, there will be 10 wheels in all. When there are 30 wheels, how many vehicles will there be? Use the following table to find the answer.

Vehicles	2	4	6			
Wheels	5	10	15			

   A. 8   B. 10   C. 15   D. 12

2. If the patterns shown in row A and row B continue, what number will be in row B below the number 5 in row A?

A	2	3		5		7
B	4	9	16			

   A. 36   B. 25   C. 17   D. 6

3. List the whole numbers that are greater than 78, but less than or equal to 82.

   A. 79, 80, 81, 82   C. 77, 78, 79, 80, 81

   B. 78, 79, 80, 81   D. 79, 80, 81, 82, 83

4. Which set contains decimal numbers in tenths that are greater than 1.9 and less than 2.3?

   A. 2.0, 2.1, 2.2, 2.3   C. 1.9, 2.0, 2.1, 2.2

   B. 2.0, 2.1, 2.2   D. 1.9, 2.0, 2.1, 2.2, 2.3

5. Marian sold 317 school booster ribbons, and Henry sold 209 ribbons. What was the average number of ribbons sold per person?

   A. 209   B. 214   C. 317   D. 263

6. Lois has 125 marbles, Jack has 174 marbles, and Anne has 157 marbles. What is the mean number of marbles they have?

   A. 141   B. 150   C. 152   D. 157

SECTION 3: GRAPHING, STATISTICS, AND PROBABILITY: PRACTICE TEST

Use the graph below to answer Items 7 and 8.

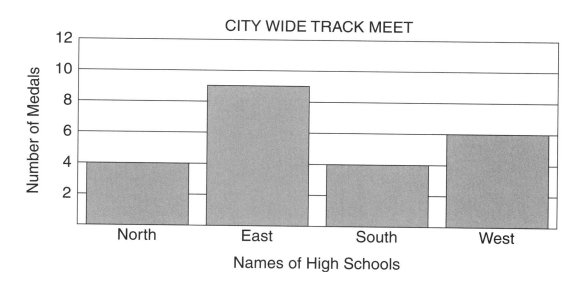

7. How many hot dogs did Ken eat at the picnic?

   A. 3   B. 4   C. 5   D. 6

8. How many hot dogs did Jose and Sonia eat altogether?

   A. 2   B. 4   C. 6   D. 8

Use the graph below to answer Items 9 and 10.

9. Which schools won the same number of medals at the track meet?

   A. North and South   C. East and West

   B. North and East   D. South and West

10. How many medals did East High School win at the track meet?

    A. 4   B. 6   C. 9   D. 10

SECTION 3: GRAPHING, STATISTICS, AND PROBABILITY: PRACTICE TEST

Use the graph below to answer Items 11 and 12.

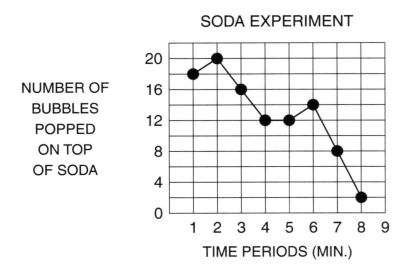

11. How many bubbles popped on top of the soda during the third minute?

   A. 20　　　　　B. 16　　　　　C. 12　　　　　D. 8

12. How many more bubbles popped during the second minute than during the seventh minute?

   A. 18　　　　　B. 16　　　　　C. 14　　　　　D. 12

13. In a total of 40 spins, to which color will the spinner shown below probably point the greatest number of times?

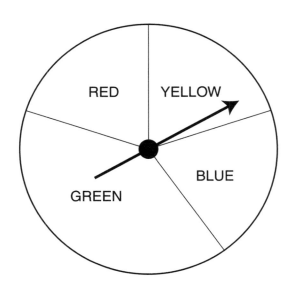

   A. Red　　　　　B. Green　　　　　C. Blue　　　　　D. Yellow

SECTION 3: GRAPHING, STATISTICS, AND PROBABILITY:
PRACTICE TEST

14. If a spinner contains 4 equal sectors and each sector is colored, which color combination for the spinner will probably cause red to be selected most often?

    A. 1 yellow, 3 red

    B. 2 blue, 2 green

    C. 3 green, 1 blue

    D. 1 red, 1 blue, 2 yellow

15. Six sticks of chalk are in a box. They are the same size but are different colors. In the set, 1 stick is blue, 2 are green, 2 are red, and 1 is yellow. If you took 3 sticks from the drawer without looking, which could possibly be the 3 sticks you took?

    A. Red, red, red

    B. Green, red, purple

    C. Blue, yellow, blue

    D. Red, green, red

16. A bowl contains 10 coins: 1 quarter, 3 dimes, 4 nickels, and 2 pennies. Which combination of 4 coins has a total value of 52 cents and all 4 coins can be drawn from the bowl at the same time?

    A. 1 quarter, 2 dimes, 7 pennies

    B. 3 dimes, 4 nickels, 2 pennies

    C. 1 quarter, 5 nickels, 2 pennies

    D. 4 dimes, 2 nickels, 2 pennies

Section 3: Graphing, Statistics, and Probability: Answer Key for Practice Test

The objective being tested is shown in brackets beside the answer.

1. D [1]
2. B [1]
3. A [2]
4. B [2]
5. D [3]
6. C [3]
7. A [4]
8. C [4]

9. A [5]
10. C [5]
11. B [6]
12. D [6]
13. B [7]
14. A [7]
15. D [8]
16. B [8]

GEOMETRY AND LOGICAL OR SPATIAL REASONING

Objective 1
Make generalizations from geometric sets of examples and nonexamples.

Discussion
The ability to compare or contrast the characteristics of different shapes is very important in the study of geometry. The very young child notices only one or two characteristics: for example, the color or size of an object. The more mature person is able to identify many characteristics—a skill that is necessary in the forming of definitions. Students need to practice sorting objects based on their common characteristics. The following activities will provide such experiences. Practice with the logical connectors AND and OR and with NOT will be included.

Activity 1: Manipulative Stage

Materials
Sets of small attribute blocks (or classroom sets of assorted small containers or commercial sets of geometric solids)

Procedure
1. Give each group of 3 or 4 students a desk set of small attribute blocks (or 8 to 10 assorted containers found in the home or of commercial geometric solids like cones, spheres, pyramids, and so forth).

2. Depending on which type of object is used, ask students to sort their set of objects according to different characteristics. Begin by giving only one characteristic, such as shape. Other characteristics to use might be size, thickness, color, existence of flat surfaces, or the existence of curved or nonflat surfaces. For example, ask students to sort out all shapes that are "triangles" from their particular set. Help them realize that the remaining shapes are "NOT triangles."

3. Repeat the process several times, using a different characteristic each time. Monitor the different groups to be sure that they are sorting their objects correctly. In some cases, students will have to decide which objects are to be considered "large" and which ones are to be called "small" and similarly for "thick" and "thin." How they decide is arbitrary.

4. Now ask students to sort according to two characteristics. For example, have them pull out the objects that are "red AND square." The shapes may be small or large, thick or thin, but they must be red AND they must be square-shaped. The two characteristics must occur in the same object simultaneously. Repeat this process with other pairs of characteristics.

5. Give students practice with the logical connector OR. For example, ask them to pull out all the objects that are "yellow OR triangular." All yellow objects should be pulled out, regardless of the shape, and all triangles should be pulled out, regardless of the color. Yellow triangles will be pulled out, but other objects will also be pulled out. This inclusive nature of the word OR is difficult for young students to understand. Much practice is needed.

6. When students seem comfortable with pairs of characteristics, challenge them with three characteristics at a time, such as "small, thick, AND red."

Activity 2: Pictorial Stage

Materials
Cards Patterns 4-1a
Scissors
Worksheet 4-1a
Regular pencils

Procedure

1. Give each pair of students a copy of the Cards Patterns 4-1a and two pairs of scissors. Also give each student a copy of Worksheet 4-1a.

2. Students should cut apart the cards on the pattern sheet, then sort them according to the characteristics described on Worksheet 4-1a. Because each card is labeled with a letter, the letter of a card will be recorded in the appropriate place on the worksheet to show that the card's design belongs in a certain group.

3. After all student pairs have completed the worksheet, have them share their results with the entire class.

4. Exercise 6 on Worksheet 4-1a is discussed next as a sample.

Exercise 6 on Worksheet 4-1a asks students to sort their set of cards according to the two characteristics "striped OR shaded." They should form one pile of cards that contain stripes, along with any additional cards that are shaded but not striped. If a card has stripes or if it is shaded, it will go in the first pile. The remaining cards will form another pile where each card does NOT belong to the "striped OR shaded" group. Have students confirm that each card in this second group will satisfy the description given on the worksheet, that is, each card will simultaneously not have stripes AND not be shaded.

Cards A, B, C, F, G, H, and K will be recorded in the blank beside "striped OR shaded" on the worksheet, and cards D, E, I, J, and L will be recorded in the blank beside "Not striped and not shaded."

Note that this is an exploratory activity at this grade level. Do not require students to memorize the logical relationship: Not (striped OR shaded) = (Not striped) AND (Not shaded). Such generalizations will be studied in later grades.

Answer Key for Worksheet 4-1a

1. E, J (H and L if eyes are counted as dots); A, B, C, D, F, G, H, I, K, L

2. A, C, F, G, H; B, D, E, I, J, K, L

3. A, B, D, E, F, G, K; C, H, I, J, L

4. I; A, B, C, D, E, F, G, H, J, K, L

5. C, G; A, B, D, E, F, H, I, J, K, L

6. A, B, C, F, G, H, K; D, E, I, J, L

7. D, E, I, J, L; A, B, C, F, G, H, K

260

CARDS PATTERNS 4-1a (cut cards apart)

WORSHEET 4-1a

Sorting Shapes
by Their Characteristics

Name _____

Date _____

Sort the cards in your set according to the characteristics listed below. Find the cards that belong to the first description of each exercise, then the remaining cards of the set will belong to the second description. To record a card under a certain characteristic, write its letter in the given blank.

1. Dotted _____

   Not Dotted _____

2. Shaded _____

   Not Shaded _____

3. More than 3 Sides _____

   Not More than 3 Sides _____

4. Plain AND 3 Sides _____

   Not Plain OR Not 3 Sides _____

5. Striped AND Shaded _____

   Not Striped OR Not Shaded _____

6. Striped OR Shaded _____

   Not Striped AND Not Shaded _____

7. Dotted OR Plain _____

   Not Dotted AND Not Plain _____

Activity 3: Independent Practice

Materials
Worksheet 4-1b
Regular pencils

Procedure
Give each student a copy of Worksheet 4-1b to complete independently. When all have finished, ask various students to share their answers with the entire class. For combined characteristics with OR or AND in items 1 and 2, ask students to explain how they decided which shape to use to satisfy the descriptions.

Answer Key for Worksheet 4-1b
1. Sample shape:

2. C

3. B (all 3 shapes are 2-D or flat shapes or polygons)

4. A (other shapes have 4 sides, not 3 sides)

Possible Testing Errors That May Occur for This Objective
- Students focus on a characteristic that is not required by the test item. For example, they select a shape that is shaded instead of one that has 5 sides.

- When the test item uses NOT, students ignore it and select a shape that *has* the stated characteristic. For example, if asked to find a shape that is NOT a rectangle, they will select a *rectangle* for the response.

- If students are asked to find a shape that has two characteristics, they will choose a shape with only one of the required characteristics. For example, if "red AND square" is required, students will select a red shape that is not a square or select a square that is not red.

WORKSHEET 4-1b

Finding Shapes
by Their Characteristics

Name _____

Date _____

Complete the following exercises. Be ready to share your answers with the entire class.

1. Draw a shape that has 3 sides and contains stripes in its interior.

2. Which set of characteristics describes the given figure?

    A. Plain AND 4 sides

    B. Shaded OR plain

    C. More than 3 sides AND dotted

    D. Dotted AND 5 sides

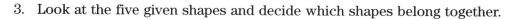

3. Look at the five given shapes and decide which shapes belong together.

    A. G, H, and J

    B. H, K, and M

    C. J, K, and M

    D. H, J, and K

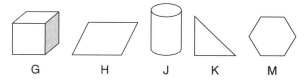

4. Look at the following five shapes.

    Which shape below does NOT belong in the group shown above? Why?

Objective 2
Use reflections to identify planar shapes having a line of symmetry.

Discussion
Students need much practice with comparing shapes before they can visually determine if a shape is symmetrical. They need to be taught methods that will allow them to compare two parts of a shape directly in order to determine their congruence (same shape, equal in size). Paper folding and grids are simple methods to use.

Activity 1: Manipulative Stage

Materials
> Worksheet 4-2a per pair of students
> Scissors for each student
> Large sheets of colored construction paper (optional)

Procedure

1. Prepare a set of 6 cutout shapes for each pair of students (see Worksheet 4-2a for samples to use). All sets may contain the same shapes if preferred. Two cutout shapes should be nonsymmetrical shapes (an irregular or concave polygon, a kidney-shaped "blob" or free-form, and so on); the other four might be simple symmetrical shapes like a heart, a diamond or a rhombus, the block letter T, or a regular pentagon or hexagon. The shapes might be precut and packaged for student use before class in order to save class time, or students might be asked to cut out their own set of shapes during class.

2. Partners should try to fold each cutout shape so that one part exactly fits on top of the other part. One part will then be a *reflection* of the other part. Tell students not to *crease* a fold until they know the two parts formed by the fold will fit each other.

3. Some shapes may have more than one line of symmetry, so students should attempt several different folds with the same shape. Encourage students to refer to the *matching* parts of a shape as "congruent" parts or "reflections of each other."

4. Once the symmetrical shapes have been identified, students should draw with a regular pencil along each correct crease found. If a shape is symmetrical, have students label the shape's crease as the "line of symmetry"; if a shape is not symmetrical (no creases should be marked), have them write "not symmetrical" on the shape.

5. Finally, have students mount their 6 shapes on a large sheet of colored construction paper to be displayed on the classroom wall. If the sets of shapes used have *not* been identical for all pairs of students, then the wall display will provide an even greater variety of shapes for students to study.

6. As a follow-up to this activity, guide students through this process. Show students a large cutout circle (circle with diameter greater than 24 inches works best). Ask them to predict where the line of symmetry might be, then begin to fold the circle into two congruent parts. Fold the circle several times, marking each crease with a regular pencil.

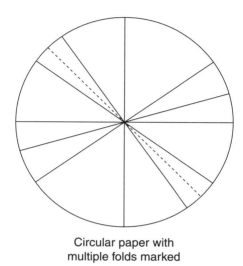

Circular paper with
multiple folds marked

After finding and marking five or six folds, ask students if there might be others. Continue to make new folds until students begin to realize that the process does not end and that unlike their earlier cutout shapes, the circle will have an "infinite" number of folds or lines of symmetry. That is, between any two folds of the circle, another fold can be found. In reality, however, it is physically difficult to find a new fold between two folds that are very close to coinciding. Any manipulative process has its natural limitations. Nevertheless, enough folds can be made for students to generalize about "infinity."

Answer Key for Worksheet 4-2a
Parallelogram (not regular), 0 lines of symmetry
Hexagon (not regular), 2 lines of symmetry
Heart, 1 line of symmetry
Cross (congruent cross pieces), 4 lines of symmetry
Blob, 0 lines of symmetry
Happy face, 1 line of symmetry

266

WORKSHEET 4-2a

Patterns for Symmetry Test

Use the shapes below with Activity 1. Cut out each shape and fold it to find its lines of symmetry, if they exist.

Activity 2: Pictorial Stage

Materials

Centimeter grid paper (8.5 inches by 11 inches; 2 sheets per pair of students)
2 different-colored map pencils per pair of students and regular pencils
Large sheets of colored construction paper for mounting (optional)

Procedure

1. Give each pair of students two sheets of centimeter grid paper and two different-colored map pencils. Each student should draw a wide vertical bar in regular pencil down the middle of her or his own sheet of grid paper, either along a grid line or through the middle of a column of grid squares. This activity will provide students with experience in testing for congruent parts by visually comparing the edge lengths and curvatures of the two parts being formed in a design.

2. Working with a partner, each student should color various square units on the *left* side of the vertical bar of her or his own grid. The "half-design" being formed on each grid should be unique and use only one color. Encourage students to use triangles in their designs by drawing a diagonal in a square unit and coloring just the half-square or triangle formed. They might also leave blank some grid spaces that are next to the vertical bar.

3. After students have completed their own half-designs, they should exchange papers and map pencils with their partners. The partner must then finish the other person's design by coloring appropriate grid spaces on the other side of the vertical bar. The newly drawn half-design in its final form should match or be a *reflection* of the initial half-design, and also match in color, in order to make a *symmetrical design* on the whole grid. Please note, however, that color is *not* a part of the *geometric* definition of symmetry.

4. After each student has completed the second half of the design, the grid sheet should be returned to its original owner, who will fold the sheet along the vertical bar to test the two half-designs for congruence. If the two parts are no congruent, the partners should work together to make the necessary changes.

5. The final designs might then be shown to the entire class or mounted on colored construction paper for display in the classroom.

Following is an example of a symmetrical design being formed (patterned interiors indicate color):

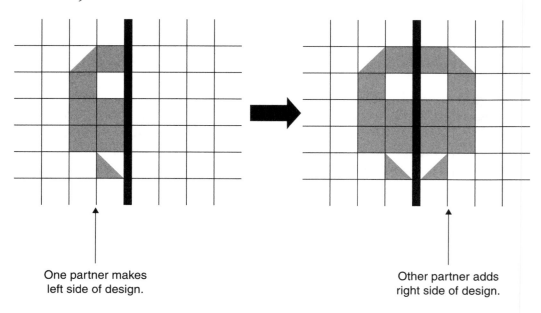

Special Challenge

Challenge partners to work together to create a design on a grid with two lines of symmetry, one vertical and one horizontal. The finished design should permit folding either way while still maintaining symmetry. Here are some possible simpler designs with their two lines of symmetry drawn on them:

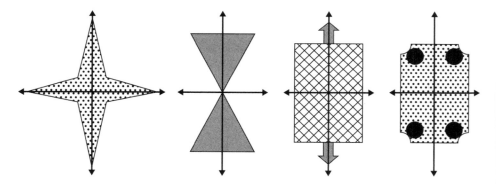

Activity 3: Independent Practice

Materials
   Worksheet 4-2b
   Regular pencils

Procedure
Students work independently to complete Worksheet 4-2b. When all are finished, discuss the results.

Answer Key for Worksheet 4-2b
   1. C

   2. B

   3. A

   4. B

   5. D

Possible Testing Errors That May Occur for This Objective
   • Only certain parts of the shape are tested and found to have symmetry; nonsymmetrical parts are not tested by the student and so are assumed to be symmetrical also.

   • The word NOT is ignored when the test item asks for the figure that is NOT symmetrical.

   • Segments that are perceived to be reflections of each other are not the same length.

   • Segments that are perceived to be reflections of each other involve diagonals of grid squares that have the same direction; that is, the segments have the same slope.

270

WORKSHEET 4-2b

Lines of Symmetry

Name _____

Date _____

Complete this worksheet by circling the best answer choice for each problem. Be ready to discuss your answers with the rest of your class.

1. Which figure shows a line of symmetry?

A. 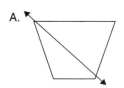   B. 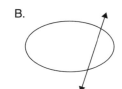   C. 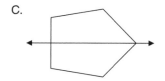   D.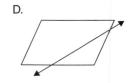

2. Which of the lines drawn on the figures is NOT a line of symmetry?

A.   B. 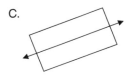   C. 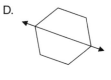   D.

3. Through which letter could a line of symmetry be drawn?

A. **H**   B. **G**   C. **P**   D. **L**

4. Which design has only *one* line of symmetry?

A.   B.   C.    D.

5. Which design has *more* than one line of symmetry?

A.   B. 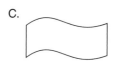   C. 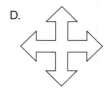   D.

Objective 3
Identify congruent planar shapes by using rotations, reflections, or translations.

Discussion
Students must know that *congruent* shapes match in size and shape, which implies that corresponding side lengths and corresponding angles are equal in measure. They must be able to recognize that two given shapes are or are NOT congruent. Young students need much experience with comparing shapes. They need both tactile and visual practice with recognizing congruent shapes in a variety of orientations. The activities described next will provide that practice.

Activity 1: Manipulative Stage

Materials
Shapes Patterns 4-3a (patterns for cutout shapes)
Lightweight tagboard (for making shapes)

Procedure
1. Prepare sets of cutout tagboard shapes, 1 set per 2 students. (See Shapes Patterns 4-3a for some suggested shapes.) Each set should contain at least 6 different *pairs* of congruent shapes. Use irregular or nonsymmetric polygons, not standard shapes like rectangles, circles, and triangles. Include shapes with nonstraight edges mixed with straight edges. Also include different sizes of the same shape. Make all the sets different so that students will have several different opportunities to match congruent shapes together.

2. When given a set of shapes, partners should work to find the matching pairs. The final test of a congruent pair is that one shape must fit exactly on top of the other shape in the pair.

3. After each pair of students has matched all the shapes in a set, give them another set of shapes to match.

Here are sample cutouts (each set should contain 2 copies of each of 6 different shapes):

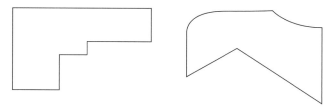

272

SHAPES PATTERNS 4-3a

Activity 2: Pictorial Stage

Materials
Regular paper and regular pencils
Scissors
Large art paper or construction paper

Procedure
1. This activity strengthens a student's ability to visually identify rotations or reflections (flips) of the same shape. Have students work in teams of 4 students each. Give each student a pair of scissors.

2. On regular paper, each team member should draw and cut out a polygon of some kind. The shape should fit within a 3-inch by 3-inch square. Encourage students to make unusual quadrilaterals, pentagons, hexagons, and so on. Both concave and convex shapes are permitted too. This is a good time to review the names of various polygons previously studied.

3. Give each team a large sheet of art paper or construction paper and have team members trace their 4 cutout shapes onto the paper in a variety of positions, using different rotations and reflections. Several copies of the same shape should *not* be clustered together. Copies of the 4 different shapes should be well distributed throughout the paper. The team should also label each *cutout* shape with its own letter: A, B, C, and D, for easy identification later. However, students should not label the various tracings of the shapes drawn on the large paper.

4. When all teams are through with their papers, have each team give its 4 cutout shapes and the corresponding large paper to another team. Then each team will compare its new cutout shapes to the shapes drawn on the large paper. Each shape on the paper should be labeled with the letter of the cutout shape used to draw it.

5. After a team has labeled every shape on the new paper, all shapes on the paper that have the same letter should be *congruent* to each other. Monitor the students' work to be sure that shapes are correctly labeled. Remind students that they may have to rotate or flip the cutout shape in their hand in order to make it fit on top of one of the drawn shapes.

6. After each completed paper has been checked, the papers (with their 4 respective cutout shapes attached) might be displayed on the classroom wall for students to study further.

Here is a sample of a portion of a *labeled* paper:

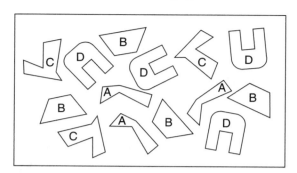

Activity 3: Independent Practice

Materials
Worksheet 4-3a

Regular pencils

Procedure
Give each student a copy of Worksheet 4-3a to complete independently. Have students share their answers when all are finished.

Answer Key for Worksheet 4-3a
1. (Grid shapes should match.)

2. C

3. A

4. B

Possible Testing Errors That May Occur for This Objective
- Students may not recognize two shapes as being congruent because one is a flipped or reflected image of the other. They need more practice with reflections and rotations.

- When a test item asks for two shapes that are NOT congruent, students ignore the NOT stated in the test item and simply select the pair of shapes that look the same to them or that are easily seen to be congruent because of their orientation.

- Students select two figures as being congruent because they belong to the same shape family, even though their sizes are different.

276

WORKSHEET 4-3a   Name _____

Finding Congruent Shapes   Date _____

Complete the exercises below and be ready to share your answers with the entire class.

1. On the grid, draw a shape that is congruent to the given shape:

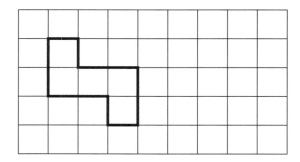

2. Which figure is NOT congruent to the other three figures?

A.   B.   C. 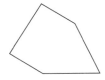   D.

3. Which two rectangles are congruent?

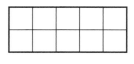   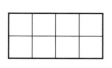   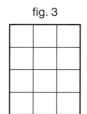   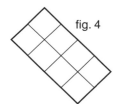

fig. 1   fig. 2   fig. 3   fig. 4

A. 2 and 4   B. 1 and 3   C. 1 and 2   D. 3 and 4

4. Which pair of figures is NOT congruent?

A.    C.

B.    D.

Objective 4
Identify polygons by their generic names.

Discussion
For students to know the different polygons by their names and number of sides requires much practice for students, especially with hands-on experiences. The polygon names—*pentagon, hexagon, heptagon, octagon,* and so on—are difficult for students to remember, especially if they do not talk about or use the shapes very often during the school year. It helps if they can learn the meaning of the prefixes: *penta* (5), *hexa* (6), *hepta* (7), *octa* (8), and so on, because these prefixes are also found in other words they may be studying in science and language arts.

Activity 1: Manipulative Stage

Materials
Geoboards
Colored yarn (or medium-sized rubber bands)
Regular paper and regular pencils

Procedure
1. Give each pair of students a geoboard and an 18-inch piece of colored yarn (or 3 or 4 medium-sized rubber bands).

2. To make a polygon with the yarn, one end of the yarn piece should be wrapped twice (or tied) around any peg selected first, then the rest of the yarn should be stretched tight and wrapped once around each of the other pegs in some order to form the number of sides needed. When connecting back to the first peg, the yarn should be wrapped twice around that final peg to hold the yarn in place. If done properly, the yarn will form a polygon.

3. To make a polygon with rubber bands, students should place the rubber band over a peg, then place a finger on the tip of that peg while they stretch the rubber band to loop over other pegs. Placing the finger on the peg prevents any "flying" rubber bands. If one rubber band is too small to loop around the required number of pegs, several rubber bands may be used like "chains," with each band connecting 3 or 4 pegs together.

4. Write the name "hexagon" on the board. Discuss the idea that "hexa" means "six," so a hexagon will have 6 sides and 6 vertices. Tell students to select 6 different pegs on the geoboard to serve as the 6 vertices of a hexagon. No more than two selected pegs should be in the same line together. Students should connect the 6 different pegs with the yarn piece (or the rubber bands).

5. Have students draw a quick sketch of their hexagon on their own paper, then write its name below the sketch.

6. Repeat the process on the geoboard, using other polygon names being studied.

7. As an additional activity, after students have built various polygons on their geoboards, have them look around the classroom to identify objects shaped like the polygons they have studied and to name which polygon each object represents.

Sample of a completed "yarn" pentagon:

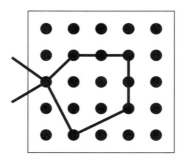

Activity 2: Pictorial Stage

Materials
Worksheet 4-4a
Rulers
Regular pencils

Procedure
1. Give each student a ruler and a copy of Worksheet 4-4a, which contains nine small diagrams of geoboards.

2. Have students draw a different polygon (with respect to number of sides or vertices) on each diagram and write the general name of the polygon below the diagram. If a polygon has a more specific name that students have studied, that name should also be written below the diagram of the shape. For example, if a student has drawn a 4-sided polygon to show a quadrilateral, using 4 equal side lengths and 4 right angles, the generic name will be "quadrilateral," but the more specific names will be "rectangle" and "square" for that same shape.

3. As an example, tell students to locate and mark 5 points or vertices on one of the geoboard diagrams, with no more than 2 of those points in the same line together. Then have them use the ruler to draw line segments to connect those points to form 5 different sides of a polygon. The name of the polygon, "pentagon," should be written below the drawn shape.

4. Repeat the process, using different amounts of sides or vertices for the other geoboard diagrams on the worksheet. The polygons to include will be determined by your grade-level curriculum.

5. For more practice, give students an extra copy of Worksheet 4-4a, and ask them to draw other polygons that have the same names but look different from the first set of polygons they drew. Completed worksheets may then be displayed in the classroom for students to see the variety of forms the same polygon name might identify.

6. For an additional activity, have students cut out magazine pictures that represent different polygons being studied. They should glue their pictures onto a posterboard or a large sheet of paper and label each shape with its proper polygon name. These sheets of polygons might then be displayed in the classroom. Be sure to include the more specific names with the generic name if a particular polygon possesses the necessary properties.

Here is an example of a generic 4-sided polygon (no special angles or sides) drawn and labeled on a geoboard diagram:

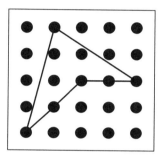

Quadrilateral

280

WORKSHEET 4-4a
Drawing Polygons

Name _____

Date _____

Use a ruler to draw different polygons on the geoboard diagrams below and write each polygon's name(s) below its diagram.

1.

2.

3.

4.

5.

6.

7.

8.

9.

Activity 3: Independent Practice

Materials
Worksheet 4-4b
Regular pencils

Procedure
Give each student a copy of Worksheet 4-4b to complete independently. When all have finished, have students share their answers with the entire class.

Answer Key for Worksheet 4-4b
1. C

2. B

3. D

4. A

5. D

Possible Testing Errors That May Occur for This Objective
- When students are asked to find a shape with "more than N sides," they select a shape that has *exactly* N sides.

- The wrong shape is selected for a polygon named in the test item, because students fail to match the polygon name with the correct number of sides.

- Students select a polygon name that is more familiar to them, for example, a triangle, even though the test item asks for a polygon with *more* than 3 sides.

282

WORKSHEET 4-4b   Name _____
Identifying Polygons   Date _____

Complete each exercise below and be ready to share your answers with the entire class.

1. Which figure will be formed when the points A, B, C, D, E, and A are connected in the given order by line segments?

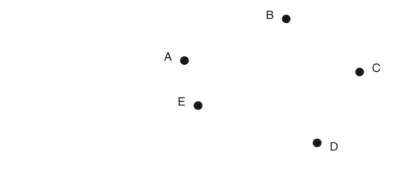

    A. Triangle   B. Rectangle   C. Pentagon   D. Hexagon

2. Which polygon has more than 5 sides?

    A. Rectangle   B. Hexagon   C. Pentagon   D. Triangle

3. Look at the group of shapes that follows:

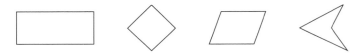

    Which shape below belongs to this group?

    A.   B.   C.   D.

4. George wants to make a picture frame shaped like an octagon. How many sides (edges) will the frame have?

    A. 8   B. 7   C. 6   D. 5

5. A decagon is a 10-sided polygon. If 3-inch pieces of ribbon are used to make sides of polygons for a banner design (that is, 1 piece of ribbon makes 1 side), how many inches of ribbon will be used to make a decagon to go on the banner?

    A. 12   B. 18   C. 24   D. 30

Objective 5
Identify right, acute, and obtuse angles.

Discussion
In order to keep the three types of angles (*acute*, *obtuse*, and *right*) separated in their minds, students need much practice finding each type in their environment. It is difficult for students to remember which name goes with which angle measure. The activities described here will provide such practice.

Activity 1: Manipulative Stage

Materials
> 3-inch by 5-inch index cards
> Flexible plastic drinking straws (with paper arrowhead taped at each end)
> Regular paper
> Red pencils and regular pencils

Procedure
1. Give each pair of students a red pencil, a 3-inch by 5-inch index card, and a bendable or flexible plastic drinking straw with a paper "arrowhead" taped at each end of the straw.

2. Tell students to bend the straw until it fits around one of the corners of the index card. The straw now forms a "right angle." Also discuss the idea that the straw represents a "straight" angle before it is bent to form a right angle.

3. Have student pairs go around the classroom quietly and locate corners of objects or furniture whose edges may or may not fit or line up to the bent straw. To test for a fit, the vertex of the corner must fit into the vertex of the straw, and one edge of the corner must line up with one part of the straw's length. If the other edge of the corner lies "inside" the straw's outline, the angle of the corner is "acute." If the edge lies outside the straw's outline (but does not form a straight angle), the angle of the corner will be "obtuse."

4. The students should try to find two or three examples of each type of angle.

5. Have the students draw, on their own paper, a picture of each object found, outline its angle in *red pencil*, and write the name of the angle under the picture. Each angle should have arrowheads drawn on its rays. An object should be drawn from a viewpoint that uses the surface of the paper as the plane of the object's angle. That is, the picture should not distort the angle.

6. As students work, it may be necessary to compare their straw with the index card once in a while to make certain the straw is still in a 90-degree position.

7. Have some of the students share their findings with the entire class.

Here is a sample of a drawing of a classroom object, the front side of the teacher's desk, with a *right* angle drawn in red pencil:

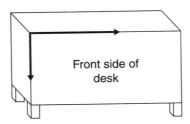

With this perspective of the desk, it would not be appropriate to draw the red arrow on the top surface of the desk. The arrow would not form a right angle to the viewing audience, as shown here:

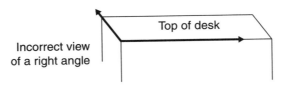

Activity 2: Pictorial Stage

Materials
 Worksheet 4-5a
 3-inch by 5-inch index cards
 Regular pencils

Procedure

1. After students have found examples of the three different types of angles (right, acute, and obtuse) in the classroom, give each student an index card and a copy of Worksheet 4-5a, which has a variety of angles drawn on it. The worksheet contains several different sizes of acute angles, several sizes of obtuse angles, and several right angles.

2. Have students work in pairs, but each student should complete his or her own worksheet.

3. Students should use an index card to test each angle, thereby comparing it to a right angle. A corner of the index card must match the drawn angle's vertex, and at least one side length of the card from the chosen corner must align with a ray of the drawn angle. The card's other side length from the same corner should be near or at the drawn angle's other ray. If the other ray of the drawn angle lies inside the card angle (or *under* the card), the drawn angle is *acute*; if outside, it is *obtuse*. A "perfect fit" indicates a *right* angle. If an angle on the worksheet appears to be "close" to fitting around the card, consider the angle to be a *right* angle; exactness is not possible with this type of activity.

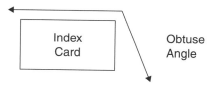

4. Have the students write the name of each angle ("acute," "right," or "obtuse") below its picture on the worksheet.

5. When all have finished Worksheet 4-5a, have students share their answers with the entire class.

6. Discuss with students that a right angle measures 90 degrees, so an acute angle will measure less than 90 degrees but more than 0 degrees. An obtuse angle will measure more than 90 degrees but less than 180 degrees. Discuss the idea that a *straight* angle measures 180 degrees exactly.

7. For additional practice, students might also measure the worksheet angles with a protractor. Student measures for the same angle may vary by 2 to 4 degrees, since such measuring is not an exact process. As long as the measure of each acute angle is still less than 90 degrees (or each obtuse angle still greater than 90 degrees), this lack of accuracy should not be a concern at this time.

Answer Key for Worksheet 4-5a

1. Acute

2. Right

3. Obtuse

4. Right

5. Acute

6. Acute

7. Obtuse

8. Acute

9. Obtuse

WORKSHEET 4-5a
Measuring and Naming Angles

Name _____

Date _____

Use an index card to help you identify each angle as *right*, *acute*, or *obtuse*. Write the name of the angle below its drawing.

1.

_____

2.

_____

3.

_____

4.

_____

5.

_____

6.

_____

7.

_____

8.

_____

9.

_____

Activity 3: Independent Practice

Materials
    Worksheet 4-5b
    Rulers
    Regular pencils

Procedure
Give each student a copy of Worksheet 4-5b to complete independently. When all are finished, ask various students to share their answers.

Answer Key for Worksheet 4-5b
1. Sample diagrams:

2. C

3. A

4. D

5. D

Possible Testing Errors That May Occur for This Objective

- If the test item asks for the name of an angle having a given measure in degrees, students randomly pick any word response because they do not know the names for the different types of angles.

- Students recognize the word names for different angles, but they do not know the allowable degree measures for each type. For example, they will select "acute" as the response for a 105-degree angle instead of "obtuse."

- Students define "obtuse" angles as being greater than 90 degrees, but they do not realize that their measures must also be *less than* 180 degrees. Hence, they consider a 180-degree angle to be an obtuse angle instead of a straight angle. Similarly, students consider a 0-degree angle to be an acute angle, not realizing that acute angles must be *greater than* 0 degrees.

WORKSHEET 4-5b

Identifying Angles

Name _____

Date _____

Complete the given exercises. Be ready to share your answers with the entire class.

1. Use your ruler to draw an example of each type of angle listed:

   A. Right   B. Obtuse   C. Straight   D. Acute

2. Which type of angle measures between 0 and 90 degrees but will not measure either 0 or 90 degrees?

   A. Obtuse   B. Right   C. Acute   D. Straight

3. What type of angle measures 135 degrees?

   A. Obtuse   B. Right   C. Acute   D. Straight

4. Which diagram shows a right angle?

   A.   B.   C.   D.

5. If the measures of two right angles are combined, their total measure will equal

   the measure of a _____ angle.

   A. Obtuse   B. Right   C. Acute   D. Straight

Objective 6
Describe rectangles (including squares) by their characteristics (sides, diagonals, angles).

Discussion
Differentiating between what is given or known and what is "seen" is very difficult for young students to do. In hands-on geometry activities, students are better able to compare and contrast the features of different shapes. They also need much practice reading and writing the symbolic language of geometry, and applying that language to a variety of shapes. The activities described here will provide practice with graphing ordered pairs, as well as with geometric language.

Activity 1: Manipulative Stage

Materials
    Geoboards with rubber bands
    Small index cards
    Rulers
    Regular paper and regular pencils

Procedure
1. Give each pair of students a geoboard with 5 or 6 rubber bands, a small index card, and a ruler. The geoboards should have the pegs labeled along two adjacent edges of the board, much like scales on vertical and horizontal axes. If your commercial geoboards are not already labeled, put masking tape along the two required edges and write on the tape to label the necessary pegs with the lettering or numbering system of your choice. One scale usually is in letters, the other in numbers. Any labeling format will be acceptable.

2. Each pair of students should position their geoboard so that the left vertical edge has a scale and the lower horizontal edge has a scale. The geoboard then becomes the first quadrant of a Cartesian graph.

3. If necessary, explain to students how to read and locate the peg (point) for a given ordered pair. For example, assuming numbers for the horizontal axis and letters for the vertical axis, the ordered pair (3, B) might mean to start at the lower left peg (the 0 peg), move horizontally to the third peg (in the column marked 3), then move vertically to the row marked B. The peg at this final location becomes the point identified by (3, B).

4. Give students different ordered pairs to locate on their geoboards before starting to work with shapes in the polygon family.

5. When all students are comfortable with how to read ordered pairs and locate the corresponding points, write a set of 6 ordered pairs on the board, which represent the 6 vertices of a hexagon. (We will explore some generic polygons before focusing on rectangles in particular.) Assign a letter to each ordered pair. Do not list the original pairs in the order in which later they are to be *connected*. One purpose of this activity is to train students to follow a list of letters in order to connect points and form a polygon. For example, write the following ordered

pairs on the board: A(2, A), B(4, D), C(1, D), D(1, B), E(3, A), and F(4, B). Then write the list of letters: A, D, C, B, F, E, and A to indicate the order in which students should connect the different pegs with the rubber band(s).

6. To make a polygon, a rubber band should be hooked on the peg at A(2, A), then stretched to hook around each of the other pegs in the order listed. As the rubber band is stretched, one finger should be placed on the first peg at A(2, A) to prevent the rubber band from "shooting off into space." If one rubber band cannot stretch that far, several smaller bands may be used so that each band connects only 2 pegs. If done properly, the rubber band(s) will form an irregular hexagon.

7. After students identify the shape's name, write that name on the board beside the list of letters used to make the shape.

8. Now have students use the index card to test for right angles. Place the corner of the card inside a corner of the shape. If the two corners seem to fit together (or almost), that corner of the shape will represent a right angle. The angle is formed by the peg vertex and the 2 rubber band segments extending away from the peg. This particular hexagon has a right angle at B(4, D) and at C(1, D).

9. Also have students use their rulers to measure the sides (from peg to peg) of the hexagon to see if any sides are equal. Measure to the nearest half-centimeter or quarter-inch mark for each length, depending on which ruler is being used (centimeter or inch). On the hexagon, sides DC and FB are equal, and sides AD and EF are equal. Notice that side AE does not equal side AD or EF in length.

10. Parallel sides may also be identified by placing the ruler on the shape between the two sides being tested. If the two sides align reasonably close to the two long edges of the ruler, the sides will be considered parallel to each other. Students may need to align the ruler with one side being tested, then slide the ruler sideways, without rotating, to place it closer to the other side being tested. In the hexagon, side CB is parallel to side AE, and side CD is parallel to side BF.

11. Also have students measure some of the diagonals of the hexagon and compare their lengths. For example, measuring from peg to peg, students will find that the distance from point D to point B equals the distance from point F to point C. Other diagonals will also be equal for this particular hexagon. Some diagonals will not be equal in length, however.

12. On their own papers, students should record the information learned about the constructed hexagon. For example, they might record any of the following: "polygon ADCBFE = hexagon"; "angle B and angle C are right angles"; "for sides, DC = FB and AD = EF"; "for diagonals, FC = DB"; "side CD ‖ side BF"; and "side CB ‖ side AE." Use whatever notation is recommended by your grade-level curriculum; geometric notation varies from grade level to grade level.

13. Using the same set of ordered pairs, continue with other lists of letters to make a variety of polygons, including squares, nonsquare rectangles, and triangles. For example, polygon DCBF will be a quadrilateral (4 sides), whose opposite sides are parallel and equal in length. The four angles will be right angles, and the two diagonals will be equal in length—all of which are characteristics of a rectangle, which is a special member of the quadrilateral family.

14. Now change to a new set of ordered pairs and repeat the process. Focus on finding congruent sides, congruent diagonals, parallel sides, and right angles. Students need to be aware of when these particular characteristics exist in a polygon and when they do NOT exist.

Here is an example of the hexagon shown on the geoboard as just discussed:

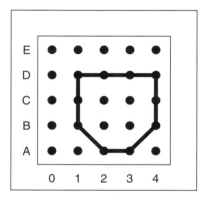

Activity 2: Pictorial Stage

Materials

Worksheet 4-6a
Small index cards
Rulers
Regular pencils

Procedure

1. Give each student a ruler, a small index card, and two copies of Worksheet 4-6a, which contains 6 small diagrams of geoboards per page.

2. Guide students to label the left vertical and lower horizontal axes of each geoboard diagram.

3. Repeat the procedures used in the Manipulative Stage, except now focus only on quadrilaterals. Students will learn the characteristics of rectangles by also searching for the same characteristics in nonrectangular shapes.

4. Students will locate and label points (with assigned letters) on each geoboard and draw line segments to connect the points in a prescribed order to form different 4-sided polygons. A variety of quadrilaterals should be drawn, but the actual shape *names* to include should be determined by your grade-level curriculum. Typical shapes to at least *draw*, and maybe name, are the generic quadrilateral, trapezoid (only one pair of parallel sides), parallelogram, rhombus, rectangle, and square.

5. In each drawn shape, students will search for right angles, using the index card, and for equal sides and parallel sides, using the ruler. Remind students that the diagonal distance between two points on the geoboard diagram does not equal the vertical or the horizontal distance between two points on the diagram. Thus, all lengths should be measured with the ruler.

6. Any specific properties discovered about a drawn shape should be written below the shape on Worksheet 4-6a, as well as its names when appropriate.

7. To give students practice with the symbols < and >, ask them on each shape to compare the measures of one pair of segment lengths (sides or diagonals), whose measures are not equal. Students should then record the relationship, using the proper symbol. For example, in the earlier hexagon in the Manipulative Stage, side CB was longer than side EF. The comparison of their measures would be written as "CB > EF."

8. When all students are through with their measuring and recording, they should share their findings with the whole class or a small group. Each student needs to practice speaking the geometric language out loud to others.

Here is an example of a 4-sided polygon drawn and labeled on a geoboard diagram, along with the discovered characteristics.

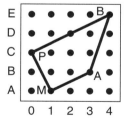

Polygon PBAM =
    Trapezoid
PB || MA
PM = MA
PB > MP
Angles M and P
are right angles.
PA < MB as
diagonals

WORKSHEET 4-6a   Name _____

Drawing Quadrilaterals   Date _____

On each geoboard diagram below, label the vertical axis with letters A to E and the horizontal axis with numbers 0 to 4. Use a ruler to draw different quadrilaterals on the diagrams. Write each quadrilateral's specific name(s) and the characteristics found below its diagram.

1.

2.

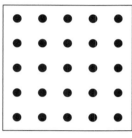

3.

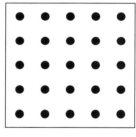

4.

5.

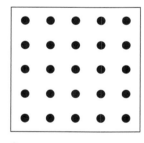

6.

Activity 3: Independent Practice

Materials
Worksheet 4-6b
Regular pencils

Procedure
Give each student a copy of Worksheet 4-6b to complete independently. When all have finished, have students share their answers with the entire class.

Answer Key for Worksheet 4-6b
1. D

2. D

3. A

4. (Shapes will vary but must be rectangular with adjacent sides unequal.)

5. C

Possible Testing Errors That Might Occur for This Objective
- If a test item asks students to compare the lengths of opposite sides of a named rectangle, students do not realize that the sides should be congruent and therefore equal in length.

- Students do not know that the diagonals of a rectangle are congruent and think that a diagonal is equal in length to one of the sides.

- When an illustration and the name of a specific shape are provided in a test item, students make visual judgments about the lengths of the shape's sides or its angles instead of using knowledge of that shape's characteristics based on its definition. For example, if all four sides of a named parallelogram "look" equal in length, students think the shape is a square, although no details in the test item identify it as a square.

296

WORKSHEET 4-6b   Name _____
Applying Quadrilaterals   Date _____

Complete each exercise below. Be ready to share your answers with the entire class.

1. A rectangle has _____ right angles.

   A. 0   B. 1   C. 3   D. 4

2. Which is a characteristic of a square?

   A. Only 2   B. Only 2   C. Only 1 right   D. 4 equal sides
      equal sides   parallel sides   angle

3. Which characteristic does NOT belong to a rectangle?

   A. 5 equal sides B. Opposite sides C. Right angles   D. Opposite sides
                        parallel   congruent

4. On the geoboard diagram draw a rectangle that is NOT a square.

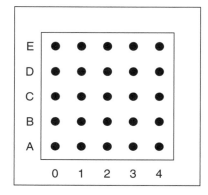

5. Polygon ABCD shown is a square. Which statement is true?

   A. AB > AC
   B. BC < AD
   C. AC > CD
   D. BC = AC

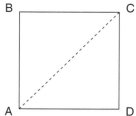

Objective 7

Identify 3-dimensional shapes (solids) by their names and by specific characteristics such as faces, vertices, or edges.

Discussion

Students need much experience with solid or 3-dimensional shapes. Commercial sets of "solids" are available that contain a variety of prisms, pyramids, cones, cylinders, and spheres. The shapes are either wooden or plastic and come in several sizes. Everyday containers that might be collected by the students are also abundant.

Children need experience just describing in their own words what each 3-D shape looks like; descriptions may be given either orally or in written form. In addition to working directly with the solids, students also need exposure to perspective drawings of such objects so that they can predict which parts of the real object are not shown in the drawing.

Activity 1: Manipulative Stage

Materials

Small plastic 3-D objects (solids)
Water-based paint or poster paint
Large sheets of art paper
Colored markers

Procedure

1. Give each pair of students a small plastic solid, a small bowl of washable colored paint or ink, and a large sheet of art paper, which will not absorb too much paint. Ink pads, small sponges in saucers with washable ink, or paint poured on the top surface of the sponge will also work.

2. Students should take each surface of their solid and press or dip it into the paint, then press the painted surface onto the sheet of paper inkblotter-style. For curved surfaces as on cones or cylinders, the entire surface should be covered in paint, then carefully *rolled* on the paper without being picked up or shifted. A sphere might be randomly rolled in several directions on the paper to create an irregular path of paint.

3. With a colored marker, students should write "curved surface" below each impression of a curved surface. Each paper should be titled according to the solid used, for example, "Surfaces of My Cone."

4. Have partners show their particular solid and its surface impressions to the entire class, as well as describe the solid in their own words. Focus on the idea that most solid shapes consist of more than one surface, but the impression of each flat surface might look like a circle, rectangle, triangle, or other polygon, and the impression of a curved surface will be a "rolled-out" shape of some kind.

Here are sample surface impressions of a cone and a sphere:

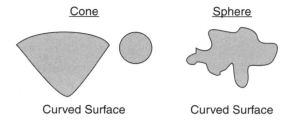

Cone   Sphere

Curved Surface   Curved Surface

Activity 2: Pictorial Stage

Materials

    Worksheet 4-7a

    Sets of Geometric Solids (same as those shown on worksheet, plus extras)

    Regular pencils

Procedure

1. After students have had experience touching and describing a variety of solids, they need to practice recognizing the perspective drawings of the solids. Give each student a copy of Worksheet 4-7a. The worksheet shows some of the solids typically studied in the first or leftmost column, that is, a triangular prism, a cylinder, a square prism, and a cone. Two rows on the worksheet have been left blank so other solids can be added, such as pyramids or spheres, that will be in the student sets for this activity.

2. Have students work in groups of 3 or 4 students each, but each student will complete his or her own worksheet. Give each group a set of solids containing the solids on the worksheet and a few solids not shown on the worksheet.

3. From their set, group members must select the solid that matches to each perspective drawing on their worksheets, then use the solid to count how many of each surface type the solid has and record the number on the worksheet.

4. Monitor the group work closely to make sure students are correctly matching each object with its drawing and accurately identifying and counting the different surfaces.

5. When all have finished the worksheet, discuss the answers with the entire class.

6. For additional practice, have students tell how many edges or how many vertices each solid on Worksheet 4-7a has.

Answer Key for Worksheet 4-7a (partially completed worksheet)

SOLID SHAPE	FLAT SURFACES				CURVED SURFACES
	☐	◯	△	▭	
	2	0	0	4	0
	0	2	0	0	1
	0	1	0	0	1
	0	0	2	3	0

WORKSHEET 4-7a

Exploring the Solids

Name _____

Date _____

Examine each object in your set of solids. Find the ones that are listed on the chart below and record how many of each type of surface each object has.

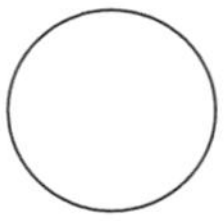

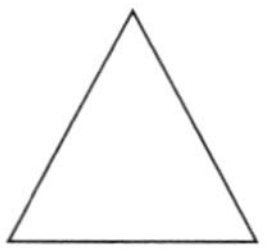

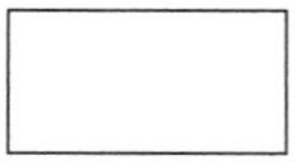

SOLID SHAPE	FLAT SURFACES				CURVED SURFACES
	▢	◯	△	▭	

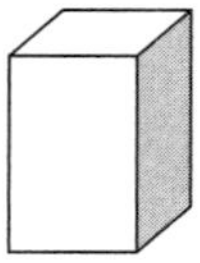

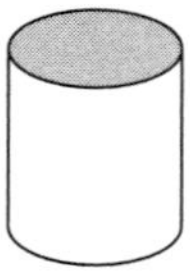

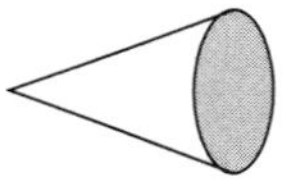

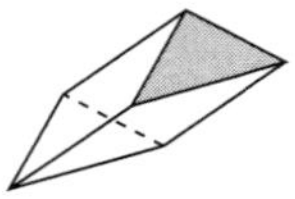

Activity 3: Independent Practice

Materials
Worksheet 4-7b
Regular pencils

Procedure
Give each student a copy of Worksheet 4-7b to complete independently. When all have finished, have them share their answers from Activity 2 with their group or with the entire class.

Answer Key for Worksheet 4-7b
1. C

2. B

3. A

4. C

5. D

6. A

Possible Testing Errors That May Occur for This Objective
- Students miscount the faces or edges of a solid that is illustrated in the test item because they do not realize that some parts are hidden in a perspective drawing; that is, they count only what they can see directly.

- If a solid's name is given in the test item but an illustration is not provided, students do not know which solid is intended so they select incorrect responses concerning the solid's characteristics. For example, if the test item requires the number of faces of a square pyramid, students might choose "6" because they are thinking of a square prism instead.

- Students have difficulty interpreting certain parts of perspective drawings as "curved surfaces." They view the drawn parts as "flat surfaces" because the parts are drawn on flat paper. Students cannot visualize the 3-dimensional form represented by the 2-dimensional drawing.

- Students often confuse the definitions of "edge," "vertex," and "face," which causes them to select incorrect responses.

302

WORSHEET 4-7b   Name _____

Exploring the Solids   Date _____

Complete the exercises below. Be ready to share your answers with other students.

1. Which figure has exactly 4 faces?

    A.   B.   C.   D.

2. Which characteristics belong to a cylinder?

    A. Only a curved surface

    B. 2 flat surfaces and one curved surface

    C. 6 flat surfaces

    D. 1 flat surface and one curved surface

3. Which solid has only rectangular faces?

    A. Cube   B. Cone   C. Pyramid   D. Sphere

4. Which figure represents a solid that does NOT have a curved surface?

    A.   B.   C.   D.

5. How many edges does a square pyramid have?

    A. 5   B. 6   C. 7   D. 8

6. How many vertices does a cone have?

    A. 1   B. 2   C. 3   D. 4

Objective 8
Apply logical reasoning to solve a word problem (with or without computation).

Discussion
Many resource books containing logic puzzles for younger students are available in local bookstores. These puzzles present situations that require logical reasoning; hence, they are often difficult for young children to comprehend. It greatly helps students to model the situations with either objects or diagrams. Here are some examples that involve such modeling.

Activity 1: Manipulative Stage

Materials
    Worksheet 4-8a
    Scissors
    Regular pencils

Procedure
1. Give each student a pair of scissors and a copy of Worksheet 4-8a. Here is the story from the worksheet followed by a discussion of a possible technique to use with students: "Four cyclists were in a race together. Sue rode across the finish line ahead of Sam. Dean was behind Laura. Sam came in second and ahead of Laura. Who finished the race in first place? In fourth place?"

2. From the worksheet, have students cut out the four small rectangular cards containing the four names of the cyclists.

3. Ask students at first to randomly arrange the four name cards in a row as though in a race. The order does not matter at this point.

4. Now begin to discuss the various clues given in the problem; discuss them one at a time. Suppose the person on the *right* end of the row is in *first place*. Then the person on the left end must be in fourth place. Since Sue was ahead of Sam, students should now put their "Sam" card to the left of the "Sue" card, if it was not there already. "Dean" has to be to the left of "Laura," because he came in behind her. Since "Sam" came in ahead of "Laura," his card must be placed to the right of "Laura." Thus, to keep "Sue" to the right of "Sam," "Sue" has to be at the right end of the row, which is first place. The ordering of the cards now places "Dean" at the left end of the row, which is fourth place.

| Dean | Laura | Sam | Sue |

5. Now have students write on the worksheet a sentence about each person's final position in the race. For example, for Laura they might write the sentence: "Laura finished the race in third place." Similar sentences should be recorded about the other three cyclists.

6. For extra practice, have students use the same name cards to solve the following problem: "Laura, Dean, Sam and Sue collect stamps. Dean has more stamps than Sam but fewer than Laura. Dean has fewer stamps than Sue. Laura has more stamps than Sue. Who has the most stamps?" This time use the *left* end of the row of cards for the person having the most stamps. The final order of the name cards should be as follows, with Laura having the most stamps:

| Laura | Sue | Dean | Sam |

Answer Key for Worksheet 4-8a

See the results described in the previous text discussion.

WORKSHEET 4-8a　　　　　Name _____

Modeling a Logic Puzzle with Objects　　Date _____

STORY PROBLEM:

Four cyclists were in a race together. Sue rode across the finish line ahead of Sam. Dean was behind Laura. Sam came in second and ahead of Laura. Who finished the race in first place? In fourth place?

　　　(Cut the four boxes apart and use them in the space below to solve the story problem.)

SUE	SAM	DEAN	LAURA

Activity 2: Pictorial Stage

Materials
    Worksheet 4-8b
    Regular pencils

Procedure
1. Give each student a copy of Worksheet 4-8b.

2. Guide students through each word problem, showing them how to use a diagram to help them solve the problem.

3. Here is the first story to discuss: "There are 15 people standing in line to buy movie tickets. Jon is ninth in line. How many people are in front of him in the line, and how many people are behind him?"

4. Below the problem on the worksheet, have students draw small circles in a row to represent the people in the line. Suppose the circle at the *left* end of the row is the *first* person in line. Students should count and label the ninth circle from the left as number "9" and as "Jon."

5. Now ask students how they can find out how many people are in front of Jon and how many are behind him. Because the ordinal numbers assign numbers to the people by counting their positions in line, the people in front of number 9 have been counted as 1 through 8; there must be 8 people in front of Jon. To find the number of people behind Jon, students just need to count the circles to the right of Jon's circle. Because the total is small, this is easy to do; the amount will be 6 circles or people. But what if the total is larger?

6. Ask students if there is a computation they might use to help them find this number without counting the circles directly. Guide them to see that the number they seek is the number of circles left after Jon's circle and the 8 circles in front of (to the left of) Jon are removed from the total set of circles. So 9 circles must be removed from the 15 total, leaving the 6 circles that are behind (to the right of) Jon.

7. Now have students label their diagram of circles so it is similar to the following:

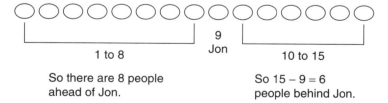

So there are 8 people ahead of Jon.

So $15 - 9 = 6$ people behind Jon.

8. To use a number line instead of circles in a row, students would simply show a mark on the line for each circle. The numbering of the marks on the line would begin with 1 on the left end and continue to 15 on the right end. The rest of the labeling would look like the labeling shown above with the circles. For larger totals, you could just skip some marks on the line and show only the final total number as the rightmost entry on the line. Here is how the number line might appear for the last question of the problem:

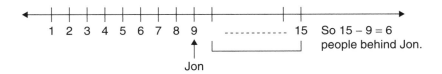

9. Continue to discuss the other word problems on Worksheet 4-8b with the class.

Answer Key for Worksheet 4-8b (possible illustrations and sentences)

1. (See the illustration given in the text for this exercise.)

2. oldest   youngest

| Judy | George | Kate | Jose |

The four students from oldest to youngest are Judy, George, Kate, and Jose.

3.

| Jim | Maria | Ray | Katrina | Sarah |

Maria sat closest to Jim.

308

WORKSHEET 4-8b   Name _____

Modeling a Logic Puzzle   Date _____
with a Diagram

Use diagrams to solve the word problems below. Write sentences about your conclusions.

1. There are 15 people standing in line to buy movie tickets. Jon is ninth in line. How many people are in front of him in the line, and how many people are behind him?

2. Judy is older than George. George is older than Kate. Jose is younger than Kate. Order the four students from oldest to youngest.

3. At the movie, Maria sat between Jim and Katrina. Sarah sat on the other side of Katrina. Ray sat between Katrina and Maria. Who sat closest to Jim?

Activity 3: Independent Practice

Materials
    Worksheet 4-8c
    Regular pencils
    Regular paper

Procedure
Give each student a copy of Worksheet 4-8c to complete independently. Ask students to be ready to share their diagrams and conclusions with the entire class. Diagrams may vary.

Answer Key for Worksheet 4-8c

1. C

2. B

3. D

4. A

5. (Results will vary.)

Possible Testing Errors That May Occur for This Objective

- Students select a response that is based on only one clue. They ignore other information provided in the problem.

- A response is selected that *contradicts* a specific fact stated in the problem. For example, the response choice "Sara is the youngest" contradicts the statement "James is younger than Sara," which is given in the problem.

- A response is selected that *reverses* a fact stated in the problem. For example, the response choice "Sara is older than David" is the reversal of the statement "David is older than Sara," as is given in the problem.

310

Solve each of the given problems. Be ready to share your answers, as well as any diagrams used, with the entire class.

1. David is older than Beth. Beth is older than James. Sara is younger than James. Which is a reasonable conclusion?

   A. Sara is older than David.   C. Sara is younger than Beth.

   B. James is the youngest.   D. James is older than Beth.

2. At the football game, Daniel sat between Pam and Kerry. Sal sat on the other side of Kerry. Leslie sat between Kerry and Daniel. Who sat closest to Pam?

   A. Kerry   C. Leslie

   B. Daniel   D. Sal

3. There are 25 people standing in line to buy soccer tickets. Morris is eleventh in line. How many people are behind him in the ticket line?

   A. 12   C. 25

   B. 11   D. 14

4. Mary, Carl, Sam, and Lisa have been collecting marbles. Mary has 30 marbles. Sam has fewer marbles than Lisa but more than Mary. Carl has more than Lisa. Lisa has 65 marbles. What is a reasonable number of marbles for Sam to have?

   A. 48   C. 80

   B. 25   D. 73

5. On another sheet of paper, try writing your own logic puzzle like those in Exercises 1 through 4. Then ask another student to try to solve it.

GEOMETRY AND LOGICAL OR SPATIAL REASONING: PRACTICE TEST ANSWER SHEET

Directions: Use the Answer Sheet to darken the letter of the choice that best answers each question.

	A	B	C	D			A	B	C	D
1.	○	○	○	○	9.		○	○	○	○
2.	○	○	○	○	10.		○	○	○	○
3.	○	○	○	○	11.		○	○	○	○
4.	○	○	○	○	12.		○	○	○	○
5.	○	○	○	○	13.		○	○	○	○
6.	○	○	○	○	14.		○	○	○	○
7.	○	○	○	○	15.		○	○	○	○
8.	○	○	○	○	16.		○	○	○	○

SECTION 4: GEOMETRY AND LOGICAL OR
SPATIAL REASONING: PRACTICE TEST

1. Look at the five given shapes and decide which shapes belong together.

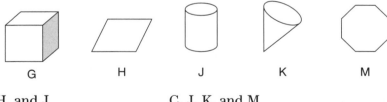

A. G, H, and J   C. J, K, and M

B. H, K, and M   D. G, J, and K

2. Look at the following five shapes.

Which shape does NOT belong in the group shown below?

3. Which figure shows a line of symmetry?

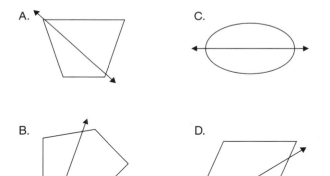

4. Which design has NO line of symmetry?

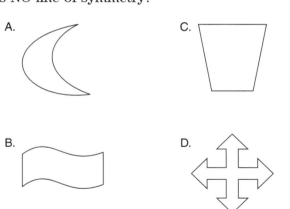

SECTION 4: GEOMETRY AND LOGICAL OR
SPATIAL REASONING: PRACTICE TEST

5. Which two rectangles are congruent?

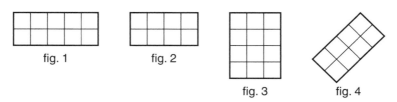

A. 2 and 4   C. 1 and 4

B. 1 and 3   D. 3 and 4

6. Which pair of figures is NOT congruent?

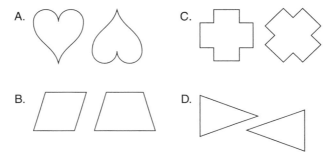

7. Which polygon has more than 6 sides?

A. Rectangle   C. Triangle

B. Hexagon   D. Octagon

8. Look at the following group of shapes.

Which shape below belongs to this group?

9. What type of angle is an angle that measures 120 degrees?

A. Obtuse   C. Acute

B. Right   D. Straight

314

10. Which diagram shows a right angle?

A.   B.   C.   D.

11. Which is a characteristic of a rectangle?

A. Only 2 equal sides   C. Equal diagonals

B. Only 2 parallel sides   D. Only 1 right angle

12. Polygon ABCD is a square. Which statement below is true?

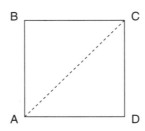

A. AB > AC   C. AD < CD

B. AC > BC   D. BC = AC

13. Which description belongs to a sphere?

A. Only a curved surface

B. 2 flat surfaces and 1 curved surface

C. 6 flat surfaces

D. 1 flat surface and 1 curved surface

14. Which solid has only rectangular faces?

A. Sphere   C. Pyramid

B. Cone   D. Prism

315

**SECTION 4: GEOMETRY AND LOGICAL OR
SPATIAL REASONING: PRACTICE TEST**

15. At the movies Don sat between Peter and Carmen. Sally sat on the other side of Carmen. Lyn sat between Carmen and Don. Who sat closest to Peter?

A. Carmen   C. Lyn

B. Don   D. Sally

16. There are 18 people standing in line to buy tickets to the school play. Mario is tenth in line. How many people are behind him in the ticket line?

A. 10   C. 18

B. 8   D. 11

Section 4. Geometry and Logical or Spatial Reasoning: Answer Key for Practice Test

The objective being tested is shown in brackets beside the answer.

1.	D [1]	9.	A [5]
2.	A [1]	10.	D [5]
3.	C [2]	11.	C [6]
4.	B [2]	12.	B [6]
5.	A [3]	13.	A [7]
6.	B [3]	14.	D [7]
7.	D [4]	15.	B [8]
8.	A [4]	16.	B [8]

MEASUREMENT

Objective 1

Estimate the length of an object, using an appropriate measuring unit (inch, foot, yard, millimeter, centimeter, meter).

Discussion

In order to make reasonable decisions about which type of metric unit to use for a measuring task, students need experience with those units. For example, the centimeter is a unit of length that is small enough so that several units, but not too many, are needed to measure the length of a pencil. It would not be an appropriate unit for measuring the length of a car or a hallway. This practical approach to measuring is also true of standard or English units of linear measure (inch, foot, yard). Students simply need to measure a variety of objects and record what they find. Such measuring activities may be organized either as a class activity or through a learning center.

Activity 1: Manipulative Stage

Materials

Assorted classroom objects
Centimeter rulers (or metric measuring tapes marked in centimeters)
Meter sticks
Worksheet 5-1a
Regular pencils

Procedure

1. Give each student a copy of Worksheet 5-1a. Give each pair of students a centimeter ruler or measuring tape. Also have several meter sticks available for students to use when needed. For length, a metric measuring tape is effective because it is flexible and will be at least 1 meter or 100 centimeters long. Curriculum catalogues also offer tapes or rulers marked off only in decimeters or only in centimeters. These are helpful for younger students because they provide only one size of unit to be counted by the measurer. Most commercial tapes or rulers are usually marked off or counted in centimeters, but they also show smaller marks, which indicate millimeters. Students must be taught how to read these measuring tools. (Note: This activity will focus on the centimeter and meter but, if preferred, may be adapted to focus on the inch and yard or other linear units instead.)

2. Have each pair of students find and measure various classroom items listed on Worksheet 5-1a and record their measurements on the worksheet. For each object, they must decide which unit is better to use: the centimeter or the meter. The classroom is full of objects that students can measure to the *nearest whole unit* in centimeters. An inflexible meter stick should be used when measuring larger or longer items like the height of a door, a tall cabinet, or the length of a classroom floor or hallway. When measuring in meters, a person is counting only *whole* meters as units. When students try to measure the width of a book, they discover that the book does not fill the full length of one meter; the book width is only a fractional part of a meter. Therefore, students must try a smaller unit like the centimeter. To reverse this situation, when students measure the length of a hallway, they find that it takes several hundred centimeters. Smaller quantities of a unit are easier to use in measurements, so a larger unit is needed—the meter. Students need to experience these sorts of "conflicts" (measuring short lengths with too long a unit or measuring very long distances with too short a unit) in order to see the reasonableness of certain units of length for certain sizes of objects.

3. After students have completed their measuring tasks, have various students describe some of the objects they measured and tell what measurements they found for those objects. For each object, ask students to give their reasons for using a particular unit of measure.

Answer Key for Worksheet 5-1a
    (Answers will vary.)

WORKSHEET 5-1a

Name _____

Measuring the Lengths of Objects

Date _____

Find the following objects in the classroom and measure the length of each one. For each object, decide which unit to use: the centimeter or the meter. Count to the nearest whole unit each time. Record the lengths found in the table below. Be sure to state which unit was used each time.

OBJECT TO MEASURE	LENGTH OF OBJECT
1. Your pencil	1.
2. Long edge of Math book	2.
3. Your shoe	3.
4. Your little finger	4.
5. Short edge of your desk	5.
6. Long edge of teacher's desk or table in room	6.
7. Width of classroom door	7.
8. Lower edge of chalkboard	8.
9. Height of classroom door	9.
10. Length of paper clip	10.

<h3 align="center">Activity 2: Pictorial Stage</h3>

Materials

    Magazine pictures (close to actual size of real objects)
    Scissors
    Large art paper
    Glue or transparent tape
    Regular pencils
    Centimeter rulers

Procedure

1. Give each pair of students 4 or 5 magazine pictures (untrimmed), 2 pairs of scissors, glue or tape, a centimeter ruler, and a large sheet of blank art paper.

2. Have students cut out the magazine pictures and glue or tape them onto a sheet of blank art paper. Now that students have had practice measuring the lengths of real objects in metric units for Activity 1, they are ready to measure distances on paper. The pictures should be as close to real-life size as possible so that students will continue to develop an intuitive sense of how long various objects might be in the units being studied.

3. Each student should now use a centimeter ruler (that is, numbered in centimeters) to measure the lengths of the pictures to the nearest whole centimeter.

4. Have students mark the beginning and ending points of the lengths they will be measuring on the pictures. Be sure that a "length" being measured reflects an actual measurable length on the real object. For example, measuring from one point on a box face to another point on a different box face as though on a flat plane would not be reasonable, even though a flat photograph would make it appear possible.

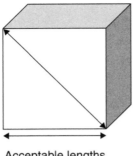
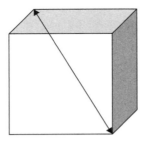

Acceptable lengths to measure   Unacceptable length to measure

5. Remind students that they must place the 0-mark of the ruler on the beginning point, then count whole centimeter *spaces* (not the notches or marks on the ruler) until they reach the ending point. Decimeters and meters will not be appropriate for the sizes of pictures involved; discuss this with the class. If the curriculum includes the millimeter, students might apply it to some of the smaller pictures.

6. Each measure found should be recorded by the appropriate picture.

7. When all are finished, have different pairs of students describe one or two of their pictures and give the measurements found. The large sheets of pictures might then be mounted on the classroom wall for later viewing by students.

Activity 3: Independent Practice

Materials
Worksheet 5-1b
Regular pencils

Procedure
Give each student a copy of Worksheet 5-1b to complete independently. Discuss the answers when all are finished. If an exercise is missed by several students, have a student measure an object similar to the one mentioned in the exercise to help students recognize what an appropriate answer might be.

Answer Key for Worksheet 5-1b
1. D
2. A
3. C
4. C
5. B
6. D

Possible Testing Errors That May Occur for This Objective
- An incorrect measuring unit is selected because students do not know the purpose of each type of unit in terms of measuring length, capacity, or weight/mass. For example, a unit of weight/mass is selected to measure a length.
- Students identify the correct unit of length to use, but they do not have an accurate sense of its actual size. For example, they do not realize that a centimeter corresponds to the width of their little finger or that a meter is longer than one of their arms. As a result, they select 50 centimeters for the length of their little finger rather than 5 centimeters.
- Students correctly recognize a given unit as a unit of length but do not consider the reasonableness of the unit for the task described in the test item. For example, a meter is a measuring unit for *length*, but it is too large for measuring a pencil.

322

WORSHEET 5-1b

Name _____

Identifying Reasonable
Lengths of Objects

Date _____

For each exercise, select a unit of measure or a measurement that is most reasonable for the given object.

1. Which unit should be used to measure the length of your pencil?

    A. Gram   B. Meter   C. Liter   D. Centimeter

2. Which measurement best describes the length of a library book?

    A. 25 centimeters   B. 50 liters   C. 25 meters   D. 100 centimeters

3. About how long is your little finger?

    A. More than 1 meter   C.   Less than 8 centimeters

    B. Less than 1 centimeter   D.   More than 10 liters

4. Which unit is best for measuring the length of your classroom?

    A. Liter   B. Centimeter   C. Meter   D. Gram

5. What is a reasonable estimate of the length of the given line segment?

    A. 30 centimeters   B. 10 centimeters   C. 5 millimeters   D. 10 grams

6. What is a reasonable estimate of the length of your shoe?

    A. 20 millimeters   B. 20 meters   C. 20 decimeters   D. 20 centimeters

Objective 2
Estimate the capacity of a container, using an appropriate measuring unit (milliliter, liter, cup, pint, quart, gallon).

Discussion
Most students at this grade level have not had sufficient life experiences to recognize just how much, say, 30 gallons is (most adults don't have that understanding either). In general, as adults we have a mental image of the size of a familiar *gallon of milk;* from there we extrapolate to a "lot" of gallons of milk when we think of 30 gallons.

Young students need much experience with different sizes of containers in order to develop "reference points" (like the gallon of milk) about various units and to practice these necessary extrapolations. This is true for metric, as well as standard or English, units of measure. Students need to measure a variety of containers and record what they find.

Activity 1: Manipulative Stage

Materials
    Assorted containers (at least some equivalent in size to 1 liter, 1 gallon, 1 quart,
        1 pint, and 1 cup; others larger than 1 quart)
    Very small containers (less than 1 cup in size, to fill with eyedropper)
    Plastic measuring "cups" marked in milliliters (250-ml or 500-ml size preferred)
    Eyedroppers marked in milliliters (or cubic centimeters, cc's)
    Worksheet 5-2a
    Regular pencils
    Plastic dishpans ("tubbies")
    Pitchers of water (or gallon jugs or classroom sink)
    Funnels (optional)

Procedure
1. Give each team of 3 or 4 students a set of containers labeled and sized as follows: A—1 gallon, B—1 quart, C—small container less than 1 cup in size, D—1 liter, E—container larger than 1 quart in size, F—1 pint, and G—1 cup. Also give each team a ml eyedropper (if container C is extremely small) and a 250-ml or 500-ml measuring "cup." A funnel would also be helpful when pouring water from one container to another if the receiving container has a small neck or opening. Each team will also need one plastic dishpan (a pouring basin) and a pitcher of water. Also give each student a copy of Worksheet 5-2a. (If preferred, measuring for this activity may be done in a learning center.)

2. Containers equivalent in size to 1 gallon, 1 liter, 1 quart, 1 pint, or 1 cup (8 oz) are easily available and might even be brought from home by students. School cafeterias often serve half-pint (1 cup) or pint (2 cups) sized cartons of milk. Curriculum catalogues also offer graduated cylinders or measuring cups marked off in milliliters or cubic centimeters, which are units not easily found in daily use.

3. On every container, a "full line" should be indicated or shown with masking tape or a permanent marking pen in order to ensure that equivalent measures are maintained. Many containers have "necks" that should not be included in the measurement of the container.

4. Younger students need to be able to fill a single small unit (like 1 cup or 1 pint) with water and pour that water into a larger container, counting the number of times the smaller unit is filled and poured out. Discuss the idea that if the container to be filled is smaller than the container initially selected to fill it, students generally will need to choose a more appropriate container from which to pour.

5. Conversely, a container might be too large and the filling unit too small. For example, when students try to measure a large container with the special measuring "cup" marked in milliliters, they may find that it takes several *thousand* milliliters (possible reference point: an 8-ounce cup holds 250 milliliters). When measuring, it is easier to count with smaller numbers, so a larger unit might be better, possibly the liter, because it will take fewer of that larger unit to fill the large container. Discuss this need to change to a different unit with students; however, still have them find the number of milliliters required for a large container (Exercise 4 on the worksheet). Students need to experience this sort of "conflict" (measuring very large capacities with too small a unit) in order to see the reasonableness of certain units of capacity for measuring certain sizes of containers.

6. As students count their pourings, they should measure the last pouring made to the nearest whole unit. For example, if it takes half or more of a pint to finish filling a large container, students should count the last pouring as one whole pint to be combined with the other whole pints of water already poured into the container.

7. As teams measure the containers listed on Worksheet 5-2a, using selected units, have them record the measure found in the column next to the name or label of the corresponding container on the worksheet. The full name of the unit should be written, not the abbreviated form. For containers C and E on the worksheet, have students write a name in the blank that describes each special container you have provided for these particular containers.

8. As students pour back and forth from one container to another directly over the plastic dishpan, some water will naturally be spilled into the dishpan. Occasionally, students will need to empty the dishpan water back into the pitcher being used as the water supply.

9. No conversion is intended between metric and standard measures in this activity. In Exercises 4 and 7, the gallon is measured in liters and milliliters simply to compare the quantities needed for the two different-sized units when filling a large container. Where several *liters* of water will fill the gallon jug, several *thousand milliliters* will also fill the same jug. Do not emphasize that the jug also contains 1 gallon in these two exercises; rather, focus on the idea that thousands of milliliters are too many to count, so liters are better units to use. Specific sizes of containers are given in the Materials section and in step 1 of the Procedure in order to minimize the number of containers needed to complete Worksheet 5-2a.

10. Additional containers may be used for more practice, if preferred.

Answer Key for Worksheet 5-2a

1. 8 pints

2. 2 pints

3. (Answers will vary, depending on the size of the container used, but total < 250 ml.)

4. Approximately 4,000 ml (to nearest thousand)

5. 4 cups

6. 1,000 ml

7. Approximately 4 liters

8. (Answers will vary, depending on the size of the container used, but total > 4 cups.)

326

WORSHEET 5-2a

WORKSHEET 5-2a
Measuring Capacity

Name _____

Date _____

Find the containers listed below and measure the capacity of each one, using the given unit of measure. In the blanks for containers C and E, write a name that describes the container. Record the capacities found in the right column of the table. Be sure to state which unit was used for each result. Round off each total measure found to the nearest whole unit.

CONTAINER	ITS CAPACITY
1. A: 1-gallon jug, in pints	1.
2. B: 1-quart container, in pints	2.
3. C: _____, in milliliters	3.
4. A: 1-gallon jug, in milliliters	4.
5. B: 1-quart container, in cups	5.
6. D: 1-liter bottle, in milliliters	6.
7. A: 1-gallon jug, in liters	7.
8. E: _____, in cups	8.

Activity 2: Pictorial Stage

Materials
Old magazines
Scissors
Glue or transparent tape
Blank paper
Regular pencils

Procedure
1. Give each pair of students an old magazine, 2 pairs of scissors, glue or tape, and 1 or 2 blank sheets of paper. The magazine should contain pictures of familiar containers found at school or at home.

2. Have students cut out 4 or 5 pictures of containers from their magazine and glue or tape them onto a sheet of blank paper (use several sheets if pictures are large).

3. For each picture, students should now decide on a unit that might be appropriate for measuring the capacity of the container shown. Consider only the unit names that were studied in Activity 1. The chosen unit's full name should be recorded next to the picture, not abbreviated.

4. Have students also estimate how many of the chosen unit might be needed to fill the container and record that amount with the unit name. To help with these decisions, hold up the various unit containers that were used for measuring at the Manipulative Stage.

5. Have students share their pictures and their decisions with the entire class. Discuss any choices that might be unreasonable or inappropriate. Some containers might have more than one possible choice of unit. For example, a container that might be measured in quarts could also be measured in liters. A small container might be measured in cups or milliliters.

   Here is an example of a mounted magazine picture showing a small bottle cap:

Milliliters
15 milliliters

Activity 3: Independent Practice

Materials
    Worksheet 5-2b
    Regular pencils

Procedure
Give each student a copy of Worksheet 5-2b to complete independently. When all have finished, have various students share their answers. Discuss whether a chosen unit is reasonable with regard to its size when compared to the size of the given container. Have the containers available that were used in Activity 1 to help students visualize the measuring units and determine the appropriateness of their choices. For Exercises 7 and 8, students will have to apply logical reasoning to find their answers. For example, in Activity 1 students found that 1 quart equals 4 cups. So if they have 2 quarts, they will have 4 cups + 4 cups, or 8 cups total. Students also learned that 1 quart equals 2 pints. So even if they did not directly pour 2 cups into 1 pint in Activity 1, they can still reason that 2 pints equal 4 cups, since both amounts fill 1 quart. Confirm these relationships for students, if necessary, by pouring water from one container into another related container, like from a cup into a pint.

Answer Key for Worksheet 5-2b
    1. B   5. 4 quarts

    2. B   6. 1,000 milliliters

    3. D   7. 2 pints

    4. A   8. 8 cups

Possible Testing Errors That May Occur for This Objective
- Students may recognize a container that holds a single unit (say, a gallon jug), but they cannot visualize how much space will be filled by a large amount (say, 20 gallons) of that same unit. They have not had sufficient life experiences to be able to make these kinds of judgments or extrapolations. As a result, they identify a familiar *small* container as one that would hold the required 20 gallons.

- Students recognize the *name* of a unit of capacity given in a test item, but they have no *reference point* by which to judge its *size*. Therefore, they are unable to identify a container that might be close in size to that unit or appropriately measured with that unit.

- An incorrect measuring unit is selected because students do not know the purpose of each type of unit in terms of measuring length, capacity, or weight/mass. For example, a unit of weight/mass is selected to measure a container's capacity.

WORSHEET 5-2b

Name _____

Date _____

Identifying Reasonable
Units of Capacity

For each exercise below, select the more reasonable response. Be ready to explain your choices to the entire class.

1. Which object is most likely to have a capacity of 8 gallons?

    A. Coffeepot   C. Washing machine

    B. Large trash can   D. Football helmet

2. Which unit should be used to measure the capacity of a firefighter's boot?

    A. Meter   C. Gram

    B. Pint   D. Minute

3. About how many milliliters of cola will a 2-liter bottle hold?

    A. 2 milliliters   C. 200 milliliters

    B. 20 milliliters   D. 2,000 milliliters

4. Which measurement best describes the capacity of a drinking glass?

    A. 280 milliliters   C. 280 liters

    B. 280 cups   D. 280 pints

Complete the following:

5. 1 gallon = _____ quarts

6. 1 liter = _____ milliliters

7. 4 cups = _____ pints

8. 2 quarts = _____ cups

Objective 3

Estimate the weight of an object, using an appropriate measuring unit (ounce, pound, gram, kilogram).

Discussion

Students need to have direct measuring experience with any unit of measure they study, so they can develop a "reference point" for that unit. For example, a centimeter equals the width of a young student's little finger (fingernail for an adult), and a millimeter is the thickness of a dime. A meter extends from the left ear, around the chin, and out to the fingertips of the right hand and arm stretched out sideways. A gram is the mass/weight of 2 small paper clips, and a small eyedropper holds a milliliter of water. It is impossible, however, to provide direct measuring experiences in the classroom with large units, such as the ton for finding weight. At best, teachers can offer some experience with the smaller units of weight, such as the ounce, pound, gram, and kilogram.

Students must be able to visualize the ton as being "much larger" than these other units of weight and therefore realize that the ton must be applied to "very large" objects like a full-sized pickup truck.

Activity 1: Manipulative Stage

Materials

> Sets of weights in grams and in ounces
> Bathroom scales marked in pounds or kilograms
> Two-pan balance scales
> Variety of classroom objects to weigh
> Worksheet 5-3a
> Regular pencils

Procedure

1. Give each team of 3 or 4 students a set of weights, either in grams or in ounces, and a two-pan balance scale. Give each student a copy of Worksheet 5-3a. A variety of scales and mass sets are available through commercial school catalogues. When purchasing or packaging weights for student use, allow for about 20 ounce units per standard or English set and about 40 gram units per metric set.

2. Teams should find 4 different objects in the classroom and weigh each object on the balance scale, using whichever type of weight unit (grams or ounces) they have been given at first. The classroom contains many familiar objects that students can weigh. For grams, use very small objects. For ounces, use small- to medium-sized objects.

3. Each object weighed should be listed on Worksheet 5-3a, along with its weight found.

4. After a team has finished weighing 4 objects with one type of unit (gram or ounce), give team members a set of weights of the other type and have them find and weigh 4 more objects with the new unit. These new objects and weights should also be recorded on Worksheet 5-3a.

5. Have teams take turns weighing themselves individually on the bathroom scale, if available. Each student should record her or his own weight on the worksheet as well, using whichever unit (pound or kilogram) is shown on the scale.

6. When all teams have finished, ask different team members to share what their teams found to be the weights of their assorted objects.

7. Discuss how it takes many *grams* for even the smallest object, but not as many *ounces* seem to be needed for similar small objects. Observe how pounds and kilograms seem to be best used for larger objects like people. Therefore, very large units like the ton must be associated with extremely large objects like cars and elephants.

WORSHEET 5-3a   Name _____

Measuring the Weights of Objects   Date _____

Find 4 small objects in the classroom and measure their weights in grams. Find 4 more objects and measure their weight in ounces. For each object, record its name and weight in the table below. Also weigh yourself. Be sure to state which type of unit was used each time.

OBJECT TO MEASURE	WEIGHT OF OBJECT
1.	1.
2.	2.
3.	3.
4.	4.
5.	5.
6.	6.
7.	7.
8.	8.
9. Your body in pounds	9.
10. Your body in kilograms	10.

Activity 2: Pictorial Stage

Materials
    Old magazines
    Scissors
    Glue or transparent tape
    Blank paper
    Regular pencils

Procedure
1. Give each pair of students an old magazine, 2 pairs of scissors, glue or tape, and 1 or 2 blank sheets of paper. The magazine should contain pictures of familiar objects found at school or at home.

2. Have students cut out 4 or 5 pictures of objects (small- to medium-sized objects in real life) from their magazine and glue or tape them onto a sheet of blank paper (use several sheets if pictures are large).

3. For each picture, students should now decide on a unit that might be appropriate for measuring the weight/mass of the object shown. Consider only the unit names that were studied in Activity 1. The chosen unit's *full* name should be recorded next to the picture, not abbreviated.

4. Have students also decide how many of the chosen unit might be needed to estimate the object's weight, and record that amount with the unit name beside the picture as well. To help with these decisions, have different students hold several ounce units or gram units in their hands to remind themselves of how heavy or how light a set of such units might feel.

5. Have students share their pictures and their decisions with the entire class. Discuss any choices that might be unreasonable or inappropriate. Some objects might have more than one possible choice of unit. For example, an object that might be measured in pounds could also be measured in kilograms. A very small object might be measured in grams or ounces. Some students might want to include a picture of a car or tractor or truck and estimate the weight to be about 1 or 2 tons.

Here is an example of a mounted magazine picture showing a small plastic vase with flowers:

Ounces
12 ounces

Activity 3: Independent Practice

Materials
Worksheet 5-3b
Regular pencils

Procedure
Give each student a copy of Worksheet 5-3b to complete independently. When all have finished, have various students share their answers. Discuss whether a chosen unit is reasonable with regard to its size when compared to the size of the given object. Have the objects and measuring units available that were used in Activity 1 to help students visualize the measuring units and determine the appropriateness of their choices. Confirm certain weights for students, if necessary, by weighing the required objects on the two-pan balance scale.

Answer Key for Worksheet 5-3b
1. C

2. D

3. A

4. D

5. B

6. D

7. B

8. Grams

Possible Testing Errors That May Occur for This Objective
- Students may recognize a particular unit of weight, but they cannot imagine how heavy a large amount of that same unit will be. They have not had sufficient life experiences to be able to make these kinds of judgments or extrapolations. As a result, they identify a familiar *small* object as one that would weigh, say, 20 pounds.

- Students recognize the *name* of a unit of weight given in a test item, but they have no *reference point* by which to judge its *size*. Therefore, they are unable to identify an object that might be close in size or weight to that unit or appropriately measured with that unit.

- An incorrect measuring unit is selected because students do not know the purpose of each type of unit in terms of measuring length, capacity, or weight/mass. For example, a unit of capacity is selected to measure an object's weight.

WORSHEET 5-3b

Name _____

Identifying Reasonable Units
of Weight/Mass

Date _____

For each exercise below, select the most reasonable response. Be ready to explain your choices to the entire class.

1. Which object is most likely to have a weight of 8 pounds?

   A. Plastic dinner plate   C. New baby

   B. Truck tire   D. Wooden desk

2. Which unit should be used to measure the weight of a bottle cap?

   A. Ton   B. Pint   C. Meter   D. Gram

3. About how many ounces will a small bowl of butter weigh?

   A. 8 ounces   B. 80 ounces   C. 800 ounces   D. 8,000 ounces

4. Which measurement best describes the weight of a large truck?

   A. 2 grams   B. 2 kilograms   C. 2 pounds   D. 2 tons

5. Which unit is not a unit of weight or mass?

   A. Ton   B. Kilometer   C. Kilogram   D. Pound

6. Which unit should be used for weighing a jumbo paper clip?

   A. Gallon   B. Milliliter   C. Pound   D. Gram

7. What might be a reasonable weight for a student in the fourth grade?

   A. 15 kilograms   B. 40 kilograms   C. 65 kilograms   D. 90 kilograms

8. If you weigh your math book in ounces and then in grams, which measurement will require more units to be counted?

   Circle one: Ounces   or   Grams

Objective 4
Define the relationship between two units of measure within the same system of measurement.

Discussion
Students should have direct measuring experience with any unit of measure they study, so they can develop a "reference point" for that unit. Some units, however, are too large, like the kilometer (several city "blocks" long), and a classroom model is not possible. Even awareness of this large unit outdoors is not there. Students' familiarity with its partner, the mile, is similarly weak. Life experiences will eventually cause students' understanding of these larger units to improve.

Meanwhile, some simple classroom activities will provide experience with a conversion method for certain metric units of length. A similar approach may be used with units of capacity or units of weight/mass in both the metric system and the English or standard system.

Activity 1: Manipulative Stage

Materials
Building Mat 5-4a
White paper strips (0.5 inch by 1.5 inches; labeled "meter," "gram," or "liter")
Colored paper squares (approximately 1.5 inches by 1.5 inches, 4 different colors; details in steps that follow)
Base 10 blocks (for teacher demonstration only)
Regular paper
Regular pencils

Procedure
1. This activity will be limited to trading 1 to 5 whole kilometers for hectometers, dekameters, or meters and any equivalent reverse trading that will produce whole kilometers. The *gram* or the *liter* may be used in place of the *meter*. The method may be modified and used in later studies of the smaller units, such as the millimeter, centimeter, and decimeter. It may also be modified to use with standard or English units of measure.

2. Give each pair of students a copy of Building Mat 5-4a. Also give each pair three strips of white paper (approximately 0.5 inch by 1.5 inches), each piece labeled with one of the following: "meter," "gram," or "liter."

3. Each pair will also need a set of colored paper squares in four different colors. Color a large dot in each column heading space of the building mats to correspond to the color of the paper square to be placed in that column. For convenience of discussion, for the columns indicated we will use the following colors with the given amounts to make the set: Kilo—5 red squares labeled with a "1"; Hecto—5 yellow squares with "10" and 20 yellow squares with "1"; Deka—5 green squares with "100," 20 green squares with "10"; and the blank heading—5 blue squares with "1,000," and 20 blue squares with "100." If possible, laminate all the labeled paper strips and paper squares for greater durability and ease of handling.

4. The given amounts of number cards (paper squares) for the student set are for trading whole kilometers back to meters or to the units between them; this

implies that only meter quantities in multiples of 1,000 will be used. Meter quantities in multiples of 100 may also be used for trading from meters to hectometers. (To be able to trade lesser amounts, each set would also need 20 green squares labeled with "1," 20 blue squares with "10," and 20 blue squares with "1." Your curriculum will determine which set to use.)

5. Before students work with Building Mat 5-4a and the paper squares or number cards, they need some review with the base 10 blocks. On an overhead transparency of the building mat design, place 100 cubes in the right column. As indicated earlier, the following examples will be limited to the meter, so write "meter" in the blank column heading on the transparency. Tell students that if "meter" is in this rightmost column, the other headings automatically include it; for example, the kilo- column becomes the "kilometer" column. (Gram or liter may be substituted for meter, if preferred.) Trade every 10 cubes, trading one group at a time, for 1 rod in the deka- column. Then trade the 10 rods collected in the deka- column for 1 flat in the hecto- column. In the following way, show students that these trades may be shown with number cards in the columns instead of the actual blocks. Draw a square in the meter column and write "100" inside the square. This represents a number card, which in turn represents the 100 cubes. Ask how many rods came from the trade of the 100 cubes. Because 10 rods resulted from the trade, mark out the 100-square and draw a new square in the deka- column with a "10" written inside the square. Now ask how many flats came from the trade of the 10 rods. Because 1 flat resulted from the trade, mark out the 10-square and draw a new square in the hecto- column with a "1" written inside the square. This demonstration lays the foundation for the trades students will be making in this activity. A 100-card in one column will trade for a 10-card in the next column to the left, or a 10-card in a column will trade for a 1-card in the next column to the left.

6. Occasionally, remind students that if 100 cubes trade for 1 flat, then one cube must be $\frac{1}{100}$ of a flat. Similarly, if 10 cubes trade for 1 rod, then one cube must be $\frac{1}{10}$ of a rod. Students need much practice using fractional language.

7. Now have students place the "meter" strip on the blank heading of Building Mat 5-4a and place 3 blue 100-cards in the "meter" column. This will be an example of "forward" trading (that is, from smaller unit to larger unit). These 3 cards represent 300 meters. Have students make trades according to the base 10 block trading done earlier. Each blue 100-card should trade for a green 10-card in the deka- column, which represents 10 dekameters; there will be 3 green 10-cards in all. Then each green 10-card will trade for a yellow 1-card in the hecto- column, which represents 1 hectometer; there will be 3 yellow 1-cards in all. As each new column total is found, it would be helpful to write that value on the board; in this case, you would have written "300 meters," "30 dekameters," and "3 hectometers" on the board for future recording by students. When students have finished their trading, they should record the results on their own papers in words in the following way: "300 meters, 30 dekameters, and 3 hectometers are equal."

8. Repeat this process, using 10 blue 100-cards in the meter column; this trading will end with 1 red 1-card in the kilometer column, since 10 yellow 1-cards are equivalent to 1 yellow 10-card, which will trade for 1 red 1-card. In other words,

10 of 100 meters (or 1,000 meters) will equal 10 of 10 dekameters (or 100 dekameters). Continuing to trade, students will get 10 of 1 hectometer (or 10 hectometers), which finally trade for 1 kilometer.

9. To go from meters to kilometers again, start with 2 blue 1,000-cards in the meter column. The trading sequence will be blue 1,000-card to green 100-card to yellow 10-card to red 1-card. The recorded result will state that "2,000 meters, 200 dekameters, 20 hectometers, and 2 kilometers are equal."

10. The next example is for a "backward" trade (that is, from larger unit to smaller unit). Have students place 4 red 1-cards in the kilo- column to represent 4 kilometers. Each 1-card should be traded for a yellow 10-card in the hecto- column, which represents 10 hectometers; there will be 4 yellow 10-cards in all. Each yellow 10-card should be traded for a green 100-card in the deka- column to show 100 dekameters; there will be 4 green 100-cards in all. Finally, each green 100-card should be traded for a blue 1,000-card in the meter column; there will be 4 blue 1,000-cards in all. Students should record on their papers as follows: "4 kilometers, 40 hectometers, 400 dekameters, and 4,000 meters are equal."

11. Continue with several other examples. When amounts such as 1,000, 100, or 10 are traded "forward" for a single unit of some kind, have students reverse their language from whole amounts to fractional amounts; for example, if 100 dekameters have traded for 1 kilometer, have students record "1 dekameter equals $\frac{1}{100}$ of a kilometer," as well as "100 dekameters equal 1 kilometer."

12. In this activity, meters in 1,000s will trade all the way to kilometers. Meters in 100s will trade to whole hectometers. Meters in 10s and 1s will not be used, because this activity is focusing mainly on trading from meters to kilometers and from kilometers to meters. (Note: As mentioned earlier in the description of the number card set, if more between-column trading is preferred, each set will also need green 1-cards, blue 10-cards, and blue 1-cards.)

Here is a sample of Building Mat 5-4a with some number cards (colors of number cards indicated by various shadings):

KILO__ ⚪	HECTO__ ⚪	DEKA__ ⚫	METER ⚫
			100
			100
			100

1	10	100	1000
	1	10	100
[red]	[yellow]	[green]	[blue]

BUILDING MAT 5-4a

KILO__	HECTO__	DEKA__	

Activity 2: Pictorial Stage

Materials
    Worksheet 5-4a
    Red pencils
    Regular pencils

Procedure
1. Give each student a copy of Worksheet 5-4a and a red pencil.

2. Students will follow the same trading procedure used in the Manipulative Stage but will draw and label boxes in the columns of the frames to represent number cards. As a number is traded, its box should be marked out on the frame and the appropriate number drawn in a box in the new column.

3. Students should complete the exercises on the worksheet. For each exercise, the result should be recorded in the blank provided above the frame.

4. For practice with fractional notation, when a trade begins or ends with a single unit of some kind, have students reverse their whole number notation to fractional notation. For example, if 10 hectograms result from trading 1 kilogram to hectograms, students should record "1 hectogram = $\frac{1}{10}$ of a kilogram," as well as "1 kilogram = 10 hectograms."

5. After all students have finished the worksheet, have pairs of students take turns explaining their methods and answers to each other. Discuss any fractional notation used with the entire class.

6. Exercise 1 is presented in detail.

   Here is a completed frame for Exercise 1: "3,000 grams = _____ kilograms." The word "gram" should be written in the blank column heading of the frame. The drawing should begin in the rightmost column under "gram," then move to the left as trades are made and numbers are marked out. Numbers being "removed" or traded should be marked out with red pencil. Instead of using word names for the final units, students might record the result with letters: "3,000 grams = 3 kg." They need practice with both types of unit labels.

KILO__	HECTO__	DEKA__	GRAM
1	~~10~~	~~100~~	~~1000~~
1	~~10~~	~~100~~	~~1000~~
1	~~10~~	~~100~~	~~1000~~

Answer Key for Worksheet 5-4a

1. 3 kilograms (kg)

2. 40 meters (m)

3. 10 hectoliters (hL); also, 1 hL = $\dfrac{1}{10}$ of a kiloliter

4. 500 meters (m)

5. 2 kilograms (kg)

6. 1 kilometer (km); also, 1 m = $\dfrac{1}{1000}$ of a kilometer

7. 5 hectoliters (hL)

342

WORKSHEET 5-4a

Name _____

Drawing Diagrams to Trade
Measuring Units

Date _____

Work the following exercises by drawing small squares on the given base 10 frames. In
the blank column heading of each frame, write the basic unit (meter, liter, or gram)
required. Use a red pencil to show any trades.

1. 3,000 grams = _____ kilograms

KILO__	HECTO__	DEKA__	

2. 4 dekameters = _____ meters

KILO__	HECTO__	DEKA__	

3. 1 kiloliter = _____ hectoliters

KILO__	HECTO__	DEKA__	

WORKSHEET 5-4a Continued

Name _____

Date _____

4. 5 hectometers = _____ meters

KILO__	HECTO__	DEKA__	

5. 200 dekagrams = _____ kilograms

KILO__	HECTO__	DEKA__	

6. 1,000 meters = _____ kilometer

KILO__	HECTO__	DEKA__	

7. 500 liters = _____ hectoliters

KILO__	HECTO__	DEKA__	

Activity 3: Independent Practice

Materials
   Worksheet 5-4b
   Regular pencils

Procedure
Give each student a copy of Worksheet 5-4b to complete independently. After all have finished, have different students share their results and explain the methods they used to find their answers. Encourage students to think in a 1-10-100-1,000 sequence or a 1,000-100-10-1 sequence, as used in Activities 1 and 2, when they make their trades. Do not stress the multiplication or the division approaches at this time.

Answer Key for Worksheet 5-4b
   1. 5,000 meters (m)

   2. 4 kilograms (kg)

   3. 2 kiloliters (kL)

   4. 300 grams (g)

   5. 60 hectograms (hg)

   6. 700 dekaliters (dkL)

   7. $\frac{1}{1000}$ kilometer (km)

   8. 8,000 dekameters (dkm)

   9. D

   10. C

Possible Testing Errors That May Occur for This Objective
   - Students think that the next smaller metric unit after a given unit is *half* of that given unit instead of a tenth of that unit. For example, they think that 1 gram equals 0.5 or $\frac{1}{2}$ of a dekagram.
   - Relationships in the metric system are confused with those in the English system. For example, because 12 inches equal 1 foot, students may think that 12 hectometers equal 1 kilometer.
   - Students know that 100 centimeters equal 1 meter, which is a 100:1 ratio, so they incorrectly extend the same ratio to other pairs of units. For example, they think that 100 meters equal 1 kilometer.

WORKSHEET 5-4b

Conversion by Trading
Metric Measuring Units

Name _____

Date _____

Work the following exercises. Be ready to share your methods and your answers with the entire class.

1. 500 dekameters = _____ meters

2. 40 hectograms = _____ kilograms

3. 2,000 liters = _____ kiloliters

4. 3 hectograms = _____ grams

5. 600 dekagrams = _____ hectograms

6. 7 kiloliters = _____ dekaliters

7. 1 meter = _____ of a kilometer

8. 80 kilometers = _____ dekameters

9. Brooks ran 5 kilometers in a race. How many meters did she run?

   A. 0.5 meter

   B. 50 meters

   C. 500 meters

   D. 5,000 meters

10. A newborn baby weighs about 4,000 grams. What is the weight or mass of the baby in kilograms?

   A. 400 kilograms

   B. 40 kilograms

   C. 4 kilograms

   D. 0.4 kilogram

Objective 5
Solve problems that involve the passing of time and the notation for time shown on a clock.

Discussion
Time is a difficult concept for young students to understand; they must first *live* it before they can totally *comprehend* it. Meanwhile, some simple activities can be used to help students at least understand changes in the clock's digital notation.

Activity 1: Manipulative Stage

Materials
    Clock and 5-minute number tiles (red and green tiles; see Worksheet 5-5a
      for patterns)
    Cutout clock long hands and short hands
    Worksheet 5-5b

Procedure
1. In this activity, students will work with time intervals in multiples of 5 minutes. Use the clock pattern on Worksheet 5-5a. The straight distance from one numeral marking to the next should be about 1 inch long.

2. From red construction paper, cut out 1-inch square pieces or tiles and write the numeral 5 on each piece (see Worksheet 5-5a for tile pattern and size). Repeat the process, using green construction paper. Six tiles of each color will be needed for each pair of students. Laminate the paper tiles, if possible, for greater durability.

3. On light tagboard, draw long (2.25-inch) and short (1.5-inch) arrows for the minute and hour hands, but cut them out in rectangular form to make the cutting task easier and quicker. Here is an example of a cutout clock hand:

4. Give each pair of students two copies of Worksheet 5-5b, a clock pattern (from Worksheet 5-5a), a long hand, a short hand, and a packet of 6 red tiles and 6 green tiles.

5. Explain that the green tiles will be used to show *increasing* time (going forward in time) and the red tiles will be used to show *decreasing* time (going backward in time). The colored tiles are to be placed around the rim of the clock face on the building mat.

6. Call out different times from Worksheet 5-5b for students to show on their clock mats with the cutout long (minute) and short (hour) hands. With each time called out, give students some amount of minutes (5 to 30 minutes in multiples of 5) to show with their tiles either as a forward time change or as a backward time change. Students should then move their clock hands to show the later time or the earlier time produced by the change. Partners should work together to show the time changes on their clock mat.

7. For each beginning time and time change given, students should record the ending time on their own worksheets. There are also two word problems on Worksheet 5-5b; these should be modeled with the clock hands and tiles as well.

8. Guide students through each problem before proceeding to the next one.

Two examples, Exercise 1 and Exercise 2, are shown next; each dotted hand on the illustration shows the minute/hour hand's initial position on the mat.

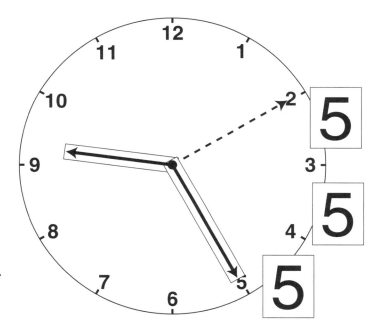

Exercise 1:
Show 9:10.
Go forward 15 minutes.
New time: 9:25
(green tiles used)

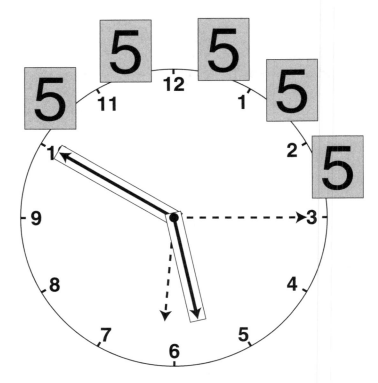

Exercise 2:
Show 6:15.
Go backward 25 minutes.
New time: 5:50
(red tiles used)

Answer Key for Worksheet 5-5b

1. 9:25

2. 5:50

3. 2:05

4. 1:05

5. 5:00

6. 10:45

7. 15 minutes early

8. 30 minutes late

WORKSHEET 5-5a
Clock and Tile Patterns

Name _____

Date _____

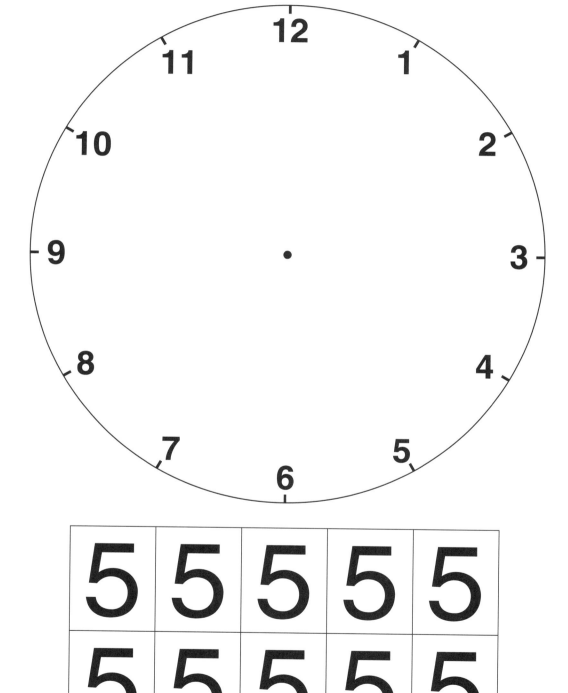

350

WORSHEET 5-5b   Name _____

Passing of Time   Date _____

Use the clock face, clock hands, and colored paper tiles to show the change in time, either forward or backward, from the initial time. Record the final time.

1. Show 9:10. Go forward 15 minutes.

    New time: _____

2. Show 6:15. Go backward 25 minutes.

    New time: _____

3. Show 2:20. Go backward 15 minutes.

    New time: _____

4. Show 12:45. Go forward 20 minutes.

    New time: _____

5. Show 4:30. Go forward 30 minutes.

    New time: _____

6. Show 10:50. Go backward 5 minutes.

    New time: _____

7. The baseball game began at 6:30 Friday evening. Maria arrived at 6:15 to watch the game. How early was she for the game?

    _____

    _____

8. The plane was scheduled to leave at 12:55 P.M., but because of bad weather, it did not leave until 1:25 P.M. How late was the plane's departure?

    _____

    _____

Activity 2: Pictorial Stage

Materials

Worksheet 5-5c (2 copies per student)
Red and green colored pencils
Worksheet 5-5d
Regular pencils

Procedure

1. After students are comfortable with making changes on the clock pattern, give each student a red and a green colored pencil and two copies of Worksheet 5-5c, which contains smaller clock faces. The clock faces will be similar to the clock pattern, except they will now have *all* minute markings shown on them. Also give each student a copy of Worksheet 5-5d. A blank space is provided at the upper left of each clock face on Worksheet 5-5c so that students can number each face to correspond to an exercise on Worksheet 5-5d.

2. For each exercise, broken-line clock hands should be drawn on the clock face to show the initial time. For forward changes, a green arrow should be drawn in a clockwise direction along the rim of the clock from the minute hand's initial position to its new position; the time change should be written on the green arrow and preceded by a plus sign. For backward changes, a red arrow should be drawn counterclockwise along the rim from the initial position to the final position of the minute hand; the time change should be written on the red arrow and preceded by a minus sign. Solid-line hands should then be drawn in the final position and the old and new times recorded next to the clock face on Worksheet 5-5c, and the final answer recorded on Worksheet 5-5d.

3. Worksheet 5-5d also contains two word problems; clock diagrams should be drawn for these problems as well. If the curriculum includes hour changes too, the same procedure should be followed; the red or green arrow will simply wrap around the clock face in a complete revolution for each hour passed, plus some additional distance for any minute time changes.

4. Guide students through Exercise 1 on Worksheet 5-5d before allowing them to work through the other exercises on their own. When all have finished the worksheets, ask various students to share their methods and answers with the entire class.

Here is an example of the first completed entry on Worksheet 5-5c, based on Exercise 1 from Worksheet 5-5d, which requires students to move the initial time forward 37 minutes (the curved arrow is drawn in green).

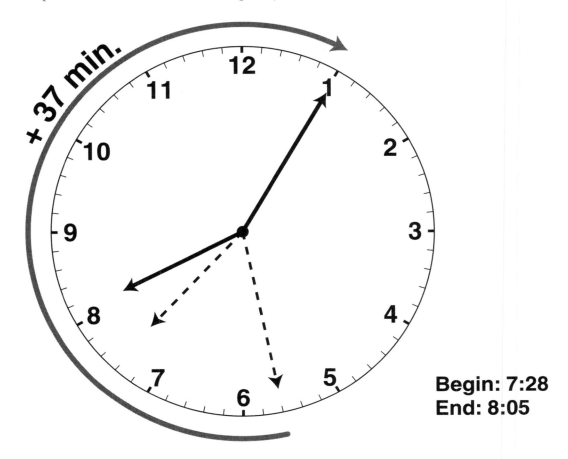

Begin: 7:28
End: 8:05

Answer Key for Worksheets 5-5c and 5-5d

1. 7:28 to 8:05 (green arrow)

2. 6:20 to 5:53 (red arrow)

3. 1:06 to 12:51 (red arrow)

4. 12:45 to 12:55 (green arrow)

5. 3:30 to 5:00 (green arrow)

6. 10:54 to 8:49 (red arrow)

7. 7:30 to 7:48; 18 minutes late (green arrow)

8. 8:45 to 9:23; 38 minutes late (green arrow)

WORKSHEET 5-5c
Drawing Time Changes

Name _____

Date _____

Follow the teacher's instructions to show various times and time changes on the clock faces below. A green pencil and a red pencil will be needed.

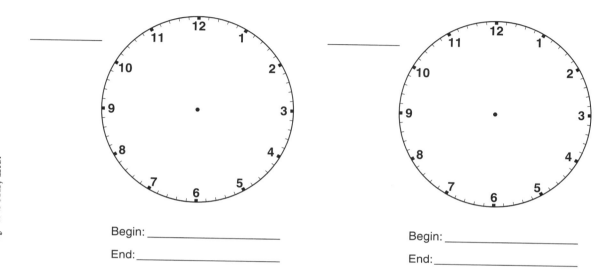

_____   Begin: _____

End: _____

Begin: _____

End: _____

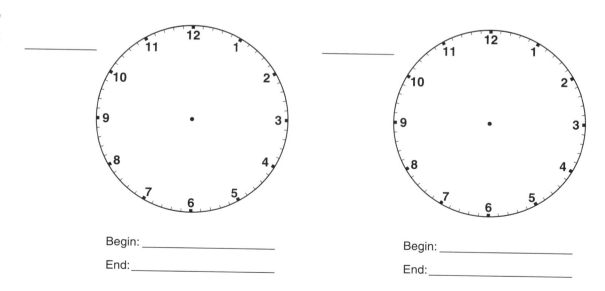

_____   Begin: _____

End: _____

Begin: _____

End: _____

354

WORKSHEET 5-5d

Name _____

Changing the Time

Date _____

Draw on the clock faces on Worksheet 5-5c to solve the following exercises. Follow the teacher's instructions.

1. Show 7:28. Go forward 37 minutes.

    New time: _____

2. Show 6:20. Go backward 27 minutes.

    New time: _____

3. Show 1:06. Go backward 15 minutes.

    New time: _____

4. Show 12:45. Go forward 10 minutes.

    New time: _____

5. Show 3:30. Go forward 1 hour and 30 minutes.

    New time: _____

6. Show 10:54. Go backward 2 hours and 5 minutes.

    New time: _____

7. The party began at 7:30 Saturday evening. Luis arrived at 7:48. How late was he for the party?

    _____

    _____

8. The plane was scheduled to leave at 8:45 A.M., but because of bad weather, it left at 9:23 A.M. How late was the plane in departing?

    _____

    _____

Activity 3: Independent Practice

Materials
> Worksheet 5-5e
> Regular pencils

Procedure
Give each student a copy of Worksheet 5-5e to complete independently. When all are finished, have several students share their results, along with the methods they used.

Answer Key for Worksheet 5-5e

1. B

2. D

3. C

4. B

5. A

6. C

Possible Testing Errors That May Occur for This Objective

- When combining an interval in minutes with the minutes portion of the digital clock notation, a computational error is made. For example, when advancing 3:15 by 8 minutes, 15 and 8 are not added correctly.

- The given interval of minutes is incorrectly viewed as the amount of minutes shown in the digital notation. For example, 20 minutes of time passing since 3:05 is incorrectly interpreted as 3:20, where the 20 in the position for minutes is considered to represent the 20-minute interval.

- Students do not realize that there is a 60-minute limit so that the minutes on a clock recycle. In error, they show 12 minutes after 5:56 as 5:68. The student does not understand that after 59 minutes, the clock returns to 0 minutes instead of going on to 60 minutes. A completed cycle in minutes also dictates an increase on the clock to the next hour.

356

WORKSHEET 5-5e   Name _____
The Passing of Time   Date _____

Complete the given exercises. Be ready to share your answers with the entire class.

1. The school bus makes a stop every 8 minutes. On the way to school each
   morning, the bus is scheduled to make its first three stops at 7:23, 7:31, and 7:39.
   At what time will the bus make its fourth stop?

   A. 7:43   B. 7:47   C. 7:48   D. 7:51

2. Kay left for soccer practice at 4:10 in the afternoon. She arrived at her friend
   Mary's house 1 hour and 30 minutes later. At what time did she arrive at Mary's
   house?

   A. 4:40   B. 5:00   C. 5:10   D. 5:40

3. A concert began at 7:30 last Tuesday evening. Charlie arrived at 8:15. How late
   was Charlie for the concert?

   A. 15 minutes   B. 1 hour   C. 45 minutes   D. 1 hour and 15
                                                         minutes

4. Which clock time is between 12:00 and 1:00?

   A. 11:45   B. 12:18   C. 1:05   D. 1:59

5. On Monday, Darla left school at 3:45 and walked home without stopping along
   the way. She arrived at her house at 4:03. On Tuesday, she will walk home the
   same way but will leave school at 2:30. At what time should she expect to arrive
   at home?

   A. 2:48   B. 3:03   C. 3:45   D. 4:03

6. A train leaves the station every 20 minutes. If one train leaves at 7:35 and another
   leaves at 7:55 in the morning, at what time will the next train leave?

   A. 7:75   B. 8:05   C. 8:15   D. 8:35

Objective 6
Find and apply the perimeter of a rectangle to solve a word problem.

Discussion
Too often, when asked to find a perimeter, students will add only the two measures given. Typically, if a picture is provided, only one width and one length will be marked on the picture. Many students will just add the two measures shown on the picture; they will not transform the picture by labeling the other two needed sides. Consequently, they do not combine all four sides for the perimeter. Students need tactile experiences with the perimeter of a rectangle so they will realize that all four sides must be involved. Otherwise, formulas have very little meaning for them.

Activity 1: Manipulative Stage

Materials
    Measuring tapes (inch or centimeter)
    Assorted objects in the classroom
    Rulers (inch or centimeter)
    Cutout cardboard shapes (polygons)
    Regular paper
    Regular pencils

Procedure
1. Provide a measuring tape, either centimeter or inch, to each group of 4 students. The tape will help students to count the number of units (cm or in.) of distance around an object.

2. In the classroom, have the groups measure around 4 different objects, such as desktops, cabinet doors, storage baskets, and front covers of textbooks.

3. On their own papers, students should make quick sketches of what they measure, then record the total measure around each object below its sketch.

4. This first effort to find perimeter should include at least one object whose perimeter is greater than the length of the tape. In this case, students must wrap the tape around the object's edges as far as it can reach, then slide the tape's 0 mark over to where the tape has ended on an edge and continue to measure to get the final number to add to the tape's initial length for the total. For example, the centimeter tape might wrap almost around a desk, but an additional 20 cm is needed to complete the wraparound of the whole desktop. Students must add the extra 20 cm to the 100 cm shown on the tape to get a perimeter of 120 cm for the desktop.

5. After students have developed a sense of "aroundness" for perimeter, give them practice with finding perimeter by combining the measures of individual side lengths. Give each group a set of 4 different cutout cardboard shapes and a centimeter or inch ruler. Each shape should fit within a 10-inch by 10-inch space but not be too much smaller than that. Side lengths should be cut to the nearest inch or centimeter, depending on which unit you prefer (but students need experience with both types); label each shape with the type of unit used in its design. Include 3-, 4-, and 5-sided polygons for the shapes, whether or not you have studied the shapes by name in class, and label each shape with a unique letter of the alphabet. The letter name allows students to discuss and write about a shape without knowing its more formal geometric name.

6. For each shape in their group's set, students should measure each edge or side to the *nearest* inch or centimeter, depending on which unit is marked on the shape. Then on their own papers, they should record the shape's name or letter, all the individual measures found, and a number sentence that shows their total (the perimeter). For example, students might write the following: "Shape B; 5 cm, 7 cm, 4 cm, 5 cm, 8 cm; 5 + 7 + 4 + 5 + 8 = 29 cm for perimeter." A quick sketch of the shape should also be made on the paper.

7. After all groups have finished their measuring and recording, have each group report to another group on what classroom objects and cardboard shapes their group measured and what perimeters they found.

Activity 2: Pictorial Stage

Materials

Worksheet 5-6a
Regular pencils

Procedure

1. Give each student a copy of Worksheet 5-6a.

2. For each shape on the worksheet, students should count the *spaces* marked off on each side (indicated with dots) and label each side with its newly found measure. For some shapes, all sides have to be measured. For others, some side lengths are given and the shape is labeled with the characteristic "opposite sides equal," so that students might *reason* through what the missing sides should be without having to count all the spaces. They should still count to measure the missing sides if they need to confirm their answers.

3. Finally, students should write a number sentence below each shape that shows the sum of the shape's side lengths for the perimeter. It is important that students write their *own* number sentences or equations and not just fill in blanks already provided. This is also a good time to apply multiplication if students are ready for it.

4. For Exercises 5 and 6, students should draw rectangles on the back of the worksheet and label their side lengths. They should also write a number sentence, either below the word problem or below the drawing, to find the perimeter of each rectangle.

5. Discuss Exercise 1 and Exercise 2 with the class before allowing students to work on their own. When all are finished, have various students share their results and their reasoning.

Here are completed examples for Exercise 1 and Exercise 2 to discuss with students (numbers with units indicate side measures):

Exercise 1:

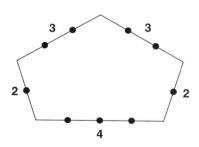

Exercise 2:

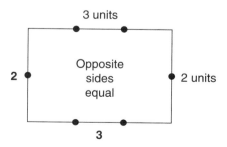

$2 + 3 + 3 + 2 + 4 = 14$ units, perimeter

$2 + 3 + 2 + 3 = 10$ units, perimeter
[or $2 \times 3 + 2 \times 2 = 10$ or $2 \times (3 + 2) = 10$]

Answer Key for Worksheet 5-6a

1. (Details shown in text)

2. (Details shown in text)

3. $3 + 3 + 3 + 3 = 12$ units, or $4 \times 3 = 12$ units

4. $3 + 4 + 5 = 12$ units

5. $14 + 12 + 14 + 12 = 52$ inches

6. $3 + 4 + 3 + 4 = 14$ feet

WORKSHEET 5-6a

Measuring Diagrams to
Find Perimeters

Name _____

Date _____

On each shape, find and label each side's length by counting the units of length marked off with small dots. Be sure to count the *spaces*, not the dots. Below each shape, write a number sentence to find the shape's perimeter. For each word problem, draw the required shape on the back of this worksheet and label its side lengths before finding the perimeter.

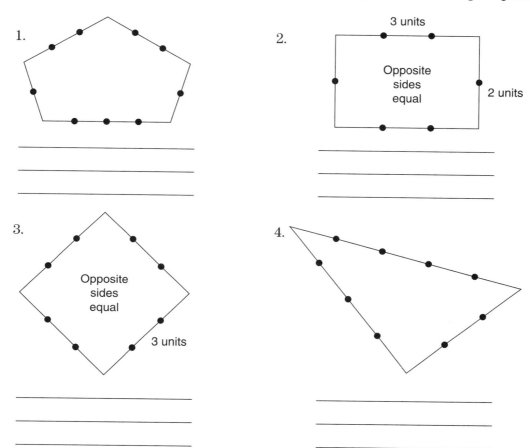

1.

2.   3 units

Opposite sides equal   2 units

_____
_____
_____

_____
_____
_____

3.   Opposite sides equal   3 units

4.

_____
_____
_____

_____
_____
_____

5. Eddie wants to make a rectangular picture frame. The longer outside edge of the frame will be 14 inches, and the shorter outside edge will be 12 inches. How many inches of framing wood should he buy?

_____

_____

6. The classroom bulletin board is 3 feet wide and 4 feet long. Miss Johnson, the teacher, wants to tack some red ribbon around the edges of the board. How many feet of ribbon will she need?

_____

_____

Activity 3: Independent Practice

Materials
    Worksheet 5-6b
    Rulers or straightedges
    Regular pencils

Procedure
Give each student a copy of Worksheet 5-6b to complete independently. All exercises on the worksheet will involve rectangles, but additional exercises involving triangles and pentagons might also be used, if preferred. After all students have finished, ask several students to discuss their methods and their answers.

Answer Key for Worksheet 5-6b
    1. D

    2. B

    3. C

    4. A

    5. C

    6. A

Possible Testing Errors That May Occur for This Objective
- Students multiply two adjacent side measures of a rectangle when trying to find perimeter instead of adding the four side measures together. For example, for a 3-ft by 4-ft rectangle, they use $3 \times 4 = 12$ for the perimeter instead of $3 + 4 + 3 + 4 = 14$.

- The formula for finding the area of a triangle is applied to a rectangle in an effort to find the perimeter of the rectangle. That is, for a 5 by 6 rectangle, $\frac{(5 \times 6)}{2} = 15$ is found as the perimeter.

- Only the two numbers given as the dimensions of a rectangle are added to find the perimeter. Thus, students use only two sides of the shape and fail to include the measures of the other two sides also needed for the perimeter.

WORSHEET 5-6b

Name _____

Finding and Applying Perimeters
of Rectangles

Date _____

For each word problem, make a freehand drawing of the required shape on the back of this worksheet and label its side lengths before finding or applying the perimeter. Use a ruler to help you draw straight sides for the shapes.

1. Josey put a lace border around a rectangular picture. She used 15 centimeters of lace for each width and 21 centimeters of lace for each length. How much lace did she use altogether?

   A. 15 cm   B. 36 cm   C. 42 cm   D. 72 cm

2. A rectangular flag measures 12 inches wide and 15 inches long. What is the perimeter of the flag?

   A. 180 in.   B. 54 in.   C. 30 in.   D. 27 in.

3. A rectangular garden has a perimeter of 16 yards. If the shorter side of the rectangle is 3 yards long, what is the measure of the longer side?

   A. 48 yds   B. 19 yds   C. 5 yds   D. 3 yds

4. A rectangle is shown with some of its side lengths. What is the perimeter of the shape?

   A. 38 ft

   B. 12 ft

   C. 84 ft

   D. 19 ft

7 ft

12 ft

5. The shorter side of a rectangle is 6 centimeters. The longer side is twice as long as the shorter side. What is the total distance around the rectangle?

   A. 12 cm   B. 18 cm   C. 36 cm   D. 72 cm

6. Jake used 140 inches of weather stripping to trim around the edges of a square window. About how long was each side of the window?

   A. 35 in.   B. 140 in.   C. 100 in.   D. 70 in.

Objective 7
Find the area of a rectangular region.

Discussions
The general concept of area as square units filling the interior of a rectangle first needs to be developed through tactile and visual experiences. Students need hands-on activities to help them differentiate the concept of area from that of perimeter. It is not enough to give them formulas to memorize; students must be able to actually measure and count correct kinds of units in order to find the area of a given shape, as well as its perimeter.

Activity 1: Manipulative Stage

Materials
> Packets of 50 1-inch paper squares (tiles)
> Worksheet 5-7a
> Regular pencils

Procedure
1. Give each pair of students a packet of 50 1-inch paper squares or tiles. A side edge of one paper square or tile will equal one unit of length, while the top surface of the tile will equal one square unit of area.

2. Have each pair build 6 to 8 different rectangular shapes on their desktop. The tiles should be arranged in rows and columns, touching edge to edge with no gaps or overlapping.

3. As partners build each shape, they should record in the table on Worksheet 5-7a the total area square units (total tiles) used for the shape, as well as the length units counted along two adjacent sides of the shape. The adjacent sides will be called Side 1 and Side 2, rather than Length and Width (which are just the *measures* of adjacent sides), to avoid confusion when Side 1 and Side 2 have the same measure, as with a square region. By using these generic labels, it will not matter whether the longer side is recorded as Side 1 or Side 2.

4. In the "Drawing of Shape" column, students should draw a simple sketch of each shape they build. Basically, the drawing will look like a grid. Under the drawing, they should write the number of rows and the row size used, such as "3 rows of 5."

5. Carefully monitor students' work to make sure they are correctly building shapes and recording their measurements.

6. After all students are finished, ask them to look at the expressions or numbers recorded in each row of their table. Do they see a relationship between the numbers in the row description written under the drawing and the number in the total area column? Do they see a relationship between the numbers for the two side measures and the number in the total area column? Ideally, they will notice that in each row of the table: (a) the given numbers in the row description represent a product equal to the total area tiles counted, and (b) the product of the two side measures also equals the total area number. Relationship (a) is the basis for counting or measuring the area of a rectangular region or shape; relationship (b) provides a convenient way to *compute* that same area. Stress the connection between relationship (a) and relationship (b). Often students will multiply the two numbers given as side measures of a rectangle to find "area A," but they do not realize that that same product is giving them the total number of square units that fill the *inside* of the rectangle, which is the *real* area of the rectangle.

7. Have students write word sentences on the back of the worksheet to describe the relationships they find. Have several students read their sentences aloud to the class.

8. Before allowing students to create their own shapes with the tiles, guide them through the building and recording of the first rectangular shape. Use the shape described next for the example.

Here is an example to use for the first table entry:

Drawing of Shape	Total Area Square Units	Side 1 Length Units	Side 2 Length Units
	35 sq units	7 units	5 units

5 rows of 7

366

WORSHEET 5-7a

WORKSHEET 5-7a

Building Tile Shapes

Name _____

Date _____

Build different rectangular shapes with the tiles. In the table below, record the adjacent side measures and area of each shape built.

Drawing of Shape	Total Area Square Units	Side 1 Length Units	Side 2 Length Units

Activity 2: Pictorial Stage

Materials

Centimeter grid paper
Bright-colored markers (medium tip)
Regular pencils

Procedure

1. Give each student a sheet of centimeter grid paper and a colored marker (bright colors preferred).

2. Partners should rotate the tasks of (1) drawing a rectangle on the grid paper or (2) counting the area square units inside the rectangle and finding the product of the two adjacent side lengths. When one partner does task 1, the other partner will do task 2 for the same rectangle. Whoever draws the rectangle will draw on the partner's grid paper, so that the one doing task 2 will record the results on his or her own grid paper. The counted total should be written inside the rectangle, and the product should be recorded as a number sentence below the rectangle. This approach will confirm that the two methods are equivalent and therefore can be used interchangeably.

3. Encourage students to draw a variety of rectangles on their grid paper: long, narrow rectangles; square rectangles; large rectangles (both square and nonsquare types); and small rectangles (both square and nonsquare).

4. Monitor students' work carefully to make sure that computation and counted area for the same shape agree and that multiplication answers are correct.

5. Discuss the example shown below with the class before allowing the pairs of students to work on their own.

(a) Count 45 square units and record it inside rectangle.
(b) Write product of side lengths below rectangle:
$5 \times 9 = 45$ square units.

Activity 3: Independent Practice

Materials
   Worksheet 5-7b
   Regular pencils

Procedure
Give each student a copy of Worksheet 5-7b to complete independently. Encourage students to draw and label rectangles to help them solve the word problems. When all are finished, ask various students to show their diagrams and explain their results to the entire class.

Answer Key for Worksheet 5-7b
   1. B

   2. D

   3. C

   4. A

   5. B

Possible Testing Errors That May Occur for This Objective
   * If the two side measures of a rectangle are given, students will simply add the two adjacent side lengths instead of multiplying to find the requested area.

   * If a rectangular figure is given in the test item and is subdivided into square units, students will count the square units around the boundary of the rectangle but not the square units within the interior of the shape. They are using a process similar to finding the perimeter, yet it counts square units instead of linear units.

   * Students will use the correct operation but will make computational errors when finding the area. Incorrect multiplication facts will be used.

   * Students will compute the perimeter of the given rectangle instead of the area required by the test item.

WORKSHEET 5-7b

Finding and Applying Areas
of Rectangles

Name _____

Date _____

Work the exercises below. Be ready to explain your steps and share your answers with
the entire class.

1. A rectangular bulletin board made of cork is 3 feet wide and 4 feet long. What is
    the area of the bulletin board's cork surface?

    A. 7 square feet   B. 12 square feet   C. 14 square feet   D. 16 square feet

2. The rectangular rug on Teddie's floor is 4 feet wide and 5 feet long. What is the
    area of the floor that the rug covers?

    A. 9 square feet

    B. 14 square feet

    C. 18 square feet

    D 20 square feet

    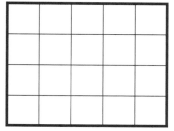

3. Which statement describes a way to find the area in square units of the shaded
    region inside the large rectangle?

    A. Count all squares inside
       the large rectangle.

    B. Count the unshaded
       squares only.

    C. Count the shaded
       squares only.

    D. Count the squares along
       the sides of the large rectangle.

    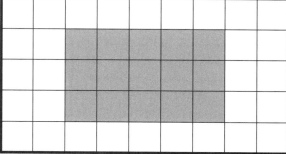

4. If a rectangular garden has a perimeter of 24 yards and a width of 5 yards, what
    is the area of the garden?

    A. 35 square yards   B. 29 square yards   C. 24 square yards   D. 12 square yards

5. If a rectangle has a perimeter of 30 centimeters, which would be a possible area
    for the rectangle?

    A. 60 square   B. 56 square   C. 45 square   D. 30 square
       centimeters   centimeters   centimeters   centimeters

Objective 8
Find or estimate the area of an irregular plane figure by counting square units or using the areas of rectangles.

Discussion
The area of an *irregular shape* cannot be found with a single standard area formula. Therefore, students need practice with various methods of finding the areas of such shapes. Basic *counting* of grid squares and parts of grid squares is a good place to start. Partial grid squares bounded by invisible triangles within the irregular shape might be combined to make "whole" grid squares, or a triangular portion of the original shape might be viewed as half of a rectangular region and its area, then computed from the area of that associated rectangle. Unless students have been trained to see the triangle-rectangle relationship, however, they will most likely try to visually "glue" parts of grid squares together to make whole ones. Practice in subdividing an irregular shape into familiar standard shapes is also necessary, but students will still need a strong conceptual understanding of the area of a rectangle in order to use this method effectively.

Activity 1: Manipulative Stage

Materials
Worksheet 5-8a
Scissors
Transparent tape or glue
Regular paper and regular pencils

Procedure
1. Give each pair of students a copy of Worksheet 5-8a, scissors, and transparent tape or glue.

2. Students should study the irregular shape shown on Worksheet 5-8a, then decide where to cut it in order to form smaller familiar shapes like triangles or rectangles. They should mark off in pencil the boundaries of new shapes they plan to make. Some new shapes may be extensions from the original shape's boundary. For example, if a triangular shape is seen as half of a rectangle, one half of the rectangle may lie outside the original irregular shape.

3. Once they have decided what shapes to make, partners should cut apart the original shape into the new shapes, including any extensions.

4. Students should determine the area in square units (grid squares) of each new shape and write the area inside the shape. Areas may be found by just counting the grid squares inside the shape; this will be particularly true when finding areas of triangles whose formulas have not yet been studied. The areas of rectangles may be computed as the product of two adjacent sides. All new shapes should then be taped onto a blank sheet of paper.

5. All the required areas should finally be added together to find the total area of the original irregular shape. A number sentence expressing this sum should be recorded on the same sheet of paper below the new shapes.

6. When all pairs of students have finished, have different students show how they subdivided the irregular shape and tell which areas they used to find the total area.

7. Discuss the example shown next with students before allowing them to cut out and subdivide the shape on Worksheet 5-8a.

Here is an example of an irregular shape that has been subdivided in two different ways. The triangular portion needed will be half of the extended rectangle.

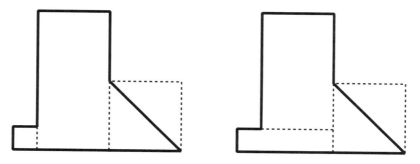

Answer Key for Worksheet 5-8a

Two triangles exist and have areas of 2 square units and 3 square units. Various rectangles are possible for the rest of the shape. The total area will be 70 square units.

372

Subdivide the given shape into smaller rectangles. Follow the teacher's instructions to cut apart the rectangles and find their areas. Remember that each triangle is just half of a rectangle, so cut out the entire rectangle at first.

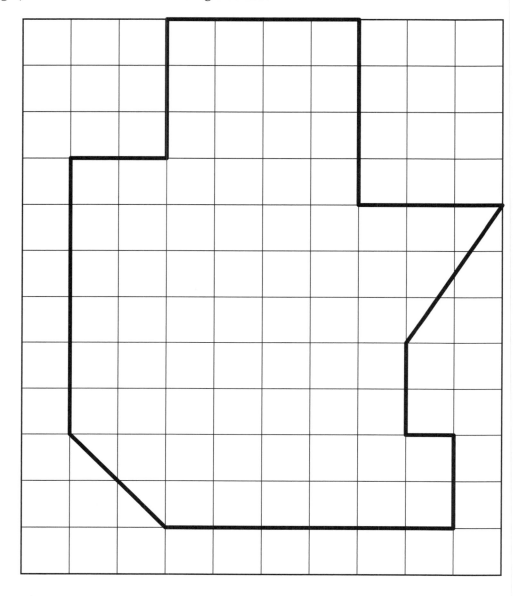

Activity 2: Pictorial Stage

Materials

Worksheet 5-8b

Regular pencils

Procedure

1. Give each student a copy of Worksheet 5-8b. Students will now estimate the area of *irregular* shapes by counting the square units in different ways or by finding areas of parts of the original shape, then adding those smaller areas together for the entire shape. Some shapes will have grids. Other shapes will have side measures shown with which students must reason to find the needed areas. If no grid is given, assume that all angles are right angles.

2. Have students work in pairs to label the sides and subdivide each shape into rectangles. When grids are given, they should count the area square units inside the shape to confirm the total area they *compute*.

3. Have different students share the ways they found their total areas.

4. Discuss Exercise 1 with the class before allowing students to work on their own.

Here is an example of the shape for Exercise 1 being subdivided and labeled to show adjacent sides of each rectangle formed. Other subdivisions are possible.

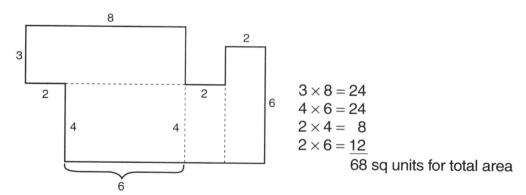

$3 \times 8 = 24$
$4 \times 6 = 24$
$2 \times 4 = 8$
$2 \times 6 = \underline{12}$
68 sq units for total area

Answer Key for Worksheet 5-8b

1. Possible subdivision shown in text; total area = 68 square units

2. Possible subdivision shown below:

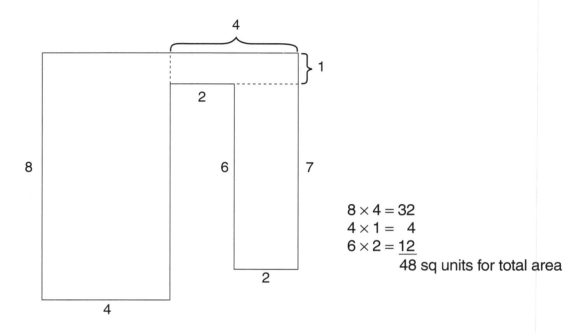

$$8 \times 4 = 32$$
$$4 \times 1 = 4$$
$$6 \times 2 = \underline{12}$$
48 sq units for total area

3. Total area = 28 square units

4. Total area = 31 square units

WORKSHEET 5-8b
Finding Areas Using Diagrams

Name _____

Date _____

Subdivide each irregular shape into small rectangular shapes. Label two adjacent side lengths for each rectangle formed. Use the areas of the smaller shapes to find the total area of the irregular shape. Use "units" for side lengths and "square units" for areas.

1.
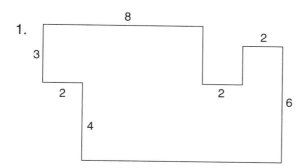

2.
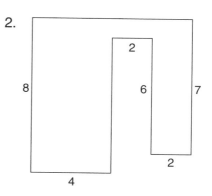

3.
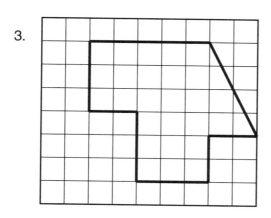

4.
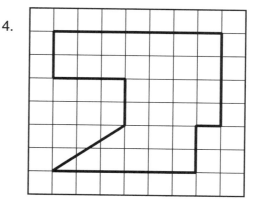

Activity 3: Independent Practice

Materials
   Worksheet 5-8c
   Regular pencils

Procedure
Give each student a copy of Worksheet 5-8c to complete independently. When all are finished, have various students describe their methods for finding the different areas.

Answer Key for Worksheet 5-8c
   1. C

   2. B

   3. A

Possible Testing Errors That May Occur for This Objective
   - If a triangle is included in the irregular shape, students will use the area of the entire rectangle, which contains the triangle, in the total area instead of using half of the rectangle's area.

   - Students will find the area of the largest rectangle contained *within* the shaded region whose area is required. They do not adjust for the additional areas of the other sections (triangles, smaller rectangles) attached to that rectangle.

   - If a grid is provided, students will miscount the square units inside the given region or will use an incorrect multiplication fact when computing the area of a smaller rectangle within the region.

WORKSHEET 5-8c
Finding Areas of Irregular Shapes

Name _____

Date _____

Answer each exercise below. Be ready to share your reasoning and your answers with the entire class.

1. What is the area of the outlined region?

   A. 21 square units

   B. 24 square units

   C. 27 square units

   D. 30 square units

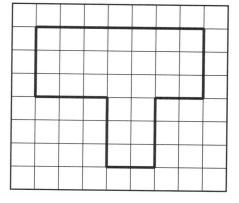

2. What is the area of the shaded region if each grid square represents 1 square yard?

   A. 20 square yards

   B. 28 square yards

   C. 36 square yards

   D. 72 square yards

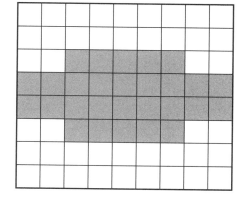

3. Anna tore a design (shaded part) out of grid paper. Which is the best estimate of the area of the design?

   A. 31 square units

   B. 39 square units

   C. 42 square units

   D. 48 square units

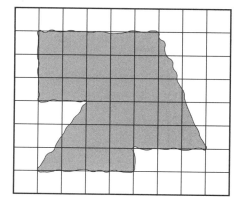

Name _____

Date _____

MEASUREMENT: PRACTICE TEST ANSWER SHEET

Directions: Use the Answer Sheet to darken the letter of the choice that best answers each question.

	A	B	C	D			A	B	C	D
1.	○	○	○	○	9.	○	○	○	○
2.	○	○	○	○	10.	○	○	○	○
3.	○	○	○	○	11.	○	○	○	○
4.	○	○	○	○	12.	○	○	○	○
5.	○	○	○	○	13.	○	○	○	○
6.	○	○	○	○	14.	○	○	○	○
7.	○	○	○	○	15.	○	○	○	○
8.	○	○	○	○	16.	○	○	○	○

SECTION 5: MEASUREMENT: PRACTICE TEST

1. About how long is your little finger?

   A. More than 1 meter   C. Less than 5 liters

   B. More than 3 centimeters   D. More than 4 grams

2. Which unit is best for measuring the height of your classroom door?

   A. Liter   B. Centimeter   C. Meter   D. Gram

3. Which unit should be used to measure the capacity of a small trashcan?

   A. Meter   B. Pint   C. Gram   D. Minute

4. About how many milliliters of cola will a 3-liter bottle hold?

   A. 3 milliliters   C. 300 milliliters

   B. 30 milliliters   D. 3,000 milliliters

5. Which object is most likely to have a weight of 8 pounds?

   A. Plastic dinner plate   C. Small dog

   B. Wooden desk   D. Truck tire

6. Which unit should be used to measure the weight of a pencil?

   A. Gram   B. Pint   C. Meter   D. Ton

7. How many grams will equal 6 hectograms?

   A. 600 grams   B. 60 grams   C. 0.6 grams   D. 0.06 grams

8. George ran 2 kilometers in a race. How many meters did he run?

   A. 0.2 meter   B. 20 meters   C. 200 meters   D. 2,000 meters

9. Jana left for tennis practice at 4:15 in the afternoon. She arrived at her friend Susan's house 1 hour and 20 minutes later. At what time did she arrive at Susan's house?

   A. 4:35   B. 5:15   C. 5:35   D. 5:50

10. The football game began at 7:30 Friday evening. Leonard arrived at 8:05. How late was Leonard for the game?

    A. 30 minutes   C. 1 hour

    B. 35 minutes   D. 1 hour and 5 minutes

380

SECTION 5: MEASUREMENT: PRACTICE TEST

11. A rectangular flag measures 3 feet by 5 feet. What is the perimeter of the flag?

    A. 30 ft   B. 16 ft   C. 15 ft   D. 8 ft

12. A rectangular garden has a perimeter of 40 yards. If the shorter side of the rectangle is 8 yards long, what is the measure of the longer side?

    A. 12 yds   B. 20 yds   C. 32 yds   D. 48 yds

13. A rectangular bulletin board made of cork is 4 feet wide and 5 feet long. What is the area of the bulletin board's cork surface?

    A. 9 square feet   C. 20 square feet

    B. 18 square feet   D. 25 square feet

14. If a rectangular garden has a perimeter of 26 yards and a width of 4 yards, what is the area of the garden?

    A. 36 square yards   C. 13 square yards

    B. 30 square yards   D. 9 square yards

15. What is the area of the outlined region?

    A. 18 square units

    B. 24 square units

    C. 28 square units

    D. 42 square units

    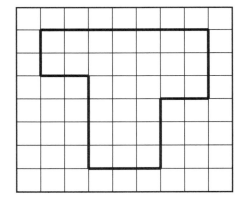

16. What is the area of the shaded region if each grid square represents 1 square yard?

    A. 20 square yards

    B. 24 square yards

    C. 26 square yards

    D. 42 square yards

    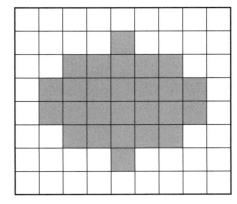

Section 5: Measurement:
Answer Key to Practice Test

The objective being tested is shown in brackets beside answer.

1. B [1]

2. C [1]

3. B [2]

4. D [2]

5. C [3]

6. A [3]

7. A [4]

8. D [4]

9. C [5]

10. B [5]

11. B [6]

12. A [6]

13. C [7]

14. A [7]

15. C [8]

16. C [8]

Other Books by Frances McBroom Thompson

Math Essentials, Middle School Level: Lessons and Activities for Test Preparation
Frances M. Thompson, Ed.D.

Paper/368 pages
ISBN: 0-7879-6602-9

"Middle school math teachers will want to take this book home with them every night! It addresses key middle school topics and provides easy-to-use activities which not only support the conceptual understanding of the topics but include links to their assessment."

-Francis (Skip) Fennell, professor of education, McDaniel College, Westminister, Maryland, former NCTM board member, and author, *Principles and Standards for School Mathematics*

Math Essentials, Middle School Level gives middle school math teachers the tools they need to help prepare all types of students (including gifted and learning disabled) for mathematics testing and the National Council of Teachers of Mathematics (NCTM) standards. *Math Essentials* highlights Dr. Thompson's proven approach by incorporating manipulatives, diagrams, and independent practice.

This dynamic book covers thirty key objectives arranged in four sections and covering numeration, computation, proportional and algebraic reasoning, geometry, measurement, statistics and probability.

Each objective includes three activities (two developmental lessons and one independent practice) and a list of commonly made errors related to the objective. The book's activities are designed to be flexible and can be used as a connected set or taught separately, depending on the learning needs of your students. All lessons are developmental in nature, allowing you to use them to either introduce or remediate the identified concept.

The three activities may be presented as a connected set, with the hands-on action leading naturally to the paper-and-pencil drawing, then to the abstract notation. Or each activity may be used separately, depending upon the learning needs of the students. All students, however, regardless of intellectual ability or diversity of background, should experience each of the three learning stages at some point.

Most activities and problems also include a worksheet and an answer key and each of the four sections contains a practice test with an answer key.

Math Essentials, High School Level: Lessons and Activities for Test Preparation

Frances M. Thompson, Ed.D.

Paper/368 pages
ISBN: 0-7879-6603-7

"*Secondary mathematics teachers will find the clearly described activities a sound supplement to standard textbook presentations. The well-designed sequences of activities proceeding from the concrete to pictorial to symbolic are especially suited for helping those who struggle with basic mathematics in high school.*"—Bill Juraschek, University of Colorado at Denver

Math Essentials, High School Level gives high school math teachers the tools they need to help prepare all types of students (including gifted and learning disabled) for standards-based mathematics testing. Each objective contains three lessons: manipulative, pictorial, and independent practice. Lessons include worksheets or patterns and answer keys, and each section ends with a practice test and answer key.

This dynamic book covers thirty key objectives found in a typical secondary mathematics curriculum, including algebraic thinking; graphs, statistics, and probability; linear and quadratic functions and their properties; and geometry and measurement with applications

This book is an essential test-prep guide appropriate for high school students, grades 9-12. Designed to help teachers align their classroom instruction with their district and state mathematics guidelines, this book offers instruction for remediation and enrichment, provides necessary scaffolding to develop key skills, and measures student progress. All lessons are aligned with the National Council of Teachers of Mathematics (NCTM) standards. For each learning objective, the book includes three activities (two developmental lessons and one independent practice), along with a list of common student errors.

Hands-On Math!
Ready-To-Use Games & Activities for Grades 4-8
Frances M. Thompson, Ed.D.

Paper/544 pages
ISBN: 0-7879-6740-8

Here's a super treasury of 279 exciting math games and activities that help students learn by engaging both their minds and their bodies. Dispensing with tired "rote" learning and memorization, *Hands-On Math!* uses fun-filled exercises that encourage your students to think and reason mathematically.

Help your students master the tools they need to solve math problems, while encouraging them to think independently with these essential, hands-on math games and activities on reproducible student handouts. In line with NCTM guidelines, this invaluable teacher's aid develops basic and advanced math skills through an effective combination of three components for each lesson: a concrete exercise (manipulatives), a pictorial model, and a cooperative learning experience.

Organized into eight sections, each covering concepts from a different area of mathematics, *Hands-On Math!* provides scores of reproducible record sheets, workmats, and other student handouts to use as often as needed. The eight sections cover:

- Number and number relationships
- Patterns, relations, and functions
- Development of written algorithms
- Geometry and spatial sense
- Measurement
- Statistics and probability
- Number theory
- Algebraic thinking

Hands-On Algebra!
Ready-To-Use Games & Activities for Grades 7-12
Frances M. Thompson, Ed.D.

Paper/640 pages
ISBN: 0-87628-386-5

For grades 7-12 teachers, here's an extensive collection of 159 ready-to-use games and activities to make algebra meaningful and fun for kids of all ability levels!

Lay a solid foundation of algebra proficiency with over 155 hands-on games and activities. Through a unique three-step approach, students gain mastery over algebra concepts and skills one activity at a time:

- Activity 1 offers **physical models** (using available materials) and easy-to-follow instructions to help learners seek patterns.
- Activity 2 uses **pictorial models** like diagrams, tables, and graphs to further help students retain and test what they have learned.
- Activity 3 encourages **exploration** and **application** of newly learned concepts and skills through cooperative games, puzzles, problems, and graphic calculator or computer activities.

Each activity includes complete teacher directions, materials needed, and helpful examples for discussion, homework, and quizzes.

Activities are organized into five sections:

1) Real numbers, their operations, and their properties
2) Linear forms
3) Linear applications and graphing
4) Quadratic concepts
5) Special applications

Other Books of Interest

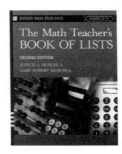

The Math Teacher's Book of Lists, 2nd Edition
Judith A. Muschla and Gary Robert Muschla

Paper/250 pages
ISBN: 0-7879-7398-X

The Math Teacher's Book of Lists, 2nd Edition, is a one-stop math resource with exciting, challenging, and quick reference materials, all supporting NCTM standards. It includes comprehensive and updated content from general mathematics through algebra, geometry, trigonometry, and calculus, useful in grades 5-12 classrooms as well as community college classes.

Part I contains nine sections of reproducible lists and offers essential, time-saving, and relevant information on over 300 topics. Part II contains a variety of reproducible teaching aides and activities to support the instructional program. The original lists have been substantially updated, a new section, "Lists for Student Reference," has been added, along with approximately twelve new lists, including "Fractals," "Topics in Discrete Math," "Math Websites for Students," and "Math Websites for Teachers."

This new edition, like the original, is designed for easy implementation. Each list is written in clear, simple-to-read language, stands alone, and may be used with students of various grades and abilities; materials can be customized to your needs. These lists are linked through cross-references and can serve as the basis for developing supplementary materials for the classroom, expanding topics in the curriculum, or extending lessons with related topics.

The Math Teacher's Book of Lists provides:

- An invaluable resource for effective mathematics instruction
- An imaginative way to help students understand the grand scope, practicality, and intriguing intricacies of mathematics

Judith A. Muschla has taught middle and high school mathematics in South River, NJ, for the last 27 years, and received the governor's Teacher Recognition Program Award in New Jersey. **Gary Robert Muschla** taught reading and writing for more than 25 years in Spotswood, NJ. This is their eighth co-authored mathematics book.